TO
HEAVEN
AND
BACK

Don't Die... Live On!

To Heaven And Back: Don't Die... Live On!

Copyright © 2023 by Paul D Walters

This book is a work of non-fiction.

Paul D Walters asserts the moral right to be identified as the author of this work. The author and publisher have endeavoured to depict events and dialogue from memory as accurately as possible. Chapter 14 has supplemental dialogue with a creative context for narrative flow. Some names have also been changed to respect the privacy of individuals. The author is not a medical professional. This book is written in good faith with intentions to help and uplift without malice toward anyone.

For information contact:
pauldwaltersauthor.uk

Book and Cover design by: Spiffing Covers
ISBN: 978-1-7393700-0-8
First edition: September 2023

Trigger warning and help

This book has themes of violence, mental health, depression, death, dying, suicide, alcoholism, and drugs. If you need help or support now or during reading this book, go to Appendix A, seek professional help or talk to someone you trust.

TO
HEAVEN
AND
BACK

Don't Die... Live On!

PAUL D WALTERS

DEDICATION

To the happy and sad people, and the human mind that's tortured me and learned to fight on. And, to suicide prevention and those affected by mental health now or in the future. To the NHS, and those bereaved as they've lost a friend or loved one to suicide.

Contents

PREFACE

*A*s a teenager, I never entertained writing a story, let alone a book. Nor did I know dark and traumatic times in my life represented an integral part of an epic, cathartic life journey.

Learning to rejoice new beginnings, light after darkness and believing it was the end form parts of my life's journey.

One such beginning, a few typed strung together sentences in 1989, formed the basic and early foundations, seeds of thought for this book, in note-form, at the start of rehab. Eight years later, from 1997 to 1988, basic stories developed into a novella. Partly as the late Maureen McCoy, MBE asked me to write about Lourdes.

Daunted by the mammoth task. Difficult topics associated with dark-times and places in my mind, I skirted around those sections. A 17-year pause enabled me to explore and contemplate those times. Places I did not wish to return to, or embrace powerful, consuming emotions.

The impasse presented a tremendous challenge as I expanded book sections, and I wrote every day from February 2015. Further thoughts sprung to mind. And areas of complexity I considered unfathomable became clearer. This brought foundation, intertwined with sense and logic.

The combined realisation analogous to joining the dots in an enormous masterpiece with coloured and blank areas with dark voids, but as an author, with words as the book separated into distinct sections and evolved with a restructure and major rewrite from November 2017 to September 2018.

With continual refinement thereafter, and during the UK lockdown because of the COVID-19 pandemic to December 2020, and from 2022 onwards, this literary task has spanned over 30 years.

A prolonged task, partly as I didn't know what else to write. I focused on other interests as I struggled for the courage how to proceed, battled mental health issues and thought of parts of my life.

Perseverance and tenacity have not been enough. Determination spurred me on to face those periods with a compulsion to write. I had to complete this book as a personal lifetime task, and for others.

This notion has motivated me as years have passed. My mind needed to be willing and ready to return to the inner depths of my mind I dared not contemplate before.

A scheme, Flourish2BU run by Dr Paul Darke and a course called Making Lemonade by Steph Cutler helped to motivate me. I am also indebted to Dave Wightman for the support, editorial guidance, and encouragement, especially at needed times and long before this, to a now late lifelong mentor from college who inspired and believed in me.

And, to my partner, Helen, for always being at my side. Yet, further experiences have been imperative for inner exploration and the mental strength to write and to present this unique book.

I have strived to add clarity to mystery to profound themes of paramount importance seldom discussed — a means of hope and wonder.

INTRODUCTION
Into Another Reality

*N*umbed with cold and can barely walk. A fun but wild night with my new, gorgeous girlfriend who'd dump me the next day, for my drunkenness. I was happy as I danced and drank, but sad as we parted, and I headed home alone toward Bilston, onto Mount Pleasant, near Mountford Lane.

White frost sparkled on parked cars by the Rising Star Club. So tired and shivery, I didn't want to drive! "Trying car doors?" A voice said. Too drunk to answer, but I tried, "I only wanted to rest and get warm."

By now at the car park, "Have my money, don't take my coat." I remembered nothing else, only the scuffle and dimly lit, leering, angry faces in the darkness.

Driven by desire, spurred on, but unaware of so much, while swayed by misguided fantasies, grandeur, and illusory dreams. The snow clouds forming on my dark path.

I walked a hypothetical tightrope. Spanning an abyss, as I teetered, tried to balance. Desperate to reach the other side — to safety and happiness.

The tightrope, the line between peace and turmoil, is sometimes a fine one. While both extremes rage and overwhelm, an arduous task, a long, all-ensuing battle between mind and body. As is the elusive search for a harmonious balance.

The consequential aftermath, a world turned upside down, flipped. Presented the ultimate test; jolted me into a different orbit from which there was no escape. Alas, many perish – I survived and despite – presented new realities.

Readers will encounter a story of survival from the perspective of someone overcome by turmoil. Who became lost, and near death but found the way, another path, strength to battle on against the odds.

This book is intended to act as a guide and resource to help those in turmoil. And for others to recognise patterns so they are more able to support. The echoed overriding message: there's often another way.

But, the book extends beyond motivations of prolonging lives. Insights into the mind, and depression form part of a physical and mental, transformational life journey. A life journey after the dawn of a stark, new reality.

This and the quest for solace and equilibrium following inner turmoil will hopefully entertain, inspire, comfort, help and uplift others that may experience dark-times. Spurring on those depressed and in despair, that believe there's no hope or choice. There is a choice.

I wish every reader well, with reading the many chapters of this book; presented to the world, and its citizens, ultimately, as a guide from self-destructive paths. And, I hope none find it as difficult as this book has been to write.

A tip: Play all songs mentioned.

Section I

THE COUNTDOWN BEGINS

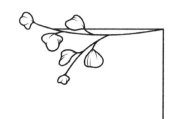

1.

SLIPPERY SLOPE

*I*t's devastatingly sad that every 40 seconds, someone dies by suicide. Almost 800,000 lives per year, lost worldwide. More alarming, for every life lost, more than 20 people attempt suicide.[1] That's a potential 16,000,000 deaths, yearly, despite the preciousness of time, and lives.

Still, how dare I mention the 'S' word that clears rooms and silences many — suicide in the first chapter of my book! Well, death is inevitable. Death by suicide is not. Do so many actually want to die? To end their lives as they consider it the ultimate answer to all problems, their mental state?

I remember wishing I was dead, depression, despair, and dark-times. Years on, as I reflect, think of my life, immerse myself in the past. It's odd to write that, and that death ever seemed an option. Sadly, it was, and despite fun days and joyful moments.

As a child, I was a constant worrier, but happy in my corduroy, flared trousers, and tank top jumpers. I loved animals, our tortoise and our blue-and-white feathered budgie, Beauty, who hatched from an egg in our kitchen.

She flew around the living room, landed on our heads and to our aloft fingers as perches, and chirped, sometimes scolded us and showed her personality.

I wanted to fly, too, and after I watched *Superman: The Movie* with my mom and brother in Wolverhampton in 1978, I believed a man could fly. With a fist aloft, I ran and jumped in the air, but didn't think I'd ever become a man.

In summer, I chased the Goodyear Airship on my bike. From

---

1. World Health Organisation: https://www.who.int/health-topics/ suicide#tab=tab_1

my garden, I listened to the speeding motorbikes on the speedway in Monmore Green Stadium.

I played marbles. Proud of my prized collection and toy soldiers. I didn't like football, but played gutter-ball. We threw a football to hit the kerb on the opposite side of the road to score points. If it didn't bounce back, the opponent had a turn.

But, I was best at Asteroids with my 'funky-shooting' on my games console. I scored six million in 24 hours, as my first endurance test.

As I grew older, I worried to a wider extent. Worried and anxious about failing, being liked, and about others, loved ones. The emotions became more intense, complex, and gradually overwhelming.

I spent most of childhood in a wonderful place. On warm summer days, I swam in the fast-flowing water of the River Severn, near Welshpool, before the trees of the woods with chirping birds, an enchanted place beside the river. Time stood still. No humdrum of a crazy world, or urban anxieties, I could relax.

During the day, and beyond to dusk, I threw my luminous Frisbee. Inspired by the UK Frisbee throwing champion and his assistant, "Buddan" in action at Hednesford Raceway when I was about 10-years-old. What a cool name I'd never forget.

And, played music from the stereo cassette player I had for my 13th birthday: Michael Jackson's *Thriller* and *Off the Wall*, New Order, *Blue Monday*, and thumping electro-funk tunes. Loud music, like a blown horn in the wilderness; the woods as I walked to the other caravan site.

Enjoying the scenic delights at a leisurely pace until I ran. Top speed, past the mill, along the railway, and through the woods, leaping over emerging tree roots and overgrown brambles. Alongside the river's dark water, like an elated cat who had found the cream.

It was a perfect summer's day in 1983, of friendship, romance, and excitement, as my second cousin, Colin, and I sat on a blanket on the grass with a newly acquainted friend, Jade, from New Zealand.

Fascinated and amused by our Black Country accents, Jade recorded our voices on her stereo and introduced us to her parents and elder sister, Paula, as she appeared. Stood in the camper doorway. Tall, shapely, gorgeous with deep-brown, wavy hair and 18-years-old, we held hands as we walked until the sun, set.

I wished I was older, more mature, and that I didn't feel like I was holding hands with my mom, but wasn't afraid as I walked back along the road in the dark. Intrepid and bold, comforted by the distant, faint torchlight and chatter, calls from the darkness, my dad.

Safe and enthralled by the pierced black cloak of darkness, wondrous blue, white pinpricks of twinkling starlight reaching and showering the Earth from the black sky. My head often trained upward to the heavens, "Ah, look at that one!" I said as I embraced dreams of being an astronaut, wishing to visit those stars.

I loved the moon and the stars, romancing, dancing, babes, and Bananarama. Tsk, impeded by shyness and self-consciousness. A lack of confidence, I hated myself on an unforgettable day, too short as I said farewell to Paula, but she was engaged to someone.

The untimely goodbye intensified emotions. Sadness, entwined with desire, as I yearned for my next romantic encounter. I couldn't meet a woman as stunning. Or be anywhere on Earth, as magical. Time passed... suddenly, after leaving school, I ventured into the wide world.

It was December 1985, the depths of winter in a faraway place so perfect. In a state of excitement and shock, unbelievable, as I strolled along a Scottish country road with a lovely woman.

Surreal as we reached the brow of a stone bridge, and looked upon a narrow stream running below us. Black running water, shimmering white, reflecting the moon's subdued glow.

Awestruck in that dark, highly romantic setting I shouldn't have been. I remembered the warmth and glow of the hypnotic dancing flames; touching moments, the thrill of a strange attraction of a dizzying intensity as our lips met.

What a kiss as we embraced! Her lips made for mine and my heart hers for it to beat so fast? It was an entranced moment preceding love as moonlit water sparkled and trickled beneath us.

But, before our first argument, "You're chucking a mental. Have you got rocks in your hid?" in a quaint Scottish accent as she trudged beside me with a red face full of anger. *What a feisty lass.* "You're sexy when you're angry," as our smiles erupted. She was my princess and I her prince, transformed into a paranoid, insecure caveman.

She was wrong, though, and I disagreed with my mom, who often said, "Where there's jealousy, there's no love." That's peers and parents influencing, moulding us to make us better citizens. To guide us with their wisdom and best intentions, and who doesn't want to live in a fairy-tale?

The best possible life based on ideals and expectations, a partner, wife, wonderful relationship, children, and a nice house, a well-paid job. I wanted all those things. And, ah, something else in my head, or rather someone, had been, the man in my mind.

Puzzled by his sudden appearance when I was eight-years-old. Elderly and smartly dressed, bald apart from two tufts of grey hair at the sides of his head.

He sat, writing at a table in an unfurnished room, surrounded by flickering fire at the bottom of the bland walls. Oddly, his lips didn't move, but he told me many things in a quiet, firm voice.

So wise, pondering, sometimes expressionless, sometimes knowingly smiling, I thought he may have been my only true and closest friend. Other influences took over as I aged. I was OK.

Contented at 17, wise, less shy and adventurous with options, I wasn't scared of anything except for glue-sniffers, gangs, pimps, and prostitutes. The best year of my life was beginning.

And, near the end of April 1986, it was strange to ride my bike, every day, on the Bilston Road. Toward the red-light district, far away from that fairy-tale world, still alone, niggled. It seemed so long ago, in another world.

No longer a hopeless romantic, I had moved on with optimism. Enthused with excitement and better prospects, starting my first job.

My past days of learning had become a distant memory since I entered the smog-filled factory. The sound of metallic objects clanking in the rotating plating barrels as I time-stamped my clocking-in-card in the machine.

The boss, Roger, showed me around and at the top end of the factory, I met Dave, a tall cheeky short-haired chap who introduced me to Brian, a stocky chap with short black hair and a moustache. Dave said, "there's a joke here. Who's the strongest, Brian, or a forklift?" Brian grabbed my overalls and lifted me in the air, held me up with one arm!

I'm in midair! Brian's lifted me as if I'm as light as a child. As I laughed, couldn't stop, but remembered tears. I was the sad clown yearning to be the strongman, just didn't realise then.

Dave said, "Put him down, put him down, Brian."

Brian said little and seemed weird as he pulled funny faces. He and Dave made a great double act.

I worked at the bottom end of the factory. Next to the clocking in machine where Tony sat proudly in his cosy portable cabin office. In a navy-blue work jacket, cow-gown, matching trousers and distinguished with Teddy boy quiff and long sideburns. The hairstyle reminded me of my dad, years earlier.

Tony, though, had a pencil behind his ear, poised to write on vast amounts of paper, all organised and important. Above this, in front of the desk, dingy windows with so much grime you couldn't see in or out the areas not covered with pink, yellow, and pale-blue cards held by chunky bulldog clips suspended from nails in the wall.

Tony was a goods-inwards guru, brilliant role model, and speedy forklift truck driver; he manoeuvred with great precision: shiny steel forks in and out of pallets, up and down, and turned the steering wheel.

I watched Tony and others zoom onto the upper levels, at the far side of the factory, via a slippery access ramp to the plating stations. Alongside vats of light-brown liquid, grey and pale-green, gaseous plumes rose, like steam from its surface and formed into a chemical smog.

The smelly clouds suffused with the air below orange glowing sodium lamps in inverted, dust covered, lampshade domes, suspended from the factory ceiling.

Tackling the ramp was tricky, and an acquired skill; like an art. The forklift wheels skidded and spun and the engine roared and smoked with maximum acceleration applied to get up, reach the top. Sometimes the front wheels of the forklift slewed sideways, requiring a precarious, controlled reverse.

I soon learned how to drive the forklift trucks and zipped up and descended the slope, transporting pallets laden with heavy pans and bolt containers. The scales a doddle, too, and I became faster than expert Tony.

After a glance, I knew the weight of jobs. Adjusted the scales to great precision in an instant, and I soon learned every aspect of goods-inwards and outwards by the time the old cabin office became a canteen, mainly for goods-inwards staff and who operated the plating stations.

They moved Tony and me to a new brick-built office extension. It was great with adjoining glass serving hatch to the girls in the office and the manager, Roger. I changed the office, made it super organised and efficient.

Whenever my superior mentor asked, "Where's the invoice for?…" I stated exact locations; answered anything. So, I became a guru! Especially when the girls opened the serving hatch to ask me about jobs.

I missed that nice, clean, efficient office, but was back in the cabin for 15 minutes a day. Breakfast, lunch, or supper with the plating workers and I looked forward to a chilled can of pop on the sweltering days, tasty warm sandwiches on chilly mornings, and warm chips from nearby shops.

I had progressed far, from goods-inwards and errand boy to becoming a zinc plater working alternating mornings (6am until 2pm) and afternoons (2pm until 10pm) for about £80, plus a £2.20 shift allowance for a basic 45 hours a week.

On the largest of four stations, Plant Two, I helped Carl. We formed an excellent two-man team on the busiest, hardest to run, and only plant with a gas oven dryer.

Another veteran plater, Mark, known as Rocky, operated the plant next to mine. Tall, stocky, with long dark hair, he was a strong, no-nonsense, often stern character who sometimes laughed. Time passed faster though, listening to Madonna's *True Blue* album and Queen's *A Kind of Magic* blasting from Rocky's stereo.

Sometimes I plated over two and half tonnes of bolts, in 12-hour shifts, but dreaded these. And shovelled and lifted all that weight; the metal for plating I loaded into large, plastic hexagonal, perforated containers with tight lids secured by plastic nuts.

As soon as I loaded a container and sent it on its way for plating, another container of plated cargo arrived to empty onto a vibrating conveyor belt to dry in the long, hot, burning gas oven. Oblong pans placed in front of the oven caught the dried cargo. Before you knew it, another container arrived.

It was a relentless race against time. Dusty, hot, exhausting, dangerous, heavy work, and stressful, in arduous conditions, and unbearable during warm summer days, I got chemical burns on my arms from the plating solutions. But, I was getting tougher.

Dave taught me how to plate at the cadmium station, too; we became friends. I learned how to run the plants by myself and fetched drums of sodium cyanide, bags of caustic soda, and buckets of concentrated hydrochloric acid with the forklift.

These tasks instilled importance as they involved hazardous, lethal chemicals. I remembered the foreman Terry with a stern expression and holding one of the white-pink sodium cyanide cubes in his gloved hand. "One of these could kill a herd of elephants."

Morbidly fascinated, too, by the pale-green chlorine fumes of the acid that sometimes entered my nostrils. Caused me to cough with a choking sensation. In contrast, the caustic soda looked like white ice.

Unpleasant tasks, but collaboration and great team spirit helped, and the music from Rocky's stereo, when he was there. I didn't laugh again, though, like on my first day. *Why am I doing such laborious, hard, and hazardous work in a factory?*

The gradual dawning preceded procrastinating thoughts and ever ominous haunting feelings exacerbated by Terry, saying, "You're clever, you am." Insinuating I could do much better and recognised potential.

I knew this and had mixed emotions since I saw the job on display at the Bilston Jobcentre, aspiring to a menial, relatively low skilled, low-paid job despite unease.

Surely, my friends weren't right to call that place a joke shop! I began with trepidation, for prestige and extra money, to save for a car. Alas, I soon became the only person there who could do almost everything. So, nothing else to learn and trapped. With no prospect of career progression or promotion, I desperately wanted a better job.

Thirty-seven and half hours a week in an office, a luxury, 60 hours in an ice-cold office, a dream, but had left college, and chosen my vocation; no going back.

But what was time? Who was I? How is it so different now? Different after such excitement, sheer pride at the start of a wonderful new era, when I began work. Well, two weeks into that first job as a man glanced at me from his car, a smart red open-topped sports car.

He sped up to overtake me on my bike but had to speed up more, so he pulls beside me, points at his speedometer and laughs. I revelled in making others laugh.

And was so fast, but not tired, the flat road, easy, faster! The roadside whizzing by, my feet spinning round in top gear, as I raced toward Bilston from work. Euphoria, with such power ¬ faster, speeding along a road I knew so well.

Invincible and on a high, I flew on two wheels. I got my wish, flying like Superman® as I turned the peddles so fast, and against the clock as I started my stopwatch at the Don Everall car showroom and stopped it at the Windsor Street turn, where my mom was born. Nearly home, but time stopped.

So sudden with shock and horror as I see my bike wheel bend on impact with the wing of a car.

My head hits and shatters the windscreen instantaneously (in the days before helmets). I continue to hurtle through the air, catapulted by the impact, and land on my hip. Argh, I lie there on the road, stunned, motionless, unable to move, not knowing what had happened.

Dazed and not wanting to close my eyes, I peer up at the sky. *My bike? Where's my bike?* Intense pain as I try to move, it's difficult. *I'll keep still; won't turn my head,* despite the sounds of traffic, and a car door opens and slams as the driver emerges from the car.

A distraught, middle-aged, blonde-haired lady, crying, as she's thinking the worst. "I pulled out; I didn't see you." She puts her face in her hands.

My only thought: *I must get up to see my bike* but cannot move. I did not care or bother about myself, or my first ever wage packet, I'd worked hard for and counted the days to get, but my bike, my bike. With help from paramedics, I limp into the ambulance. Devastated as I see my prized bike, wrecked!

Many miles in a bygone summer. No mountain beat me and nearly a King of Snowdon. Then, dismounted on the King Street junction, but the Volvo® 343, was badly damaged, too.

It's inexplicable, in an ambulance, to the Royal Hospital. Back along the road, I had travelled along with a woman from Wolverhampton at the start of that year. And sped along moments earlier.

There was no time to scream. The sudden shock and such cruel confusion, despondence entwined with pain after elation, fantastic euphoria, and power.

That evening I arrived home, still in pain, with a dressing on my hip. So sore and achy, my head hurt. Nothing felt the same! Dishevelled, dejected and beaten. I no longer had my faithful steed; I removed my heavy armour and bled.

That larger than life, chirpy charisma destroyed and all-optimism. None of this mattered. My emotions and state of mind, meaningless, bandaged, and they dressed physical wounds. That's all that mattered!

I hobbled to work the next day, plodded on, although I could hardly walk because of the pain. Everything felt different, as if detached, separate, not even there. I did not belong or deserve. Earlier times of depression, tame compared to now.

I became more withdrawn, depressed, melancholy, after being

so upbeat — nothing to enjoy or fight for anymore. Not even being reimbursed for a new bike roused me. It wouldn't have been the same.

The invisible, incalculable mental scars, and aftermath were beyond any price. At least my pitiful, insignificant £45 wages are safe in my back pocket. And my wrecked bike, a trophy-memento of past accolades, never to be again.

Still, that first £45 and wages afterwards enabled me to buy my first car for £80, a gold-coloured Vauxhall® Viva from Pensnett.

Rust on the body, and brown rotting rust holes on the wings, but I saw the potential, and cankered, oxidised alloy wheels. *I'll paint those, make them shine.* Dad drove it back while I beamed with delight in the passenger seat. *I've bought my first car.*

The engine wasn't powerful; it needed a new clutch, but Dad fitted many parts, worked hard, and got my car roadworthy. He and friends as qualified drivers sat with me, while I proudly drove around with dreams of passing my driving test.

I even drove to Rhyl, North Wales for practice, and for the first and only time with my cousin, Dava, to sample the nightlife. Extra special, a novelty, as I wasn't with my parents.

As we walked back to my car, and in my car, we chatted and I felt proud to be there and in a secluded car park. Although cold, so hard to sleep, even though fully clothed, as I eventually closed my eyes, I went back in time.

Drifted away on the waves of the sea I loved. I always looked forward to seeing the sea and visiting the beach. Loved digging in the sand.

Mom and Dad said I could fetch an ice-cream as long as I came straight back to them. It was delicious, cool, and refreshing. Great, but I wasn't ready to come back to the caravan yet.

I'll walk further and easily find my way back. Mom and Dad will be pleased and impressed, hearing about my adventure. Eager to look at the sea, I walked further and turned. But faced walls of metal between long aisles of grey tarmac.

No people or sounds, except for the gentle roar of the breaking waves. Further and confused, every avenue looked the same. Stay calm – I'll find my way back – but how? I didn't know what to do, except keep walking. *How have I become lost? I haven't gone far.* Tears stream, cool on my cheeks, salty as they wet my lips, after I tried to stay calm. I become worse; inconsolable as I hear mention of the lost little boy from a Tannoy®. *That's me; Dad will shout, and he and Mom are looking for me.*

But, intrigued as I approach a caravan door, and hear Jimmy Cliff, *I Can See Clearly Now,* playing from a radio amid chatter. The music soothes me, and calmed by the friendly occupant's chatter, although not our caravan, and strangers, not Mom and Dad.

I don't remember who took me to reception, a guardian-angel? That place, cool and welcoming, shaded from the sun. Still anxious as I waited.

The moment Dad saw me, he lifted me into the air but didn't shout; he cried. Puzzled, but elated and joyous at being reunited with my mom and dad.

I was an adventurous four-year-old then. The fear wasn't being lost. It was of being alone and Dad shouting, but he must have loved me as he cried.

Dawn soon came, and I woke with similar fears and insecurities as the wind gusted and seagulls cried.

Saddened with malaise on a deserted Rhyl car park with strewn litter, and I remembered the disco lights from the night before. I turned the key in the ignition to return to Bilston and never went to the sea.

On the third driving test, my heart sank as the unnerving robotic, emotionless driving examiner who'd failed me twice met me at the Bilston test centre. *He'll fail me if I drive perfectly! I'll just drive* and I passed.

Yes, my car's on the road, with a fabulous second-hand auto-reverse tape deck, blasting Shalamar, and other favourite, funky-tunes, as I drove. It was April 21ˢᵗ, 1987, a year since my bike became the trophy-memento.

I cruised around with *NOW Dance 86* cassette tapes playing. Tremendous, but the last song got to me, made me melancholy.

I liked a few slow songs, Phyllis Nelson, *Move Closer,* George Michael, *Careless Whisper* and loved Rufus and Chaka Khan, *Ain't Nobody,* just seldom asked any girl for a slow dance.

Anyway, I preferred dancing to faster songs. Jaki Graham's *Set Me Free,* Madonna *Into the Groove,* Paul Hardcastle, *19,* Colonel Abrams, *Trapped* and more. But too shy, and always drunk well before the slow music played in clubs.

Unlike some of my friends, engaged after one slow dance! What was wrong with me? I had given up on romance. Did no-one want me, or my heart?

I longed for the weekends. Visited pubs and nightclubs with my old friends – obsessed with the excitement – heart pounding as music thudded and lights illuminated lovely ladies looking at me.

Arousing rhythmic sights as I became part of the harmonious rhythms. Addicted to the enjoyment as I danced in trendy places, beckoned by vibrant, packed dancefloors. And drank, stayed until the end, walked home, up at 5.30am for work.

Sometimes, during the week, to Harry's wine bar in Bilston, open until 2am. A long time since my first pint at The Moxley Arms as Dazz Band, *Let It All Blow* played. I became like an alien, a reluctant party goer in foreign lands. Places I didn't want to be.

It was total madness. A strange turmoil, with another realisation, as I looked in a mirror. *Why am I in this flat?* Who was that person confused by laughter? The face staring back at me I didn't know? They'd forgotten how to smile.

Groggy, sore and in pain from my throbbing chipped tooth, a black eye and cut face, white flesh where my eyebrows used to be. The pain in my mind hurt more.

Funny, I remembered laughter as daylight illuminated the still closed curtains and woke me! In a lounge armchair I fell asleep, dreaming of the women on the dancefloor. How the night should have been.

Anger as I tremble and warm liquid, a tear rolls down my cheek. No, it's blood, oozing from below my eye after being momentarily dazed by a sudden, hard, sharp knock on my face. Hit by a fist or head.

Furious, as I had done nothing, or hurt them. I wanted to retaliate, but couldn't see who hit me! *A jealous, ugly bastard. Did they hate me so much?* Was I the ugly one? Although I didn't even have any spots?

But, what was beauty? I still hated myself like I did as a youngster into my teen years. When I cried, listened to sad songs, when alone. Depression and curiosity, wanting to sleep, escape from the lingering inescapable fear, the dread deep within of future pain of a different kind.

Despise, self-hate, but I had my secret endurance test. It may have been harmless, but with new extremes and escalating curiosity as I had endured and survived. Power, control, no-one knew, that instilled a strange comfort, solace in a lonely world I didn't belong.

Eighteen now, and as I drove away from Tamworth toward Bilston, the emotions, thoughts were still there deep within but amplified and ready to surface. *Worthless and alone Are my friends really my friends?*

I make everyone miserable anyway. Used to becoming ever more insular knowing I had chosen my path and become tired of the madness of that world.

I didn't need anyone, or pretence. Strangely upbeat, but oblivious to the war raging and turmoil in my mind, drifting to memories of times when I still dreamed and battled.

But I was alright. Although I knew no-one would, or could, understand. I had to find a way to change that.

My anger intensified, as it wasn't enough to feel alone. Something or someone always spoilt things. At least I amused them — their laughter, more important. I was happy when I danced and break-danced to electro-funk years earlier.

My friends insisted on Tamworth. I drove us there. *Bilston was better. I'd have been fine there, and walking to Harry's or Piper's wine bar to dance.*

Respected more, too, with boosted popularity there. My car was rarely empty. My driving license rekindled ambitions. Broadened opportunities, while long-forgotten aspirations and dreams I once had, were ignored. *Yes, I could do better!* And had a plan. I was OK!

My old boss implored me not to go. "Sales is a mug's game." He said, as I shared my plans in his office. He and my old assistant manager phoned nearly every day, asking me to go back; they struggled without me; I was hardly ever at home.

I respected them and their opinions, but with mixed emotions, I had left my plating job and more. Strangely, I cannot remember if I ever returned to help. Maybe I did, in many dreams.

I pursued grand ideas on an alternative career path. Allured by exciting prospects and the glitz and glamour of sales.

High earnings, £500 a week for selling amazing multi-functional vacuum cleaning systems. As we pulled away, the slick team leader pointed to a smart new Range Rover® in the car park. "That's Mike's new car, our top sales guy."

Enticed by fancy ideas and novelty. Being driven around by an ultra-cool guy, our team leader, in a black Audi® Quattro. Wearing a shirt, tie, and trousers was a pleasant and welcome change from drab chemical-soaked overalls and steel-toed shoes, too. No comparison, my choice, and best career path is obvious!

Most turned us away. Some let us in, agreed to a free demonstration of the system. With the cleaner out of the box and display materials, I recited my well-rehearsed lines.

It sucked shocking amounts of dirt and grit from even the cleanest of carpets. More shocking, magnified images of dust mites scared even the toughest of the tough.

My new mad job, every morning The Pointer Sisters, *I'm So Excited* played, a catchy, upbeat song, as the sales people sat in a room. Those who had sold units walked onto a platform at the front and told the sales audience how they clinched the sale. Someone playing the drums and bashing a cymbal followed this.

Door-to-door sales were tremendously difficult. Mega-impressive, though, and a must have household device and substantial progress until mention of the price. It was downhill from there. They'd show you the door.

Still, some sold two a night, twice, sometimes three times a week. Unbelievable — what was their secret?

Surely, I wasn't that bad, so inept? What did they have I didn't? Was it luck, charm, charisma, cheek, boldness, ruthlessness? Mega rich people in the houses they visited and paupers in the ones I visited, or sensible ones?

I had joined a cruel mug's game. A mad job, or was I mad in a normal world? The advice of my wise old boss, shunned without mentioning the possibility of a pay rise, and despite niggling feelings, he might be right. Ahh, I wanted to prove him wrong.

And had tasted a different life, the splendid life of leisure, sales: dream-chasers, easier money, drumrolls and feel-good pop music, instead of hard slog! The 5.30am, early morning rides to the factory every day in all weathers.

I'd had enough of plating and that factory. Determined not to return to that life. Returning with egg on my face, not an option. Fond memories, though, and excellent friends. I'd miss having a beer with my dad in The Villiers Arms after work, 'the last pint' before closing time.

Alas, the glitz, and glamour of my new career, lustreless, sales did not meet expectations. Maybe the crux, I just didn't believe in the product, or myself. Oh well, I hoped for more success as a double glazing salesman, but can it be any easier selling windows?

I was one of two trainees to start at the Dudley showroom. The other trainee, more flamboyant, and outgoing than me and my self-esteem, low, I didn't bother to complete the training, no confidence, or belief in myself!

So sad, yet sensible, and in full control. But how could I be unemployed? Whatever had gone wrong to make me a drop-out? *My life, nothing how it should be, a one in 10 like in the UB40 song from 1981, incisively real and true!*

In that era of a Conservative government, with Margaret Thatcher in charge, I depressingly understood why many of my friends called the Jobcentre the joke shop and said Bilston became a ghost town after the steelworks closed.

My dad and granddad worked there. The steelworks defined the essence of the Black Country.

The best thing about Bilston, Woolworths, Cotterill's toy shop, Major's Chippy, and the market. I loved it there, and the job I had. Nothing left in Bilston.

With each joke shop visit, we gazed upon endless rows of cards with despondence, £3.00 an hour, £4.00 an hour for skilled and the never-ending text, ringing in my ears and my mind, "Experience needed". So, we looked in a big folder of vacancies further afield.

They weren't for me. Wasted golden academic opportunities, and deviating from the learning path, the sobering reality as my school form tutor's words rang in my mind, exclaiming with passion: *"You're the cream of the school and can be whatever we want to be."*

No, I disbelieved this and who cared? So what, the reading ability of twice my age at age seven? Many had much higher aspirations of me. I shunned them all. *University and education, is only for those with loads of money, elsewhere.*

Besides, to me, reading was so easy, boring. I couldn't understand the point of reading, or reason, anyone should read. My superhero comics were more stimulating and thought-provoking.

Anyway, I preferred numbers and complexity to reading. The bloke in my mind knew this. I touched the corners of tables, diagonals, and other places and doors; there had to be symmetry.

I tapped my forehead, counted and repeated, and timed my stride perfectly as I walked home from school. Doing these things eased my mind, for a while. Otherwise, there'd be unbearable heartache.

Something terrible would happen. It would all be my fault. There was no other choice!

The pressures, the worry, the nurturing seeds of depression I didn't recognise, or realise I had provided an early basis for a dangerous formula. Still, I visited the joke shop with the remote hope the place no longer peddled cruel despair.

It was the same, no opportunities for me, just ever shifting goalposts of unachievable attainment. I wanted to go back in time. To a year earlier, to happier times, a time I had options. But I had to go forward.

And never went back, although I walked, drank, and tried to resist, regroup my disarrayed, troubled mind. Reminiscing as the world and everyone in it changed. Maybe it was my altered perception. It was always time to return home so soon.

Back to the monotony; still no job, career, or constructive plan. Bilston, the ghost town with its zombie glue-sniffers and joke shop. I no longer smiled. Discontented, depression, and woe, never far away.

I couldn't be happy. Laughter and pain, laughter, and pain, and I couldn't cry. Despair at the rage after contentment. Rebellion, I tamed as the sensible, calm pacifist who never caused trouble. The simmering mental turmoil, out of control, emotionally unstable and paranoid — I never knew.

The spontaneous, erratic, unpredictable me that did anything to make others laugh became nonchalant. Reflective, emotionless and tired, although I should have kept on battling. Magical days flew by; gone and never to return.

Then, as I rested on my bed looking up at the model airplanes I built, painted, and suspended from the ceiling with cotton. Why not follow my dream, and inspired as I watched *Top Gun?* I've always loved space and airplanes, flying. So, I passed the aptitude tests to join the Royal Air Force®.

But, as I enjoyed a TV programme around that time called "Nozzas" and loved swimming. Wonder if I'll pass the entry tests for the Royal Navy®, too?

Inspired and enthused, as I considered a future at sea. Contemplated being a sailor, not necessarily with a girl at every port!

I had fallen for Paula and others after, and kept on falling. My feelings had become too deep for the world, and I didn't know. How can it be nothing excited or comforted me anymore?

College and former aspirations leading to grandeur became a distant dream derided by time. Niggling frustration at wasted opportunities. So many avenues and doors had closed. My schooldays seemed even longer ago. The cream quality pupil, now long-sour and rotting, grand plans, hopes fading away.

Realisation, a cruel, tempting illusion of things, never came to pass so long ago. The always sensible, level-headed optimist in me may have thought I can backtrack, ascend if I had to, or chose to, no rush. I could join the navy if I wanted. They'd whisk me away to learn a trade and see the world.

Fooling myself with false comfort and pipe dreams. I hated the gymnastics in the recruitment video.

Negativity and ambitionless ideals, lonely times and directionless, with no options, prospects, or job so soon after I left work, led to feeling dejected, and deflated.

No charisma any more with the weight of social stigma associated with downbeat times. Every day I walked around, "dossed" the apt word.

My friend and I bought cheap, out-of-date alcohol from a local supermarket, cheaper and stronger, the better. To drink and dream of pastures that could never be as we sat on a high grass embankment overlooking a vast football field, near Bilston Football Club. Shared empathy, and a kindred-companion, I was less alone.

Funny, my first taste was on a similar but windy grassy hill, on my back, gazing upward at stars from a spinning world. Stars, I so wanted to reach at the speed of light a lifetime ago.

If only I had realised the chance to escape; of redemption, by looking for the treasure, acclaim, foolishly thrown away, but never realised.

No, I was P! The one, the former prefect, press-up champion and Prof., but I missed my nickname of "Spaceman", and remembered other names, from "Sweet P" to "Badass". Cruel nicknames, too, that swayed me, misguiding negativity onto another path.

Such power, maximum speed, on the edge, as extremes became the natural norm, and I loved the thrill of speed, car, or my bike, but not fast enough and now wise drunken fool.

Drunken stupor brought solace, a means of escape, but escape was illusory and temporary. A sobering, dull reality always returned with a vengeance and too soon as the bottle emptied.

Alas, too far from the river and the stars, and alone, as rocket ships launched, boats sailed without me, I missed them all.

Thus, the cycle continued. Became a routine, a way of life. An existence as I became rooted to that hill, and only lonely, place. Dank, dreary with temporary discontented solace and no other life, way out, or pasture, as if I entered a dark whirlpool of negativity, fallen and unable to escape.

Like a particle swirling around a massive black hole, the ever insular me in an endless, inescapable, diminishing circle as drink fuelled depression and despair as I dwelled on shattered dreams. Oh, how things might have been. A cycle so hard to change, but I tried so hard and changed.

I even bought my second car, a sky-blue Vauxhall® Chevette, as it had a great engine; fast as I drove it along Prouds Lane, passed the Grapes Pool and the same hill. Dad planned to exchange for the old engine in my Vauxhall® Viva, and knew everything about cars, could fix any problem.

A job turns up, too, in a factory for half the money I earned as a plater. Still, it's a ray of hope, and not shift work. No morning drumrolls, cymbals, or music, hot gas ovens, chemical odours, and burns, but I missed the friendships, camaraderie, and team spirit.

The people were mostly stern, abrupt, unfriendly, at least to me, the new lad. But I settled, learned. Made new friends; *I'll be OK. At least it's a day job, much closer than my old job.* It beats dossing on the dole, walking the streets, drinking.

After a few days, I felt fairly happy. Went to work on an ordinary morning, a normal day. It was the end of summer, nearly autumn, as I plodded on, oblivious to living in a detached world of enveloping darkness.

A cold wilderness in disguise, where harsh winds whipped cold snow, lashed and embraced the ground, muting the raging fire of the sun. Fading light, darker, colder days — the long summers suddenly became cruelly fleeting. Winters ever longer, until summer and winter became indistinguishable.

I didn't fear the darkness of a different kind enveloping me anymore with a curious clarity. And, although I longed for warmth,

I felt grateful for solace; coldness that numbed my emotions and warped-time within a clockwork but mysterious universe.

Strange, my earliest memory, was sitting on my grandma's knee, fascinated by two red pieces of long, triangular card attached in the middle by a kiss pin on a white round Dairylea® lid.

A toy clock, but knowing nothing about time, its relentless march, how fast those fingers would spin. The onset of a long, cold, dark winter that became eternal, impinging on that last ray of hope; the dwindling golden glint of the pendulum of time as it swung in rhythm with its hypnotic tick.

Such niggling and joyous memories of precious moments encapsulated in time, and the countdown had begun. When would it stop? How long would I live?

I thought I knew that answer and might have had a desperate plan beyond logic. But what was I thinking? Was I indestructible and fearless as I raced ever faster, steadily gained momentum on a downward spiral to oblivion?

I wouldn't remember calling my best friend and telling him what I was about to do, or my other friend who left me in tears and said, "You won't do anything daft, will you?"

What a question that was. I wasn't OK.

Section II

OTHER REALMS

2.

BEYOND THE WORLD

*U*naware of my acceleration into the unknown, the sky's no longer blue, but grey. My greatest fear, being alone, made me strive to reach the stars and other prizes beyond reach, or meaningless.

The deluded notion of being in harmony with nature drove the fulfilling moments in meeting zany challenges. Believing I was in control, despite being wild and wise as I knew how to count. But I was on a countdown to self-destruct, and an imminent launch.

At the mercy of gravity now, and so tired as I succumbed to the tide. Swept away in a strange, unknown and unique orbit; my lonely path, analogous to a renegade meteor, hurtling through space, ever faster, ever further away, I became lost; ever colder as I yearned for warmth, to see golden rays of sunshine.

I wanted to freeze time, unable to halt its inexorable march, salvage precious moments I craved to savour, forever in a race against time. Frightened, but bold amid frantic diligent efforts to rescue a human soul. To wrench them back from the brink of oblivion as the raging turmoil abates.

Grateful, but I'm slipping ever further out of reach. No-one could catch me now. The renegade meteor, well on its way, as I rocketed to a new reality. The journey had begun to other realms, beyond the esoteric boundary of tangible, materialistic life.

To mysterious places that had beckoned for so long. Had I reached the twirling, twinkling stars? A place where dreams and reality reside as separate, sometimes entwined entities.

Unfathomable meanings to belabour or disregard as the beautiful, intricate cosmos continued to tick. Its occupants continued playing their parts. In the places they had always belonged. But without me now.

My brother had called the now speeding ambulance, blue lights flashing, sirens mercilessly piercing the air.

Dad followed with a foot to the floor. His car in hot pursuit, unable to let go or bear to be any distance from me, desperately hoping, asking why, while they wonder whether I was alive or dead, trying to not contemplate the latter.

Had the demons won? Took me from this world? Or was it a more divine power in a fight between good and evil, against time and fate?

The world I had transited from contained loved ones, bitterly upset. Stunned into a static state of shock with ironically racing thoughts as they tried to contemplate, cling on to hope.

Then a family entourage, huddled round, congregating for support. Trying to find out what had happened; to understand, while compelled to watch and listen to the rhythm, the lifeline trace on the ECG (electro cardiogram) in unbearable suspense, as they try to grasp the raw reality.

As they relish and gain comfort in the uncertainty whilst trying to embrace the enormity. The realisation I may have gone forever; at least the person they knew now before them, their body still warm, soaking up the sorrow; the tears in a cold world. Plugged in, connected to tubes, electrode pads providing the only means of communication.

Struggling to accept whilst savouring each second, knowing my beating heart, my life, that thin line represented all of me, and that at any moment, my heart may cease to beat, heralding the end of my life on Earth. How was that possible? Where was I?

My unique orbit, my escape velocity so great I had left that physical world. Onto another path, and in transit to other realms whilst my physical body in stasis. In infinite deep sleep, with stillness far deeper than any trance, dormant and waiting to perish or emerge from suspended animation, like a butterfly from a chrysalis.

They and I perceiving sensations as distinct realities, in altered guises, by virtue of subjective awareness of worlds, as a nurse implores my dad to fetch more family.

"Whatever you do, don't turn off the machine!" his tearful reply as he left me. Fearful I may fade further, but not knowing I had already departed that world in tumultuous disarray.

My physical self at X and Y coordinates on a logical, three-dimensional geometric earth as I lay. Where was my soul, my mind, my consciousness — the very essence of me and all that defines me?

My mind was beyond-all-reach, adrift in a vast ocean, far from the cruel world, the relentless tug of war, the battle to save me.

Science, medicine, would that be enough or shall divine higher powers ultimately decide my fate, perhaps my fate, more complex than that, the question: How much of a fighter? How determined; can anyone reach me from far beyond this physical dimension?

My brain swelling, nervous system in trauma, yet deep within the depths, my mind was active, although not aware. The next 48 hours, critical and incognisant of many doing their utmost to save me from the brink of oblivion.

Relentless efforts of doctors and nurses who worked frantically. Rushed around, chasing the glimmers of hope. In contrast, prayers, and words from priests of several religious denominations gave support with faith. Efforts, regardless of whether I'm beyond rescue, at the end of my life.

It is hard to grasp or comprehend the magnitude of those emotions. Or imagine how heart-wrenching and distressing it must have been. To see and hear the last rites uttered for someone so dear.

Were those words of pure faith absorbed, lost in the ether, or were they like ripples created by raindrops falling into a pond? Ripples sent out to the universe to reverberate to the heavens, to God himself?

I was on the edge of now confounding, mystifying realms, the cusp of a bewilderingly complex labyrinthine world from which return infinitely difficult, or even taking one tiny step.

Immense obstacles, challenges of profound importance to

brave and endure as survival or doom is at stake. The depths or upward to the stars? To escape or dwell in that complex maze within a grander, intricate maze, with doors as portals to fresh pastures – not for me, but I yearn.

Lush pastures, others, barren, devoid of comfort, toward dead ends. Empty closets of despair, trapdoors to dark, terrifying oblivion, opening and enveloping me as I became caught up in the essence of warped-time, although beyond time and physical perception: a new reality. Time has no concept or value now.

It's nothing like eternal winter in the previous world. The sunlight of another day struck my face, my eyes, like an alarm clock, but more subtle, tame, silent. Exhausted, motionless, dazed, I daren't move because of strange bewilderment; try not to contemplate anything as I survey the horizon and the ground.

The landscape, bland, desolate and inhospitable, resembles desert; except for where dark, distant peaks met high, wispy, white clouds in an unblemished, deep blue sky, like an ocean trying to cool a blazing golden yellow ever rising sun; a furnace that has baked the ground and the tarmac road beneath me and the stony, jagged wall behind me.

An immense cliff of brownish red rock, so high I cannot see the top. And surrounded by orange, brown sandstone.

Had I fallen onto that dusty tarmac road? It is weird and scary on my own, unable to move and drained by the power of the sun mercilessly beating down from high.

I lay motionless on the roadside at the foot of that sheer rock wall, facing the uneven horizon beneath a now cloudless-blue sky. It's hot; I yearn to revel in the glorious sunshine.

In a strange limbo, in a lowly, unknown place that evoked feelings of emptiness, fear, and despair. I had reached the bottom, but on a trajectory beyond the physical world. It continues without me as I realise I am in need, injured, by a road accident in Malta, a place an ex-girlfriend admired.

An ambulance with a red cross painted on the side arrives for me. Intense, blue-white light illuminates all but annoyed, as I'm taken from that sunny place, into darkness, on board the ambulance, on the stretcher.

The doors close, shutting out the warm daylight, annoying me further, but I feel terrible and lost. It's warm; I'm so thirsty, in desperate need of a drink. So weak, as if fading away.

Befuddled and unable to comprehend fast chatter. A foreign dialect, like Spanish, and interesting as the ambulance follows the road, gently rocks and sways. The bed is cool against my skin, and I smell clinical smells. The ambulance men's chatter stops and continues as they speak again.

I cannot speak back or even open my eyes. My thirst now consuming, overpowering me, but I'm not frightened as I sense myself falling into an ever deeper sleep. Calm as I rest my weary mind, but still so thirsty.

Sensing the ambulance is in motion and travelling at high-speed as I hear the shrill noise of the siren. I enter a state of utter comfort unperturbed by the gentle swaying, descents then ascents. Onward to an unknown destination, dwindling, fading as I become unable to contemplate or care.

I emerge in another place, but didn't recall arriving anywhere. And, while I experience altered perceptions and unfathomable, deep sorrow, my eyes were closed, yet open somewhere in my mind, in a mysterious realm, as Fleetwood Mac, *Little Lies* plays. Will I ever wake, return to the world?

Was the ambulance really in Malta? Or the world I had departed? Maybe it was my limited perception of the actual journey to hospital, I don't know. Regardless, the turmoil exchanged for other battles and pain.

3.

ANGELS AND STARS

*S*uch strange, exciting confusion and wonder as I stand in awe on a firmament up high. Intrigued, too, surrounded by white all around — clean and serene. *Am I in heaven?* It isn't how I had imagined.

Mesmerised by the stars twinkling magically in the black night sky. So high and way beyond the clouds, but it seems one could nearly reach up and touch the stars, or poke them with a long staff. Well, the large stars that seem close, yet not quite reachable.

To be there, high in the heavens, instils tremendous warm feelings of excitement and electric joy. I am puzzled but pleased, though. School friends are there – but not accompanying me – they are gods.

In the other world, both of them exceptional athletes, I considered them the two best lads at sports in the entire school. The fastest runner and best footballer, others, including me, tried to aspire to their level.

The athletic sprinter, Mercury, and the other, Cupid. Mercury has pure blonde hair and wears a magnificent shining robe of white; but the blondness and whiteness becomes a mere blur that merges into a white streak, as that god darts around at unrivalled superspeed no mortal or god can match.

He can get anywhere in an instant with just one flap of the pure white wings that adorn both ankles, making him fleeting, swift with great agility.

Cupid is as prolific, but in a unique sense. With a white quiver of pure white arrows attached to his back, and possesses a magic of his own. People begged for Cupid's attention, for him to take aim and strike them with one of his arrows, and adoring crowds follow. Unstirred by advances, the deity's face, serious but full of joy.

He frequently reached to his quiver and gracefully placed an arrow in its bow to shoot them up into the stars. It was a wondrous sight. The stars glowed more intensely and pulsated; hearts pounded with besotted true love. The arrows never fell and always reached their targets — the stars and lucky hearts.

Mortals, and sometimes even angels, gasped in awe and admiration at Cupid's aiming skills. No-one admires me in that dwelling place for wondrous super-beings. My presence puzzled and intrigued me; I am there too, but far from wondrous.

In stark contrast, I was Plutonium Man. An ominous character who fascinated me in a favourite comic: DC Comics. (May 1976) *Metal Men,* as a kid. I feared plutonium, a radioactive element, and its association with nuclear bombs.

Very slow as I'm heavy. It's extremely difficult to walk. I cannot run. Inabilities that deeply saddened and frustrated me, as I yearned for admiration. Pitifully, I had no skill, and could not boast any prowess.

I envied Cupid and Mercury being so nimble on their feet. It's as though I didn't belong there, a mere spectator, an admirer of things that I cannot ever become? Of friends who had become gods and achieved acclaim.

They're worthy of approaching the angels beneath the stars. I'm so near to the angels, but so far. In awe of the magnificent white staggered stage, like a staircase of shallow steps, each stage is for an angel. Twenty-two staggered platforms of sparkling white marble where 22 angels in heaven slept.

The 22nd angel belonged on the highest platform. The other angels slept on the lower platforms, descending to number one, where the most beautiful number one angel slept.

But it was a matter of opinion, taste, and desire. They're visions of loveliness, perfect beings with the purest hearts. Profound captivating beauty, and faces that can compel and hypnotise anyone to instant love. A mere gaze upon their faces is an ultimate prize.

To earn an angel's heart required immense skill, poise, and concentration, a hard task; a feat impossible for mortals. The heavenly prize, fuelled by desire and necessity to shoot the stars from the heavens, then catch them.

A star for an angel's heart and nothing less! A precious prize, as each star encompassed infinite beauty of its own, a genuine gift in exchange for the love of an angel.

My special gun for making the stars fall intrigues me, but I'm not sure what it shot, or how it worked. A perfect aim and poise for any hope; pinpoint accuracy for the star to disappear and fall to the ground.

I tried and tried in vain to hit them, but was a hopeless shot. Cupid and Mercury, in contrast, shoot even the smallest stars from the sky effortlessly and had a lot of fun and romance.

The stars aren't as precious to them as to me, as I longed to get an angel's heart. But the task seemed impossible. Perseverance led to delight, though, as I shot at a line of emerald green stars.

Hitting one, and knowing I had because it disappeared. Elated and cannot believe my luck, as I aimed again, at the next star in the line, and it too disappeared.

I focus and carry on shooting at the stars and hit 12 stars, one after the other. Ecstatic with excitement as a sizeable crowd gathered nearby because of my unexpected success and apparent skill.

These will please the angels, although green, and the largest in the sky. So the easiest to hit, but associated with bravery, and I hit 12 stars!

To my dismay, specks of light appear where the stars had been, as they gradually reappear. It seems cruel as spectators gasped. No longer did they have animated expressions, but pitiful as they roll their eyes and walk away. The emerald green stars weren't precious and wouldn't impress the angels.

The blue topaz-coloured stars were considerably smaller than the green stars. Next smallest, the red that shone the most magnificently, emitting a ruby-red glow. The blue and red stars symbolised hearts, and were more exquisite; precious.

I didn't give up at trying to hit the stars. My ultimate goal, please and win an angel's heart. Any angel to love, such determination driven by an insatiable yearning.

Eventually, I shoot down and retrieve both a red star and a blue star; achieve success and acclaim. Proud, and in humbling delight, I become excited as I approach the staggered platforms to present my prize.

I cannot possibly approach the highest angel, or the prettiest number one angel. My gift may have seemed meagre, as the gods and everyone else presented them with the most stars. I loved and pined for every one of them but preferred one particular angel.

Uncanny, she slept at the same platform number as my nan's house, number seven. That angel, my favourite as she had such beautiful eyes, long brown shimmering hair and lips I craved to touch upon mine in a soft kiss; a smile that made my heart pound and melt.

As I walk over to the chosen angel, as quickly as I can and careful not to attract attention of rival and swifter admirers presenting their stars, I hope rivals won't beat me to my ultimate prize, or spoil the precious moment.

My excitement mounts as I near the platform, to present her with a cool blue star and a ruby-red star, a spectacular prize.

Sheer beauty, a perfect complexion, and seductive brown eyes twinkle and reflect like mirrors as I give the very stars to her. Gazing upon and my eyes meeting that number seven angel filled my heart with love and bliss as my face beamed a smile of joy; overwhelmed with emotions.

All I can give, and all of me totally hers. I belonged to her; would have given anything for her. But had given even the stars in the sky, as symbols of my heart. Pining, transfixed by her face: perfect, pale, sweet and unblemished.

She looks sleepy as her lips open, then elongate to a gentle, lovely smile. To my dismay, she closes her eyes and falls asleep. My efforts were in vain. Should I wake her, or did her heart belong to more worthy gods?

Despondent with an aching heart, I walked away from the

angels, towards a large opening as M|A|R|R|S', *Pump Up the Volume* plays with Asian style singing.

A young Asian lady with black, shiny, tied back hair and dressed in a long, elegant multicolour sari came to me. She's holding a large white plastic open-topped container as she approaches.

Alarmed and confused by the vessel's contents as I look in and see a dark-red heart beating; the chambers moved, expanded and contracted, pumping blood. The lady sings the line in the song and offers me the heart. I am bemused but accept the gift, and hold it in my hands; it's slippery, warm and moist.

It continues to beat. *How can I show gratitude for this precious gift?* I cannot remember what I did with the heart. It reminds me of things I had experienced in the other world, in the butcher's shop I worked. Was the heart symbolic of something?

To visit a place so divine is an ultimate privilege. *Am I only a visitor? A naughty intruder, with so many inhibitions?* Reluctant, as I leave the angel's sleeping compartment. Melancholic and dejected, to have failed in my quest to get an angel's heart.

And to leave gods that were once friends. *I do not belong there,* as I step onto a white path, white sky in front and above; it's warm and uncannily no breeze.

Beckoned and coaxed by dance music, Was (Not Was), *Walk the Dinosaur* that becomes progressively louder, as I walk along the pathway, and on a gentle descent. Into a vast expanse, toward the music, and an intermittent glow of coloured lights.

Excitement as I reach an opening beside an enormous dancefloor. People in smart nightclub attire skip around in patterns, across the multicoloured, chequered dancefloor as dazzling lights shine from beneath the floor. Flash in sequence to the music; alluring and truly spectacular. It's a great place.

More excited, my friend Jamie is there. A good pal of mine, and one of the best dancers I knew. As I remember going out to nightclubs, and loved dancing, but feel awkward as I cannot dance now; and so heavy as I am Plutonium Man.

The dancefloor clears, except for Jamie. It's great to see him, but funny; he's standing on five razor-blades, sharp edge facing upwards. He waves and cups his hands to his mouth to project his voice, "You're on Mars, P, I can kill a dinosaur with five razor-blades."

Wow, Mars, at the chequered disco as the song about the dinosaur plays again. Many dressed in smart nightclub clothes emerge from the shadows on both sides of the dancefloor. They skip across it in a crisscross pattern as a dinosaur appears out of nowhere.

I look up at it in astonished disbelief. Someone's riding it. *How have they got up there?* The dark-brown reptile is a brontosaurus. A long, thick tapered neck, a rounded head, a long tail; like in the dinosaur book I had as a kid.

Intrigued, but sad, I'm so heavy, immobile and unable to dance, despite immense effort. I can only manage a slow walk and tired and unwell; distraught and frustrated by my ineptness compared to everyone else.

A bright light to my right instils curiosity; I turn and approach. See silhouette figures. Familiar people, but I cannot think why.

Perplexed and tormented, being in that disco in another realm is fabulous. I'm reluctant to leave that fun, funky place, although I cannot dance. I soon recognise the figures as my mom with three of her sisters, my aunties.

They're standing by a door in a wide corridor. *Is it a hospital ward?* Light shines on them, illuminates them, they beckon me, call me with their hands.

Should I return to my family or stay in the wondrous, but lonely place, torn as I realise it's a choice? Yet, I couldn't go back. Beguiled, intrigued by adventures that had just begun, I didn't intend to leave the party.

I choose to join my family, though, and love them dearly, but am so ill and weak; it's so difficult to walk. *I won't reach them in time, but don't wish to upset them. I'll walk toward the family figures.*

They seem pleased and shout words of encouragement. It's hopeless, but I continue walking toward the light, and the door despite pain and being slow, laborious. It closes as I reach it, and the sound of sobbing fades like ever-distant church bells as the light illuminating my family dissipates to darkness.

The door, as a portal, closed. So, I stay in the other realm. It doesn't seem possible to return, though. *I'll have to find another way. If I choose to return.*

Again, I look to my right. Excited and curious as lights flash in a variety of colours. *Disco lights, or an alien spaceship?* The party will continue as a cool breeze blows from another opening behind me; I made the right choice as I turn around to investigate.

And, as I emerge from the opening into a vast, desolate, icy wilderness of harsh howling winds, frost, and snow, *I am somewhere different. On another planet,* as I think of my mom and aunties, but too late. We are in separate ever-distant, mysterious, unreachable places.

Along the snowy path, I trudge. A cup with steaming liquid on a table near a large white upright freezer delights me as I taste delicious, hot chocolate. I drink this before climbing into the freezer that's so comfortable as I fall asleep.

The most beautiful woman I've ever seen opens the freezer door. She holds my hands; guides me from the freezer. Stunned by the sights and a glacial, white, barren landscape.

Strange, I'm not cold. Surely my indecision about whether to come back to my family isn't in vain. The reason for that match, made in the stars, as shining jewels in heaven.

We embrace, hold each other tight, forming a magical bond, entwined. By looking into her eyes, I instantly fall in love. *She's the one I must marry.*

My heart belonged to that woman with lovely ebony skin, blue eyes with white icy flecks, so enchanting. A most fleeting gaze is priceless, forever not long enough, an embrace like a dream.

Such powerful emotions, desires, as if besotted. Who was she? How can any being be so beautiful to evoke such deep love? Am I a worthy suitor? Forsooth, I had to be, as contemplating anything less would break my heart and torture my soul.

I was unaware that stunning woman belongs to a race that possesses superhuman strength, an alien civilisation that had waged war and conquered many.

4.

ICEMAN

*F*inally, I become happy. Glad to become Iceman's friend, too, with a family bond of togetherness and deep love for his daughter. In those realms, Iceman, a companion, and ultimate protector who takes me under his wing, and to mysterious places and other worlds.

He has the means and technology to travel through time and to other places. Iceman travels back in time with me to 1924. To an unfamiliar place, but I'm on Earth.

We are in a street covered in untouched, pristine, freshly fallen snow. Dim streetlights create an incandescent, crystalline glow as snowflakes fall and settle on the ground and on abandoned, desolate shops on both sides of the street.

Iceman leads the way. Into a building, with a long white corridor that's like Bilston Baths. Alarmed by the noise of a growling dog. *Is it fighting and vicious?* We walk along the corridor toward it.

Below us is a pit with white walls, like a squash court; I see the dog, a bull terrier, writhing, jumping. It even attacks, dents, and throws a metal tray into the air.

I fear dogs, especially that breed, but my anxieties ease, as another door blows open on the pit. Biting cold, howling winds from outside instantly tame the dog.

Further along the corridor, I hear a door opening and shutting, buffeted by the wind. We go through the door and enter a dark, squalid, deserted room, a butcher's shop, I assume, because of the white marble countertops, tarnished by dirt and time. *Why have we visited that place?*

So cold, desolate, harsh and with its ghosts perpetuating and instilling fear, but I did not fear. Iceman is my friend, and we're only visiting. His mere presence caused the snow and ice-storms, a mini ice-age like in his distant world.

A bitterly cold planet between two remote suns, in another galaxy I didn't know. But I'd seen his conquering wrath, immense, merciless power.

He appears to be an ordinary human being. Young, stocky, muscular with black, short, but wild, curly hair, even sounded human, with a soft but deep, jovial voice. Kind, hazel eyes with twinkling, white flecks are the only alien distinction.

In the old world I wanted a warm, beige sheepskin fur coat like he wears. This shields and disguises his almighty power. Whenever Iceman became angry and takes off his coat, desire for conflict evokes a transformation into an immensely strong, formidable being.

Sheer fury and power, and an instinct to conquer, destroy, inflict pain, entire worlds shudder, shake with each thunderous step he treads.

Indomitable with terrifying force, the might of 100 men encapsulated in one being. He could halt and knockout a rampaging rhino with his fist. Knows every fighting move.

Iceman is a superhuman, alien being. But is more formidable, if cold, as thick, cubic, opaque, crystalline shaped white icicles with edges and points sharper than the sharpest blades and stronger than the most lethal daggers form on every muscle and part of his body. Icicle spikes harder than diamond make him invulnerable.

His hair turns as white as frost and power to slice through the hardest iron with one strike from his hands, yet tame, calming, mysterious eyes that glow like the sun. Hazel, darkening to black then turning white and glowing as beacons whiter than the whitest purest snow as he focusses.

It's an honour to be his friend. Solace at last, companionship, and love in an unknown place in an unknown, and mysterious place in the universe. I'm happy although so far away, and I looked forward to visits from Iceman and his family, to whom I became well acquainted.

Particularly the mother who was friendly and nice to talk to, and I idolised the daughter, and intended to marry her.

We intended to live between worlds, on planet Earth and sometimes on the distant icy world. And, I'm glad to be back on Earth, years in the future, and not in 1924. I even lived in an enormous house with thick, solid wood, doors. The walls, decorated with dark wood stained, carved timber; so elaborate and ornate, as were the ceiling beams. It's a delightful house for my future wife and I to live.

They travelled from their world in a long, white-coloured, old-fashioned open-top flying car I avidly watch as it descends against an overcast sky. But they don't need spacesuits. Their sheepskin coats shield them from the frigid temperatures of outer space.

Eager expectance as I await super-beings, my fiancée, and sweetheart, and the car lands. She opens her car door, turns to me and smiles; my heart pounds. *A gift from the angels for the stars I gave them?*

They get out of the car and take off their sheepskin coats as I wait by the door of my house and greet them. "Come in," as they enter and I hug my adorable sweetheart; she kisses me on the cheek.

It's wonderful to see her, and we stroll to a sizeable living room. My sweetheart and I sink into a comfortable, thick, dark-brown sofa.

We clasp our hands together as the parents sit in the matching chairs and then lean and perch forward as I made polite conversation.

It was difficult knowing what to say; their culture and lifestyle are so unlike that on Earth. Nervous with the awkwardness, but that didn't matter; I loved the daughter so much.

Her grip on my hand tightened, and she looked at me with her enchanting eyes. I so wanted to lean forward and kiss those soft, irresistible lips, and imagined our wedding day. The wondrous vision in my mind of a perfect, longed for day. A day I had romanticised and envisioned.

Mystified by the sudden change, as the parents became agitated. Upset by the way we held hands, our lingering, longing stares and affirmations of affection. Different and conflicting cultures as we express love.

Iceman abruptly stands up. "We're leaving. The wedding's off," as he reaches the door.

Her loving hand unclasps mine as she places a soft tender kiss on my lips and she whispers, "I'm sorry."

The mother stands up. Tears glisten in my sweetheart's eyes as we both stand and hold each other tightly.

"Wait, don't go, stay." As I seek to prolong the embrace, hoping it's not the last one or to contemplate the sorrow of parting. We hold hands. Look into each other's eyes; I remember the first, lingering and enchanting stare.

Indubitably, not the last time I gaze into her lovely eyes. Distraught as the handgrip loosens again. A state of sheer disbelief at their sudden churlishness as they storm out of the house. Get into their car, and the engine roars as they leave.

Anxious, as I watch their stern facial expressions, looking forwards, hoping for one of them to turn to look at me; none did. Even my sweetheart didn't avert her gaze to mine or even wave as they ascend into the sky, higher and higher, destined for their home planet.

Stunned and upset at the sheer speed of events, unbelievable. I sit on the floor, slumped against the door to not only gather my thoughts, but to surmise what's gone wrong. I loved my future wife so much, missed her and ached to be in her presence again, to wrap my arms around her.

Once they realise how hasty and unreasonable they have been, they'll return. Heart-wrenching events, but I dared not even contemplate what may happen next, the fate of myself, our planet.

Half an hour later, I hear the roar of the car engine and a car door slam. Then the dreaded bang on the door, and I stare, ponder. One knock, alas, excitement precedes disappointment: he hadn't brought my fiancée and didn't stay to talk. I didn't hear her sweet voice.

Still, I open the door. *No.* Iceman is hurriedly speeding off into the sky's upper atmosphere yet again.

A white piece of jagged notepaper pinned to the door filled me with dread. Written in large, black, capital letters "PAUL MUST DIE!"

Oh no, but surely, he doesn't mean that; I'm no match for the aliens. The strongest human on Earth was no match, even 100 times stronger. The alien ice race was immensely strong, their society much more technologically advanced than our own.

They want to destroy Earth because of me! Their rash actions are utterly unfair. *How can my sweetheart and future wife leave so easily?*

Such troubling thoughts, trying to rationalise, knowing there's no escape from a mortal enemy, once my only protector. *What can I do to defend myself against Iceman? I cannot reason with him. He wants to kill me! Do I deserve to die?* Iceman was my friend. I was on the verge of marriage. Now I'm doomed.

Out of options, I mentally prepare for an inevitable and fatal confrontation. *Friends might help me, my tough friends. Paul is a best friend, a year older than me. Rocky from work is tough, well-built and often boasted of his fighting achievements.*

Still, I'm not optimistic. Even at the front of an immense brick building, I assume, is a military complex.

With lined formations of camouflage-coloured army tanks with huge, long artillery barrels assembled in front of me. In addition, armed soldiers, and police officers in face of, and in-between, the tanks, primed, and ready to take aim; defend me and the planet, forces determined to repel Iceman.

Impressive, and military aircraft are on standby, from many nations. Overwhelmed and encouraged by the support. Particularly as Paul is with me and his tough older brother. *But the mightiest force on Earth cannot protect me.*

Iceman came as expected, descends from space in his car. Military jets zoom past the car, escort it to the ground. He lands in front of the tanks, in defiance of Earth's might.

And, as Iceman stays in the car. There is camaraderie among the troops, and loyal friends.

"Don't worry, Paul. We'll protect you, all these tanks, soldiers, police, the planes, and friends. To get to you, he'll have to get through us, no chance!"

I didn't share their optimism. Just did not wish to contradict or dash their hopes. I had seen Iceman's power, watched him conquer and destroy worlds.

Iceman opens his car door. Nonchalant, as he climbs out, causing those who didn't know him to gasp at his brazenness in the face of Earth's best weaponry and resolve. He smiles, then stares at the obstacles in front of me; several tanks, many soldiers. Wild, raging eyes glow as Iceman takes his coat off, transforms into the ultimate weapon.

All alarming, more so as he boldly walks; ever briskly, stomps, and barges his way through the tanks, tipping one over longways as if it's a caber. He knocks another 30ft away with one swipe of his icy hand, before bashing and pummelling another as if it's a cardboard box.

He continues, straight towards me, despite the impact of heavy calibre machine-gun fire from helicopter gunships. The guns rattle as they launch flaming projectiles that hit Iceman and the ground; making him angrier and stronger.

An air-to-ground missile launches from a distant jet. The troops watch in false hope as it menaces, approaches, roars ever louder. Iceman opens his arms and smiles as he lets it explode on him, as a show of might and defiance. An immense explosion and fireball absorbed and extinguished in a microsecond.

The message: no escape from his wrath! The icy spikes pulsate, glow white as winds howl, ever colder, thick, intense, relentless snow, a blizzard.

My friend, Paul, stands firm in front of me, brave and valiant as he smiles, offers protection. He punches Iceman several times. It has no effect. Iceman punches Paul back in the stomach, winding him, and puts him out of action.

He holds his stomach and lowers his head as Iceman punches him again, in the face. Paul falls to the floor and becomes unconscious. His brother tries a subtler approach. "Why do you want to kill Paul? He's got no chance against you. What's the point of killing him?"

Iceman does not respond; he comes straight for me and punches me repeatedly in the stomach and the face. The pain is excruciating. I fall on the spot and close my eyes, hoping Iceman will stop the brutal attack.

Luckily, he does. He might have thought I was dead, job done. I wake up in hospital, in intense pain and sore, but relieved that Iceman stopped when he did. Chuffed too, Paul and his brother come to my bedside, try to cheer me up, lift my spirits.

Downbeat, they put on a brave face, although limping, hobbling, and bruised and battered as they hold their stomachs. "We have ruptured spleens, but don't worry about Iceman," Paul says.

But they've realised I am doomed, and the planet. Iceman is such a powerful adversary, retaliation is futile, impossible to fight; he has no weaknesses or vulnerabilities. He could defeat 1000 men with one slap of his hand or even by him removing his coat.

Sadly, and inevitably, the only choice is to accept the punishment, endure the torment. Nothing anyone can do, except for hope. Hope that reason will prevail. This is false optimism, there's no reason to hope.

Iceman soon learnt I still lived and waited outside the hospital, below my upstairs window. He knows I'll leave the ward eventually, and as I recover and walk outside; he continued to practise his rage. Relentless persecution with one sole aim: obliterating me.

Merely destroying me is not enough! A quick death is inadequate, too kind, rather a slow build-up, to inflict as much pain as possible to monger fear and prolong the suffering, the terror; as I wait, knowing at any moment, the next attack may be the last.

Again, he puts me in hospital, but not fatally injuring me. Iceman had the power and brute strength to kill me instantly; well, that is what I believed. Was I more resilient than he thought? Did he want to kill me, though? Or even couldn't? The ordeals continued. All efforts to repel the attacks were woefully inadequate.

After a while, God intervenes and sentences Iceman to

10-years of hard labour on a distant planet. I become elated and so grateful to God for giving me respite, peace after persecution, but I still couldn't escape the icy wrath.

Iceman's brother comes after me, seeks and is intent on revenge for my part in causing his brother's absence. He's a much more powerful adversary than Iceman, impossible to reason with, savage and ruthlessly cruel. In despair, I try to evade the persecutor; it's futile.

So contemplate a hopeless end as I sit, cornered and alone in a dimly lit jumbo jet. Abandoned long ago, dust suspended in the air and on the seats. Harsh, howling winds blowing across a frosty, white, barren landscape and the swirling snow of a blizzard, I see from the aged, dirt obscured semi-opaque windows.

Despair as I hear a powerful motorbike engine and see Iceman's brother in a beige fur collared jacket, black leathers, and a horned Viking-like helmet. He races and skids around the plane, leaving tyre tracks in the snow, as I sit in powerless anticipation of an imminent attack, or to starve.

There's no food on the plane. It's long since rotted away and poisoned, although it looks edible. No escape from the impending doom, as I slump back in my dusty airplane seat and close my eyes. But should I clasp my hands together, to pray, as Scarlet Fantastic, *No Memory* plays. A strange song I hadn't ever heard.

Iceman and his brother were formidable enemies and obstacles to love, happiness, and the solace I sought. So alone, as in the past world, I departed. How could I fight such enemies, or begin such a quest? I'm no match for them or any other, to fight or love.

Would my mind find answers? Was I still capable of logic?

5.

MOON AND WATER

I loved the moon in the old world. Yearned for romance under moonlit night skies, and scenic, watery locations. It's strange and exciting to be above the sea, on a platform in the sky. A lower part of heaven and a special privilege, although different to the wonderful place I experienced earlier.

The surroundings aren't as white or as clean. Partly because of a black night sky, but still upon a white platform of clouds, they're spongy as I partially sink into them. The texture is warm around refreshingly cool air, a pleasant sensation.

Openings on the white platform allowed beings to gaze upon the Earth from the sky. Inquisitive as I look through one hole in the clouds, peer below, to the Earth and upon a vast, black sea.

Intrigued by a ship that looks like an ocean liner on the enormous expanse of water. Black water of the sea, glistening moonlight and white light shining from many portholes added a yellow tinge to the waves.

The water's calm, just the sounds of the gentle movements of the sea. It's a deserted scene with no people, or landmass, only shimmering blackness.

I miss the earlier part of heaven, other worlds, the love for my wife that never was and tormented by loneliness as I remember the angels and their magnificent beauty. *Why am I in this place? Will I see the angels again? If I did, how can I impress them? Might they be watching me as I sit, pondering?*

I yearned for them, even gazing upon them for the briefest of moments, and was always thinking of ways to please and impress the angels; it's my dearest, and only mission. But, competition is so intense.

Most mortal men had the same aims. What can I do? Something no other suitor can? Something so amazing, it sets me apart from the rest, shows my loving heart. Above the sea, though, there are no stars to give, or any gifts.

I become excited, though, by a marvellous idea that might achieve my aims, and not just please the angels, but delight them. Fill them with wonder and maybe instil a desire to meet me, who made so much selfless effort; thought into a heavenly task to woo and wow?

A rainbow might get the angels' attention. It's just very difficult, perhaps impossible, at night. *Can I still succeed and ascend to the stars? Be with the angels,* as I gather up various coloured transparent precious stones and lay them on the cloud floor near the opening over the water.

I adjust the stones' positions carefully until they pick up the reflected rays of sunlight from the moon; to create dazzling, pure, bright colours, like mini stars as the moonlight entered and filtered through the crystals.

And, I sit by the hole in the clouds. To my delight, and the angels', a rainbow formed in a perfect arch. The coloured beams of light entered the black water below. Instilled with pride, I devised such a method of forming a beautiful spectacle of nature: a rainbow at night, although not entirely because of Mother Nature.

A captivating, breath-taking sight before a wondrous sight: the pure, white glow against a black sky, as the angels come from above, and hover for a moment. As they flap their wing's elation grows entwined with ecstatic joy as I gaze upon their beauty.

Lovely faces, incandescently glow in the moonlight, and perfect lips mortal men dreamed of kissing shine. Their gorgeous eyes evoke instant love. Long, flowing hair in a range of colours, blonde, brunette, black, and red strands of hair parting and swirling as they gracefully move.

The softest, gentlest of breezes, as soft as the tiniest bird from their white feathered wings. And, soft, flapping sounds suffused with the sound of the waves as they sit around, by the hole, and beside me.

White, silk shimmering dresses complement shapely legs, some kneel, and sit back on their legs, another sits with their legs outstretched and one dangles her legs over the soft edge of the hole. Delighted, they gather round, in awe of what I had created.

Proud, and humble, and elated as I turn to them. "I made this for you." *No mortal or deity would have thought of my idea. Given such a gift or that delight.*

The rainbow looks magnificent. Blessed to see their gentle smiles at the rainbow. *I hope one of them lifts their head, gazes upon me, and smiles.* Saddened, none of them do; more so as the rainbow dissipates. But, to my surprise, one angel lifts their gaze to mine.

Loving, crystal-blue eyes, bluer than the deepest ocean, look into my eyes. As she smiles tenderly, I become lost in swirling whirlpools, as if under a spell of love.

As she opens her wings, I experience sheer joy suffused with adoration as the angels ascend into the sky, toward the moon. The higher they ascend, and with each flap of their wings, the more my heart aches as I yearn to be in their presence. I wish they had taken me with them, to the higher heavens.

Thoughts and visions of the lovely face, perfect complexion, warm blue eyes flood my ravaged mind. *Had she seen my soul, felt the love in my heart, or even read my mind?* My transfixed gaze, as I avidly watch those beloved angels ascend.

Strange, it's as if I am deep underwater watching glorious angels swim to the surface, toward the moon above the water. But I'm in the sky, on the clouds, with air, and the night sky above, the black sea below, and air.

The blackness instils sadness as the rainbow dissipates. It changes from something astoundingly beautiful to something less pleasant to look upon as the coloured bands lose their definition and colour. I realise it's because of sewage leaking from the ship at sea level.

Disheartened, my efforts are in vain for such brief moments of joy. Beauty destroyed by mischief, selfish humankind. Yet, the wondrous spectacle lives on in my mind, the visions of those angels I delighted for such fleeting moments.

I so want to make another rainbow, and I hope that humankind, humanity, misguided, cruel humans; ignorance doesn't selfishly destroy. Although the special feat of making a rainbow at night was akin to mimicking and distorting nature.

Created not by a god, or God himself, but by a transcendental being. Someone who didn't know who they were, only their sole purpose, doing their utmost to bring joy to the angels.

To win just one heart, a divine heart, I know will be true. Yet, content with a mere smile, as these are more precious than gold, even the stars themselves, my survival is a secondary goal, and infinitely less important than trying to bring joy.

I wanted the angels to recognise me as being different, above all other men. Not unfairly classed as a mortal man. Or considered as part responsible when it wasn't me who destroyed the rainbow, or disrespected nature itself.

I sensed a transition and so want the angels to accept, want me, love me, so I become worthy of heaven and of my heart belonging to an angel. I'd shown ingenuity in terms of the loving endearment and had delighted the angels.

As if by magic, I am aboard the ship, inside the open-plan, gigantic vessel. Large vats full of liquid in the centre and at both sides, similar to the plating solution vats at work, where I stand.

Small metallic, light-grey painted cubicles to the sides of the decks intrigue me, present a further ominous mystery, and the unknown destination.

No sailors or people, but in the shadows of subdued light, life-size embossed white figures of saints live on to steer the vessel by telepathy. The ship has a huge red cross medical symbol painted on the side, a hospital ship.

Have the patients survived? There's silence now, apart from the gentle sound of the sea and the occasional distant drip of water onto metallic decks, and my thoughts, as I imagine, screams.

A complex sensation of humbling eeriness makes me shake and focus as I step, precariously along the edge of the large vats, as a test of bravery. I'd rather be in the sky as I listen to lapping waves change, causing a momentary distraction and I glance out at the black sea.

As I look back and forth at the black void, I see more of the ship. There is a girl in one cubicle. She has jet-black, straight, shoulder-length hair; I recognise the features, but a black-and-white guinea pig is in her hands?

Its nose and eyes glistened. The scene, like in the sketch I drew in art class at primary school. I loved art and was proud of my picture.

The girl is motionless except for, she's trying to comfort the guinea pig, as it fidgets. It's so strange, spooky. I decide it's safer to jump into the water than walk along the edges of the vats.

The water's warmer than I expected, and calm as I swim away from the ship. Along an enclosed stretch of water with two other blokes that swim toward me and accompany me.

It's dark except for a distant, white glow, we swim toward. There is metal around us and water droplets trickle from the walls and fall from the ceiling above us with a gentle splashing sound.

It becomes clear I am one of three soldiers on a secret mission. In front of us is a platform.

Seconds later, to my horror, we hear dogs barking behind us. Although tired, I quicken the pace of my stroke and increase my speed as adrenaline reserves kick in, propel me ever closer.

Each stroke, each kick, edging me tantalisingly closer to safety, hopefully away from the swimming canines in relentless pursuit as they snap at us. Just as we approach the platform, nearly within touching distance, a canine grips my boot, but I kick hard.

Luckily, we reach the end of the dark, inland channel, and clamber out onto the platform, into a place resembling an office. I run to an old wooden desk, in the middle of the room, and open its drawers, look for secret papers to aid the war effort.

We freeze though as we hear voices and the engines of a motorboat, cruising along the channel, toward us. Trapped and frantic, there's nothing we can do except face the enemy in unbearably awkward circumstances.

The voices, those of German soldiers who soon mounted

the platform, surrounded and outnumbered us with rifles and handguns; trained on us. The leader is stocky, muscular, with shaved hair, and battle-hardened face, a scar on his cheek to below his jawline, and wide, hate-filled eyes as he glares.

I stride to the front of the desk, toward him as he said in a German accent, "We meet at last. Do you know who I am?"

"No, should I?"

His subordinate soldiers laugh. He looks across at a fellow, meeker soldier. "Tell him."

"The boxing champion of Germany." The soldier stands more upright with pride. I stay still and silent as the boxing brute walks to the desk, opens a draw and gets out a map of Germany, which he studies then points to a place, presses a stubby finger on a town, "Did you release 20,000 fleas and ticks on this town?"

A sane man facing such an adversary would've lied.

"Yes." I said with pride and defiance.

On an aerial mission, I released the parasites over the land to irritate the Germans.

"You're brave, but foolish. Men, take him to the platform." Three German soldiers prod my back with their guns. "Walk." Leading me to a wooden podium as the boxer puts a boxing glove on his hand.

I step up and intuitively know I must endure, and that people rarely stayed conscious after being thumped half as hard as he'd hit me, an intruding enemy soldier.

How can I psychologically prepare for the punch? With anger and defiance, as his fist hit me like a hammer to my head. Shaken, but I still stood. Defiant as I stared into the boxer's wild, but surprised, eyes. Did he think: *Who is this? How can he not fall? Or even shudder… is he human?*

Gasps of surprise and muttering echo in the room, but I smile; Iceman's punches hurt more. He hits me again in the stomach. I tense my muscles and don't even flinch.

Unafraid as we stand poised, enemy to enemy, a tense stand-off facing each other. The enemy could have shot us. That would have been too quick, easy.

The soldiers let us go, but prod us with their guns and laugh as we walk toward the water. To swim the way we came, although the dogs await us as they growl. Releasing us is a greater act of nonchalant power, as they force us to face a more intense fear than being shot, even torture.

Reluctantly, we jump into the water and swim back along the channel. *We'll have to face the vicious dogs.* Terrified, but somehow, I outswim the dogs. My heavy boots offer some protection as the dogs nip at my heels.

Drained as I swim in my clothes, but I have hope as I notice a faint blemish of light on a distant horizon. Wearily I swim toward it, through the salty water on a sea of black treacle.

The wind picks up, making the waves lap and spray against my face. *Will I reach the light?* It's so distant; my legs, and arms as heavy as lumps of lead, like when I swam a mile at Bilston Baths.

Each breath, a gift – *If I stop and sink* – *it may be my last.* I make it to a channel of water, though, warmer, calmer water, toward a distant glimmer of light through sea mist, light shining from a distant building on a riverbank.

It's a strenuous, never-ending swim. An immense effort as I clamber out of the water, shivering and tired, so heavy because of my water-logged clothes.

I enter the building, into a labyrinth of white corridors. Thick plush white carpets on the floors and such warmth, contentment, and comfort as I rest on the carpet. More to my delight, I'm in the dwelling place with ladies.

Ravishing, pretty U.S. Navy women? As they walk toward me, longing zeal in their stares. "Aww, such a sweet man." Said a tanned lady with long, blonde wavy hair in a black, silk negligee; her soft accent makes me swoon.

Excited, stunned as a blonde with bobbed hair and a long-haired brunette lies beside me; strokes my hair, teases, and the brunette's lips brush mine. "Where did you come from, sweet man? You're all wet and cold. Let us take off your shirt and pants to dry." Awestruck, I cannot answer.

More ladies approach, focus their attention on me and undress me; as they undo my shirt buttons. One strokes my chest with her fingertips as she kisses my cheek, tantalising and seductive. "Mm, sweet man, you swam to us?"

Her hand wanders ever lower, unfastens my trousers, then reaches even lower, touching me and so sensuously. So aroused, desire, yearnings. I wanted her; I wanted all of them.

Nervy as they focus increased attention on me. *These girls must have fellas,* as I hear a motorboat and shouts, the naval boyfriends. So, I panic.

The girls try to calm me in soft, seductive tones. "Hey, relax, don't worry. We'll look after you."

The voices grow louder, the navy boys rush in and don't take too kindly to my presence, each of them trains their eyes on their girl.

Most of them walk toward their boyfriends, but two stay beside me, one with her arms draped round me, the other with her hand on my chest. Somewhat reluctant as I get up to leave the girls.

Frantic, I run along the corridor, lightning-speed, out of the door, and dive into the black water, submerge and hide underneath a black rubber capsized dinghy.

I hear their muffled voices and wait as long as I dare to swim back. Into the open river, through the darkness toward the sea, relieved to escape. But, I face more sinister terror, buffeted by underwater pressure-waves.

It can only be sharks. The immense power of their fins and tails as they try to bite me. Dread as they're relentless in the enveloping blackness. *Will I survive until dawn?* So tired, swimming into a vast expanse of blackness, I remember the navy girls, but yearn to be with the angels.

I close my eyes and keep swimming, kicking and lifting my arms from the water, my rhythm slowing and hoping for daylight, or to see the moon when I open my eyes. *What time is it?* As I touch a solid object. My stroke halts, my eyes open.

Bright orange flames dance upon the sea. It's a ship. A huge, black, metal structure protruding from the chilly water.

A ship in a warzone, the sea ablaze with burning oil on top of the water, but I clamber onto the ship even though it's tilted and sinking because of being struck by a torpedo. Black water is engulfing the black ship beneath a moody, ravaged black sky.

The orange oil fires, as bright and as hot as the sun, reach upward like long yellow tongues lashing the sky. Acrid grey smoke bellows upwards and lingers across the ominous black, calm sea. A dank setting, the only comfort, the dull part-obscured white reflection from a bright but tarnished full moon, large in the night sky.

So tired, I fear I won't survive that hostile warzone, and hold on to a floating piece of wood in desperation as I drift with the waves. Happy and relieved to look at the sunrise. On a cerise, orange horizon and for a cloudless sky, and to breathe as I'm woken by a noisy engine of a boat.

I wave as it approaches, parting the smooth waves, swaying and bobbing up and down on the blue water. Firm, brawny hands grasp my shirt, pull me from the water, over the side of the boat, onto the deck with a thump.

The smells, so distinct, pungent, fish, engine oil, and chemicals, but I am glad of the rescue from that chilly, unwelcoming water.

So, I become a passenger at sea on a noisy old boat. Noxious fumes spewing from the unknown cargo, and there's caustic soda on the decks. I don't realise the boat is heading inland, into an estuary, onto a wide river that becomes narrower.

Lush green trees flank either side of the riverbank and help to ease the raging soreness of the burns from the caustic soda. The boat enters an open underground enclosure with high, drab, grey jagged rocky walls on both sides, and above, leading to an incline in the distance as I stand.

Relieved, and pleased to reach dry land, and to leave that toxic smelly boat. *Why has the captain lifted me from the water, saved me, and gave me free passage?* Wary as I jump from the boat, onto dry land and sink into the soggy, silty ground as I walk onto the incline.

The brown soil is great to walk on after being at sea. *But who's there?* The silhouette of figures at the mouth of the cave inlet.

"There he is. Get him." I look in the voice's direction and the figures become distinct.

A scruffy, unshaven old man beside large blue drums, containers and various coloured bottles at the top of the incline being pushed by menacing unknown figures, and white sky beyond them.

Cornered – no escape – I turn to face the menace and step backwards along the incline, entering a grey stone cave. Edge back, but can go no further as I reach behind me, touch the wet jagged stone of the base of the cave inlet.

The gang roll toxic blue drums of chemicals toward me, like the sodium cyanide drums at work. Hurl, poisonous, fizzing and fuming deadly concoctions at me.

Puzzled as my old neighbour is the gang leader, and as he shouts, "You've had too many girlfriends, too much fun... We'll make you suffer." *This couldn't be a motive to inflict such a malevolent, evil attack. What's the real reason?*

Horrified and alarmed as they continue to throw hazardous chemicals. The lethal projectiles hit me, explode on the stone cave wall behind me, splash on me, fizz and dissolve the rock, making ever more noxious toxins. I fall to my knees, cough, and splutter.

Saddened and terrified by the senseless, relentless chemical onslaught. But startled by the dull roar of a loud engine of a large black motorbike. The gang disperses and flees as it speeds toward me. It's great to see a determined, brave friend, Brian, from my (Youth Training Scheme (YTS)) work placement.

A black-purple scarf is over his face to shield him from the toxic fumes. The bike skids to a halt, as chunky tyres skid on the soft soil in a churned semicircle at my feet. "Quick, jump on the back," as the tyres melt and hiss, and we zoom away, swerving past the deadly, rolling drums, leaving the jeering, hostile gang, and that gloomy cave.

Pleased and grateful for that brave, daring rescue at high-speed. Toward daylight with tremendous G-force and acceleration.

Faster and faster as Brian changes gears. Builds speed on the liquid oxygen fuelled motorbike.

There's an exhilarating rush of fresh air, open road. A blue, hazy, but cloudless sky welcoming us, in contrast to the dark, poisonous cave, as we zoom along the coast, and a blue-grey sea with breaking waves, then inland.

We have to refuel, anxious at the distinct possibility of a determined pursuing gang. Frantic as I remove the fuel cap and unsure how much fuel to fill the tank with, I guess.

Continuing inland with a wheelspin and screech of rubber, changing gears, we accelerate to a top speed. "They won't catch us now!" I said. A moment later, the motorbike judders and violently explodes with tremendous force, sending Brian and me hurtling through the air.

We land apart from each other. After overcoming being momentarily dazed, I crawl towards Brian. His eyes are closed, as if asleep. "Thanks, that was awesome... Don't die." Too much fuel was in the tank. It's my fault.

Mixed emotions fill my mind, sadness, and anger whilst amazed Brian rescued me from the chemical gang. I feel terrible. If it weren't for the motorbike explosion, Brian would be okay.

Thoughts and emotions that change to loneliness and despair. But the angels take pity on me, overwhelmed and joyous with my efforts to please them. They grant me a precious gift: one of my dearest wishes and yearned for dreams, and a further heavenly encounter.

6.

AT HEAVEN'S GATES

*I*t seems the most wonderful experience imaginable. I cannot believe I'm in bed with a gorgeous woman. A joy to behold, perfect in every sense, a moment's glance evokes instant eternal love.

We're not in an ordinary bed. It's inclined at an obtuse angle, and well-padded with white material, softer than cotton wool.

To our left are two large, white, elaborate, ornate gates. To the right of these gates, two white marble platforms. On top of these podiums, sublime, perfectly carved statues of pure white marble stand facing each other.

They were 7ft tall, elegant and muscularly defined, partially clothed men, standing poised and stooped with one leg in front of the other. The dormant but magnificent, prolific statues seem to be bodyguards, guarding the gates of heaven.

With immense strength, and named Simon and Garth. They came to life when needed to fight and repel unwelcome, possibly evil intruders. The boldest, craziest demon dared not provoke their wrath.

The woman beside me is like no-one I had ever dreamed of in my wildest dream or fantasy. The epitome of beauty and evokes powerful emotions with deep desires of an intensity never experienced. We are lying side by side.

My arm placed around her and her arm draped around me; as I tingle with excitement, immensely attracted to my newly acquainted partner. It's obvious we are to make love. My male instinct and intuition takes over; passion and desires to quell, and mutually please, but I'm relaxed with no sense of urgency.

I know, though; it signifies a moment I must use my entire

knowledge and experience for any chance of remaining in heaven. Her perfectly shaped body, her breasts look soft and white. She is gorgeous; lovelier than anyone I had ever seen. Long, brown hair embellishes a perfect face, and stunning eyes that captivate and entice. I purse my lips and tenderly kiss her breast, teasingly kissed her soft white flesh, smoother than velvet. Around a curvy breast and edge nearer toward her neck and lips as her breathing deepens, and she caresses my inner thighs.

My heart pounded and bleated for her. I move my head higher up her body until our lips met. Soft but deep sensuous kisses as our lips touched and as we embraced; hugged each other as she placed her leg across my legs.

Disbelief and wanton desire filled my body. It seems like a test, though, and unnatural. A test on my part to determine whether I'm affectionate enough to be a suitable match for the female beside me.

Even if the bodyguards were dormant, the enormity of the task evokes nervousness. The stakes are high; it's my chance for bliss in heaven.

If only I didn't have inhibitions, wasn't so shy and embarrassed, immature. If I could have put 100 percent effort into showing affection. My insatiable desire and yearning weren't enough. I'm an unsuitable match for that divine woman.

Inadequate and unworthy of entry into heaven, no soulmate on Earth or other worlds, so alone again. Dejected, I walk through the open gates onto a pure, white surface. *How could I have failed?*

It was such a profound transition maybe I wasn't ready for. Loved ones wanted me to return to Earth, their power overcoming and superseding the power of desire and lust? Such painful and harsh, yet exotically comforting truths.

I wanted more, anyway. A loyal, dependable partner to love, who will love me, and share life with, together. Despondent, too, gaining entry to heaven was akin to a wonderful, esoteric, divine privilege.

Fascinated as a red single-decker bus arrives to my right. It parks a distance away and is packed with people. *Who are they?* Those with the purest hearts — those who'd suffered? Or reached the end of their lives on the physical Earth?

Which category applied to me? What will my next task entail and will I succeed? I cannot see any angels, but see women on the bus, and other males who mill around, then stand, poising themselves, holding special guns.

As am I, and as the buses arrive, I realise I will soon play a heavenly dating game. A bizarre, but exciting game of high-stakes, where the ultimate prize is bliss, made and matched in heaven.

The ladies skip across the platform as they get off the bus. They form lines and cross other lines of ladies.

Sometimes, one gaze is enough, and such looks make one's heart pound and evoke instant feelings of intense love. My gun's different to what I had for shooting the stars in the first part of heaven I visited. It is white and shoots projectiles of love, heavenly arrows, like darts.

Competition is intense. But the game rules and methods become instinctively clear with the notion, mortal hearts to win after failing to win angelic hearts. I watch adorable women with long hair and dressed in loose-fitting, flowing, white robes, skip across my path, to tantalise and to woo.

Occasional eye contact fills me with delight as a pretty matched woman skips toward me, evoking 1,000 dreams of eternal love. Alas, despondence as they skip past to another.

To my delight, one of my heavenly arrows hits its target. The chosen lady with long, straight brown, flowing hair and stunning brown eyes falls in love with me; her eyes focus on me as she smiles. Elated as I know, the heavenly matched couples could live in heaven.

Another hits the target, though, a truer aim, instilling deeper love. The heavenly mate changes direction, destined for the arms of another.

Confused and frustrated by my lack of success; each arrow I shoot misses its target. Or did it, but somehow, inexplicably, my chances of success – thwarted. But male rivals aren't my only obstacles to bliss.

My efforts, finding partners in heaven, annoyingly sabotaged by Bill, an old workmate, and fellow plater, more senior in age, with light-brown tufts of hair and a receding hairline.

He doesn't speak, but often points with one of his grimy, chemical stained fingers, sometimes laughs and scolds, and seldom smiles.

His nickname in heaven, Poison Bill. He glares at me, watches in his dirty, dark-blue, chemical stained dungarees, shaking his head and pointing his spindly, grimy finger at me as if I shouldn't be there, have no right.

More dismayed as he aims his black poison gun that shoots black arrows. Betrothed women fall out of love if hit with the projectiles. Skip on to another as I pine. If only Poison Bill hadn't hindered me with his vindictive stare.

Torn between growing anger and dwindling delight at seeing a familiar face and workmate as his motives puzzle me. Is he an ally, or an enemy? Is he actually there for a purpose, a mission to return me to Earth?

I wonder, as red double-decker buses arrive on a pure white road, bringing many lovely ladies, adding to my frustration. They run and skip across my path and I stand, poised. Contemplative, as I watch bus after bus, and the female occupants, stunningly good-looking.

Some dressed in white, short, frilly skirts, tighter skirts, loose tops, and have long, flowing hair. My efforts, though, to win a heart seem so utterly futile. As if it's not my destiny, at least not yet.

Inept and lonely, but glad to be away from the wretched gangs, although that place and fruitless efforts caused a different yearning pain. I tried so hard in my quest to find a delectable soulmate in heaven, and like all entrants to heaven; I had three chances before descending to Earth as a spirit, but cruelly failed.

It is strange returning to Welshpool, a familiar place. The garage opposite our caravan, just how I remembered it. I reminisce as I look at the trees in the woods and elated as an ex-girlfriend walks toward me in a delightful, long, white dress that shines like silk. It's a wedding dress.

Surely, she couldn't be marrying me! In the other life, I'd

romanticised getting married. But never imagined it, or being worthy of anyone. Thinking I'd find nobody who'd want to marry, or love me enough, made it even stranger. I'd stopped expecting to find love, or to find solace, respite from the persecution, the gangs.

Was it another trick? *How could Debbie have been my sweetheart?* As she smiles, my new bride is incredibly beautiful in every way. I just want to look upon her face forever; lovely blonde hair, wonderful blue eyes adorned with bright-blue painted eyelashes.

Pink painted, perfect lips, I craved to kiss for eternity and an incredible, warm smile. We hold hands, chuckle with excitement and expectation of a lifetime together in each other's arms.

My dreams have come true. *I'm in seventh heaven*, utterly and totally in love. Elated as I walk up the aisle in my smartest outfit in a quaint, old church.

Weird to be using walking sticks, but I'm determined to walk to the front, although shaky. To my horror, I hear growling, barking and vile scratching claws behind us, and ever closer.

Such intense searing pain, a moment before several dobermans scamper ahead. I feared them. They return, jump up at me, bite my legs. Still, determined to marry, I walk past benched pew seats, up the aisle with my bride, despite the savage and unwelcome dogs, biting us.

We continue walking with sheer defiance. In desperation, I clutch my walking sticks despite my legs being relentlessly bitten. Terror, pain, and despair; sorrow at the cusp of bliss, as my beautiful, future wife passes away.

My bride isn't at my side, though; I only see her as a dream, waiting for me. It is confusing, as I discern I'm merely a spirit.

A contented spirit though, as I'm free to roam, and although heartbroken. Another fellow and love rival marries my sweetheart. I am left in the lurch. They smile; I am happy for them, and knowing she's safe and well.

I didn't deserve to be with her. Since I kissed another woman.

Alone again and far from that world. Dreams dashed; aching desires, by such a cruel travesty.

Distraught, sad and in pain, I rest at our caravan and hope I'll be safe there, in my favourite room, too, the kitchen and bedroom. A backdoor opens toward the backwater, and a sheer drop onto an acute-angled bank of greenery and many stinging nettles to the backwater.

My dad and I stood there while listening to a never-ending, perpetual patter of rain on the aluminium caravan roof and watching the rain. Mom often said, "Shut the door. The rats'll get in." Dad took no notice.

This opened door presented scenic and audible delights. Perfect circular, concentric rings formed. Randomly, radiated outwards on the water, then dissipated, and beyond the backwater to the trees of the woods, the sounds of birds, singing.

The river and country' smells and rain-refreshed air, fresh with the scent of plants, in gratitude for the rain.

It was weird to be there without Mom and Dad, to hear strange voices. The voices of two women, I assume, are witches as one cackles as they enter the room, and although not dressed how I expected witches to dress. They're wearing ordinary, casual clothes. One has long, straight blonde hair, the other with shoulder-length, brown wavy hair.

I know one of them is good. They have a sweet, kind voice I instantly fall in love with as she chats and chuckles and although neither are as pretty as the angels. I like her brown hair, too. The other, I know, is bad; intent on causing me harm as she glares at me but doesn't speak: the two opposites, conflicting contrasts.

Wary, but hopeful the good witch is the more powerful and can somehow tame the bad witch as she sticks needles in me, pushes them into my knee and arm joints, paralysing me. It is frightening, like when I knelt on the carpet and one of Mom's sewing needles stuck in my knee as a child, but nothing compared to the dogs.

I cannot move now as the bad witch cackles and scowls. The good witch soothes and comforts me, though, "Aww, you'll be all right, Paul. Don't worry. I'm here, and people love you" as she holds my hand and caresses my face as Terence Trent D'Arby's *Dance Little Sister* plays.

I think of my futile quests to win hearts. Were the witches nurses in a world I am oblivious? A world I'm no longer a part of and had departed?

I yearn to hear the sweet voice of the good witch. Had she enchanted me with her soft voice, the sweetest I had ever heard?

She evoked such powerful emotions, deep love; had won my heart. But, with strange undefinable love, lust, desire, yearnings, compared to love of the angels, the gorgeous other women, and to the horrid witch.

Yet, my deep emotions now signalled an even deeper, eternal love of an addictive flavour and entwined in a magical bond unlike ever experienced.

The experiences and adventures puzzled me, but part of me deep within is just beginning to understand the true meaning of intangible, loving emotions. As for good and evil, love, and hate, I would soon become even more confused and torn as I leave the caravan and see Dad.

He's driving a red Ferrari®. Wow, as he revs his car, the rear wheels spin, tyres smoke as rubber burns, and he speeds past me on the dusty driveway. It's a sleek supercar, a stunning sight.

In contrast, Mom is driving a smaller, less powerful white Rover® car, dainty in comparison. *They're trying to influence my actions. Do I have to choose between them?*

I love them both the same. Why should I have to choose? Is my dad evil with a red car, Mom good with her white car? They argued sometimes — in the old world. Fierce arguments, but powerless, and unable to bear living without either of them. I felt awkward, afraid, in between, as I do now.

They love me, but how deeply? What do they expect me to do? How can I express any preference without hurting one? If one is evil, I still love them. Maybe I should love one more than the other. I feel sorry for them as I cannot choose or speak to either. It would hurt the other.

My next adventure would touch on yet another kind of love, perhaps because of the heart-wrenching choices I couldn't bear to make.

7.

ROBOT TRICKERY

Times in parts of heaven seem so long ago. I had become a part of a long, cruel war. It had been raging for years; a technological war with crude pain inflicting elements that continue as I became entwined in the conflict.

At a strange encampment, I'm sleeping in a green canvas tent, like I had stayed in Mid Wales, but different. Now, I'm a soldier in a camouflage outfit and army boots. My solitary tent is on the left of a huge, white polished, flat floor which sits at the side of a vast open-plan expanse up high, above distant buildings and hilly scenery.

Bemused, as I peer out from my tent and hear the distant whirring sound of what I assume is a helicopter. The sounds of its rotor blades and a dull, low-pitched engine become ever louder and distinct.

Surely enough, in the distance, a circular blur changing to an elliptical blur becomes distinguishable as spinning rotor blades. Grey rotor blades, above a black object that tilts and sways as it rapidly approaches. It's a black helicopter against a collage of the grey overcast sky mixed with wisps of white cloud.

I watch in intent fascination, and wonder who the occupants are. Even as the helicopter lands on the platform, the engine stops, and the rotor blades gradually slows. Wonder becomes intrigue and excitement; my heart filled with delight as my mom and dad climb out of the helicopter.

Dad is wearing gold round-rimmed glasses, and looks much older; not how I remembered him in the alternative world. Piloting a helicopter now, and relieved he's not driving a supercar. He and Mom, are elated as they hug me, as am I, and they bring gifts.

Overjoyed, as I hadn't found them. So lost and alone in this strange place, I believed they had passed on long ago, or forgotten me. The gifts are strange, especially the toy babies.

Other gifts, the yoghurt, the mirror, and a comb, are very ordinary, but as my parents enter the tent a fellow soldier puts me wise, before I join them. In fact, the gifts are highly dangerous and ingenious devices.

The yoghurt, poisoned and the teeth on the comb meant to fall out, and the mirror shatters into razor-sharp splinters. Most despicable, the toy baby is a shrewd bomb in disguise.

I disbelieve the soldier, *Mom, and Dad wouldn't bring me anything dangerous*, but wonder if my doubts are unfounded as Mom and Dad act strangely. Perturbed and confused, too; they're emotionless and don't stay as long as I hoped or expected. It's been a long time, though.

Saddened as my parents leave my tent and climb into the helicopter. The rotors spinning ever faster as they takeoff, hover in the air, and I wave. But, to my dismay, they don't wave back, and their facial expressions change, as though laughing evilly.

As they hover and ascend, I am stunned and shaken by an almighty blast as the helicopter explodes in a massive ball of flames that plummets to the ground. The heat, intense from the explosive fireball, and I crouch to avoid flying debris. My parents were not who they purported to be.

The hug was wonderful. They looked real, but they were Japanese robots disguised as my parents. Robot androids, designed to mimic and infiltrate the most formidable enemy defence, as cunning weapons of war.

To penetrate the deepest emotions and demoralise. Sadness by the torture of one's mind and soul, but not destroy. Such false joy, then heartache, loneliness, and despair. Was I fighting a kind of personal battle? Wrestling with a question too painful to contemplate: Will I see my actual parents again?

Would they find me, or will I find them? Mere, doubtful dreams and filled with even more dread. *The enemy could cause more harm; inflict even greater psychological pain.*

Have those evil robots or other Japanese agents left a toy baby gift somewhere else, a despicable, deadly exploding bomb? My sweetheart is in a nearby chalet, on the holiday camp site, left of the embankment on high. I must get to her, run at top speed, although my efforts will be futile.

Increased desperate blind panic and dwindling hope as I pass a swimming pool, but as I near the first chalet, there's an earth-shaking detonation. Intense – immense plumes of yellow flame illuminate the sky from an almighty explosion – I am too late.

The deadly weapons of war were potent enough and brought such destruction, heartache, with intensified suffering.

Still, parent impostor robot androids signify a higher and more ominous motive in an already despicable physical and psychological war, to new, wider levels with no boundary or respect, even for tortured souls.

How can an enemy be so evil, clinically cruel? Such devious, sinister plans of intricate precision filled me with deep dread.

What diabolical forces was I battling in vain? Will this cruel war ever cease? No place or solace, only emptiness. No love or hope, only deep loneliness and despair.

I longed to see my parents, my real parents, as I remembered them, and without having to make any choice. Yet, maybe the earlier choice between good or evil, a sham as my mom and dad were not them, anyway.

The events, emotions, felt like being trapped in a vast, cruel, wilderness. A wilderness I longed to leave made ever crueller, as I cannot find my parents, or anyone, to love. I yearn to see the angels, or to hear the good witch's voice, anyone not evil.

I walk away from the campsite, toward the seafront and smile and wave as I know the girls' swimming captain from school. She's in camouflage, too, and in a dinghy, near the shore and she waves; beckons me to join her.

It's great to be in a black, rubber boat together, floating out on a blue-grey sea. Waves lap against the boat, it rocks and undulates as we float. A black, rocky shore in the distance below a white overcast sky, a reminder of pain, but at ease and pleased by a familiar face.

For a moment, I forget about the wars, the heartache, and strife, smiling instead as we reminisce past triumphs in other worlds.

A sudden distant rumbling sound prompts us to look up at the sky and we focus on the outline of a plane. A black plane flying high above us, and we become increasingly anxious. We see objects being released from the plane.

Deadly cargo, and we are the target. Should we swim or hope? It becomes obvious there's no escape, regardless of the choice between the water or boat. In panic, we paddle the dinghy, try to avoid thousands of rapidly descending objects.

An orange, oval-shaped ball lands in the dinghy. One of many that land on the surrounding sea with gentle splashes before they submerge slightly and rise to the surface.

A sound, like compressed air being pumped into a football as the balls expand in half a second, is ominous. But in despair, as the expanded balls explode and release millions of deadly spores.

The floating spore bombs explode around us, frantic-desperation as we try to puncture the ball in our dinghy before it expands and explodes. Neither of us can halt that explosion, covering us in deadly spores.

Nothing we can do – except wait in despair – but grateful to not die quickly or alone. Lost in my rudderless boat on the sea I'd loved since I was a child at Rhyl, as I hear the lapping waves and see the distant shore we'll never reach.

I so wanted Mom and Dad to find me; I'm much further away now. Beyond reach, as I drift away, but I don't remember dying, just the lingering sadness of war. And a poisoned planet I must leave, as I'm destined for another world.

8.

SPACE ADOPTION

*T*ired of the heartache and little solace. Being alone with no place in the universe, dimension to belong, and enduring despair. Sadly, I was just beginning to experience the despicable evil.

While this realisation evokes deep sadness and despair, I'm disturbed by such malicious intent and the cruel trickery, in the form of parent impostors, as it shows new, ever more sinister and escalating depths.

There's respite, happiness, though. Elation, contentment in a distant world with a family who loves me; I have somewhere to belong.

I enjoyed living in a house as the adopted son of a Jamaican family. It's wonderful to be part of a family, and not alone.

A corridor adjoins two cubicle bedrooms with bunk beds, uncannily like a place I stayed at in Scotland, in the other, long-gone world.

It's strange as I climb onto one bunk bed to rest and discover a cigar. I light it, and smoke, out of curiosity. I'm so careful, but accidentally burn two, small holes into the bedsheet. *Oh, no, but it's OK, the holes are small. Hope the brothers will understand, though.*

I hear them return, chatting as I watch TV in the room at the corridor's end. It's a stressful wait and as expected, the brothers fling the doors open, storm in and aren't at all happy.

The eldest trembles as he lunges toward me. "What you doing smoking my cigar, the holes in my sheet? It's time for you to leave this place. Go back to Earth, or wherever you came from. Nobody wants you here."

I bow my head and lower my shoulders. "Sorry, I am sorry." *You've resented me since I arrived. Jealous as your parents adopted me, love me as much as their own children. I love them, too, but don't belong to be with them. I'm an alien in this world.* And, had to leave that dear Jamaican family.

Heartbreaking sadness, lost and alone again. The father I wished to call my own, but did not deserve to, cries. The other brothers and sisters cried, too. Such sad faces, and melancholy, distraught, but they, and I, powerless. My actual parents are lost to me in a distant world and perhaps even another dimension.

Contentment, solace, and a sense of belonging, found in a distant alien world. Yet, again forced into a lonely, cold, cosmic wilderness. Impostor parents, then substitute parents and a family I love and tried so hard to fit in with, so they will accept me as a son and brother.

Dejection as I walk on the grass beside a stream and notice a dark-green canvas tent. I walk towards it, become surprised and comforted as I hear an ex-girlfriend's voice. My emotions change to sorrow and despondence at laughter as I realise she's taking drugs and having sex in the tent.

Cruelly, reminded of emotions I grew tired of from a world I once belonged, but escaped from as a slow, melancholy song plays, LL Cool J, *I Need Love.*

Strange how apt the words were, how they intensify yearnings for solace and love, but I wasn't beat. Still determined, but drained, listless as I return to another world. Unsure if it's a replica of Earth or in another dimension.

Next, I am part of another dating game, exciting but dangerous, the first part of a wondrous gift, possibly from the angels.

9.

SEESAW BALANCE

*E*xcited as I stand on a platform, high above a roaring, fast-flowing torrent. A large alien sun, high above the sky to my right, sends warmth mixed with the cool, misty spray from the water, and adds to the suspenseful drama.

The sounds remind me of Welshpool. It's like a platform ledge of the railway bridge I had stood. This place is more hazardous. The only way off, is to jump across the water, onto long planks of wood, tilted like seesaws.

Seesaw planks along the platform and on stone pillars, on the other side of the river, and I smile as I see the girls I played kiss chase with at school. Attractive girls, I recognise as old flames and kiss chase partners, sometimes teasers.

Adorable, tantalising smiles as they glance at me before they jump across the treacherous rapids below, and balance so well on the seesaws.

I realise it's a dangerous dating game to pair up with girls standing on other planks on another platform. A lottery, as the girls may jump across to me as I jump to them.

In anticipation of timing my jump, as I walk along a few planks; waiting for the opportune moment and using all my strength for an almighty leap. I land perfectly, but the plank overbalances as they jump off simultaneously.

I didn't fear as I fall from the seesaw, into the river with the plank. Beneath the cool water I plunge, surface, then swim in the torrid torrent of fast-flowing water.

Dismayed, falling without a date. The swim, a consolation as the girls wave from the seesaw and blow me kisses.

Downstream, I reach a quieter section of the river. Calm,

trickling water, beside lush vegetation and scenic views of green fields, and hear a loud *boing* sound on the riverbank and see a bright white flash of light in the sky. I clamber up to see a circular trampoline on a grass field near the river.

A trampoline with a red and white target painted on the elastic canvas, angled toward the sky. As I approach, I hear the sound again, accompanied by a brilliant flash of light, above the trampoline, and beam of light to the sky; it's no ordinary trampoline. *Is its simplicity an elaborate illusion disguising its immense power?*

Curious, I climb onto the trampoline and sit, then jump. Nothing happens until I jump higher and higher. Each descent improves my landing accuracy. The trampoline vibrates and elongates, and with a *boing* and flash of light as it launches me on an instantaneous trajectory to another dimension in space.

Amazed, as I float amidst an exquisite panoramic three-dimensional tapestry of stars. Stars that shine and gleam, like diamonds adorning blackness, and enthral me as my gaze shifts to a group of stars.

As I focus, they move into clusters and form a white, glowing arch. It resembles a cosmic bridge. An arch that spans across space, distant galaxies and multicolour swirling nebulae, and is astounding.

Even more beautiful, a white streak of light emerges from the nebulae and crosses space; becomes more defined as it travels. Transfixed as I realise, it's an awe-inspiring gift. The streak is a majestic, white horse, Palomino, as it canters, and leaps across that cosmic gulf between the stars, then gallops into outer space.

Sublime and pure wondrous beauty as Bruce Springsteen's *Brilliant Disguise* plays, but my mind interprets as "bridge in the skies."

I am surprised to be in a bland room, with one enormous window, no furniture. Euphoric, my friend, Paul, is there, but curious as he's dressed in a blue, red, and white Lycra® costume that reminds me of Superman®, I'm delighted the two lovely, kind ladies I worked for on Bilston Market are also there. The ladies loved travelling and were always cheerful as they spoke of holidays to sunny, earthly places.

They're so excited now. "Hey, it's lovely to see you, Paul. You're on planet Krypton, and there's a black hole, CYGNUS X1, above this room. It's an inter-dimensional portal back to Earth, and to activate it, all you have to do. Is touch the button up there." They look up at a large, red button in the room's corner.

Frustrated, and embarrassed at my ineptitude as I reach upward in desperation, but cannot quite reach it; hopeless, although my best friend is there. Who I'm doubly delighted to see as he's tall and can reach the button.

And I am so proud he's my friend, but become mystified. He acknowledges me with just a nod and smile as he lifts an arm, punches the air and zooms through space like an elite god hurtling toward the swirl of stars around the black hole's centre.

He orbits ever faster, spinning around the black hole at nearly the speed of light, creating a blur of blue and red. Euphoric and in awe as I travel through space to Earth, but saddened to leave that marvellous place where I had seen friends and magnificent celestial beauty.

Paul was a superhero at the edge of time as *Hey Matthew* by Karel Fialka played.

10.

SAVAGE JAWS

*I*t's strange to be back on Earth, such a contrast after a wondrous, disorienting journey. In a dark, deserted supermarket, my breath is visible as a misty fog as I breathe, and rub my hands together to warm them. The air is cool, clammy and damp and the shelves are bare, but meat hangs from S shaped steel hooks. *Am I in a freezer section?*

An unnerving atmosphere of fear with an eerie silence, broken by the sound of footsteps. Then Dava whispers between anxious breaths, "Good to see you, P. Don't make a noise."

His voice puts me at ease. I'm pleased; *I'm not alone.* The moment he finishes speaking, there's the terrifying sound of growling dogs and fast scratching of their sharp claws as they run towards us.

No escape and outrunning them is futile, but we try as we run for our lives. Out from the supermarket, into the night, besieged, desperate to escape the agile dogs. We run into a railway station and onto a stationary train and slam the door shut. Still, two dogs harass us as they enter the carriage, barking and snarling, coming at us.

Breathless, as the train engine starts up, and it moves. We hear footsteps, ominous taunts and shouting from above, on the train roof; vandals are trying to kill us. We flee from carriage to carriage to escape their wrath, but the pursuing dogs are more terrifying.

Amazingly reaching the end carriage but our efforts to evade the gang have been in vain as we hear them on the roof, shouting abuse in their harsh accents. They taunt us from the train roof and stamp their feet as they try to intimidate and demoralise us to the extreme.

And, throw lit fireworks into the carriage. They bounce and ricochet from the carriage walls as they hiss and shoot a bright multicoloured array of hot, smoking sparks, illuminating the black carriage. Scorching the floor and seats where they land and smoulder. Acrid smoke makes us cough; there's so many fireworks entering the carriage, our perilous refuge.

Intense heat and a brilliant flash as a hot firework explodes near my leg, coloured fiery sparks sear my skin. There's no escape from the pain and terror. I hope another spark doesn't hit me and that I don't see the most terrifying things I can hear.

Alas, the barks, growls, of the dogs snarling; as the fireworks hiss, fizz, bang and the coloured sparks and fire illuminate the dogs' eyes. They whimper and whine, tamed by the fear of fiery sparks and loud bangs, and scamper away.

Not even those enemy creatures to accompany us as the train pierces the misty darkness of night as it speeds onwards, its carriages sway. The train was nowhere near fast enough. Such pain and fear on a journey that seems endless. So, pleased as dawn breaks, the sun's rays welcome us as we cross into England.

It's great to be safe, away from the dogs, the fireworks, and gangs. Relieved as I hope there won't be further persecution, and I walk out of a deserted Wolverhampton Railway Station and say farewell to Dava.

I am so tired and must have stopped to rest and fell asleep. Disoriented and in despair as I wake and touch cold steel with a machined but pitted surface, with my hands, and the forged links of thick chains binding as I pull on them until my knuckles turn white.

I cannot believe what I am chained to, a large, red painted, World War II bomb. The bomb is long, heavy, and cylindrical, with a rounded point at the front, four large fins at right angles at the rear.

A man's voice says, "He's awake. He won't get away this time," laughter follows from whom I presume is another gang.

Sheer terror, suffused with utter confusion and anguish as I tremble and struggle to get free. Desperate to slip through the binding chains, I cannot break. There's no escape; my efforts, futile and fruitless.

I scream the moment the bomb explodes, intense white heat

and hot metal fragments pierce my body; intense pain and terror, but still, I live on, despite chunks of metal embedding deep in my body.

Dark-red, jagged, chunks of metal from the bomb casing pierce my skin, covered with horrific wounds. Still, they point their fingers, "Look at him," as they laugh, double up, hold their stomach's, unable to stop as they taunt again, "Let's see if the bastard survives this."

The gang push a large, red bottle of propane gas toward me, and run with it as it rolls, pin me to the ground and chain me to the propane bomb. Gas hisses from the valve as it opens, and they leave a lit cigarette lighter on the ground beside me as they run to a safe distance.

Its blue flame, the sound of flammable escaping gas and smell, terrifies me as I frantically struggle in a last-ditch attempt to get my arms free.

They bellow, "Don't fucking struggle," but I keep fighting, in defiance: "Stop me, then! Come on? Fucking scared?"

"Ooh, big man." As they jump and dance with excitement at their cruelty, my pain.

The gas continues to gush and with the cold metal of the cylinder upon my skin, but I slip free of the chains and run in sheer panic. Each second is like 100 years as I'm gripped. Subjected to the utter terror, then an almighty blast.

Intense heat and fire melt a mini crater in the tarmac, as dust and smoke congeals with fire debris, and high-speed metal shrapnel pierces my skin and the heat and power from the blast propel me through the air at great speed. Excruciating pain, and momentarily stunned by the blast and events.

Anger and defiance fuel my determination to get back up from the ground onto my feet to show them they failed! I walk away from the gang as they jeer and taunt, "Why won't he just fucking die?… Let's see if he survives this?"

As I struggle to get up, an engine roars in the distance. I soon realise, as I turn, it's the engine of a black van that, to my horror, is hurtling towards me. The engine becomes ever louder as the gears change.

No time to run or escape, as I am in a vast car park. Curious, I wait to see who's driving and glimpse at a cohort of the gang. I am knocked down; run over, I see the underneath of the van. Smell old engine oil and am so worn out, disenchanted, in pain and fearful.

Surely, *I cannot survive this! Their ruthless violence, sadistic bastards* as I arch my head upwards and see the van zoom away, bellowing black smoke.

It reverses, turns, and hurtles towards me again! Maniacal, hatred and anger in his eyes as he accelerates, frenzied as he repeatedly revs the engine, as there's a screech of rubber and I smell it burning, congealed with pungent, thick, grey smoke.

He runs over me a further six times. I still live! The madman and the evil gang were annoyed, not happy with me as the van zooms away. They jeer as I plod away.

Again, I hope they'll leave me alone, but as I walk along the pavement toward my old school. Again, the gang taunt and shout, from behind me. I try to stay calm, pretend I didn't hear, staying silent and don't turn around as I hear closer whispering, "Shush, quiet."

Then mischievous laughter as I fall to the ground with searing pain, as a large knife pierces my back. A knife thrown by the gang. In desperation, I struggle to crawl on my knees, terrified, as a second knife enters my back.

Driven by despair, anger, and sheer defiance. I crawl on my front, alarmed by the warmth of my blood oozing from my wounds.

Another thrown knife enters my back. I keep on crawling up an incline despite their taunts and more knives. "Why doesn't he just stop moving and pretend he's dead? We'll stop throwing the knives?"

I continue crawling up the slope, as the gang mercilessly throw their knives into my back, but think, *If I stop moving, they'll stop the attack.* So I don't stop as they taunt, "Why won't he just stop and die?" I carry on and on fighting, never giving up as I want to astonish them with my defiant resilience and that I'm still moving.

The evil gang were relentless in their efforts to kill me; they failed! Sinister efforts continued, though; the next twists, more subtle, sophisticated, less barbaric, but just as lethal.

They throw me in the back of a white truck. It's dark, as it doesn't have any windows. I am alone and sense the truck moving and something uncomfortable in my ear, like a small tube. Tiny ball bearings inside my ear touch my eardrum, causing pain, mind-numbing pain, and there's nothing I can do.

It's an awful sensation. In horrified despair, I try to remove the ball bearings, and realise they're made of lead from the dull texture.

A terrifying punishment as lead ball bearings poison me through my ear. Each ball bearing hurts as it touches my eardrum. *Are they poisoning my brain?* Struck with fear of that fate, but powerless to resist. There's nothing anyone can do, the punishment and mechanism of evil behind the actions, unstoppable!

The gang cannot destroy me, so try to erode my mind, my will to continue to resist; the true source of my strength as the truck slows and the doors open.

I am in Welshpool. On the dusty drive beside the caravans but am so weak, much slower, the lead poisoning, effective, fills me with dread, although it's wonderful to be in a familiar place but no birdsong, as it's dusk.

In this secluded place, I'm an easier target as I stroll and hear footsteps treading on the loose stones behind me, by the caravan. *Is it another gang member, a stalker? A professional assassin paid to finish me?*

The pain, intense, excruciating as a bullet pierces my leg and touches my knee. I stumble to the ground and try to crawl, grasp loose stony ground, my wounded leg out straight, but I do not beg, as I hear footsteps approaching from behind.

Not even as I am repeatedly shot in my back, each bullet, with a terrifying bang, moments later, searing pain, despair. *Please, no more. Why, why,* but I stay silent. Have to keep on moving in defiance. I must live, never give in, but become so slow, so weak, I can barely move.

Tired, defiant, yet, I continue, even as I receive a sharp kick to my body from the assassin. From the sound of his footsteps, walking away from me. *Whoever's tried to murder me thinks I'm dead, or close; they've left me here to die!*

Beaten and in despair but happy to live on in sheer defiance, I continue to move, daring the assassin to come back as he failed to kill me, and although terrified. Soothed by the gentle rushing sound of the river, I long to see beside the backwater, and woods.

It's strange being shot considering I fired a shotgun near there, in my previous existence, and other world.

The assassin denies shooting me but was just a puppet, tricked by the gang, who told him I was a highly dangerous terrorist. I just want solace, but the gang becomes even more annoyed and determined as doctors extract a lead bullet from my knee as proof. Their onslaught continues; they become ever more cunning, despicable, and devious.

Each attack becomes more terrifying, and I hope is the last. But each failed attempt to murder me makes them more determined and resolute. Even when there's a lull and I return to Bilston. *What might be next, and will they succeed? Why do they despise me so much?*

Again, I am filled with dread near my old school. A rough, scruffy looking family follows me, another gang in an unfamiliar area, and I am glad not to see any weapons, but they have intense hatred in their soulless eyes as they taunt. "He thinks he's indestructible! Let's see how tough he is!"

I watch in horror. The gang kick and roll heavy drums of hazardous, lethal chemicals along a slope towards me and throw enormous stones at me; I try to evade. The attack is identical to an earlier attack. Except isn't in a cave, and more sinister.

They intend to kill me. This time there's no rescue. I am left for dead. The long arduous battle for survival, lost, but could I still win? The faintest glimmer of hope: A last show of defiance in the form of a despicable wager.

11.

RACE FOR LIFE

*W*ith my last ounces of energy, I drag myself up a hill. To a place I knew well. A road like a racing circuit, long straights and adjoined by roads at both ends, called Central Avenue. I drove around there in my friend's car in the other world.

Just ghosts and silence now as the gang watches. Wait for me to stop, fall, and die as the low-pitched noise of a motorbike engine distracts me and becomes ever louder, and is extraordinarily comforting. Elated to see the rider is my dad, approaching on his motorbike.

He has found me. Joy and solace after so long, although there's nothing he can do to thwart the evil gangs. No rescue or deliverance from death.

Still, they run toward us as I sit on the back of Dad's AJS motorbike; I'd never seen in the other world, but he often reminisced. The motorbike stalls, but starts as the gang reaches us and the leader lunges to pull me off the motorbike. "You're dead but do two circuits and live till 10.00 o'clock and you win."

So tired, beat and close to death, but glad they gave me an important task I must complete. The gangs gloat in triumph and dance, celebrate on the grassed areas of Central Avenue.

They think they have succeeded, but can I make one last stand of defiance to sour their sweet but twisted victory? I cling on to my dad as he rides his shiny, black motorbike around the circuit, and the observing gang.

Exhilarating, fast and thrilling, as the gears up-shift, leaning on the corners, heads down, braking and accelerating, zooming fast until the ground becomes a blur, then gradually defined as we decelerate for the corners.

Thrilling, but scary as the stakes are so dauntingly high, I must be defiant until the very end. So tired. Fading away, but must hold on, not fall as the race continues. A never-ending race; as I cling on, hold on tight to my dad's black jacket with its warm white fur collar.

Dwindling consciousness, as my heart makes its last beats, as I endure my lament, rebellious as I try not to fade away. To hang on in defiance — and win.

The bike comes to rest as Dad pulls up by an open-plan shop. He stops the engine and helps me from his motorbike and onto the grass to lie down, but I cannot rouse to celebrate our victory.

We won, but there's the profound ultimatum. I lie on the grassy ground willing myself on even though I have lost the long battle... my heart must beat until 10.00 o'clock. "Hold on! Don't die!" Dad says. Alas, I have lost the battles.

I gaze up at a topaz-coloured blue sky with fluffy white clouds that instil calmness and peace. For a moment my heart fills with love, thinking of the angels, sweethearts, and so many battles.

Alas, triumph in the race for life is tainted with such sorrow. My time is short. To die so soon after, being reunited with my dad, cruel, but my heart hasn't stopped yet.

We both intently follow the second-hand of my dad's watch, ticking toward the top number 12. As the watch finger reaches 12, I know I can rest; we won. I won the last race, that decisive encounter, and defied the gangs, the evil.

I cling on somehow until they acknowledge that we've won for definite. My eyes close as my heart ceases to beat, and I slip away from that realm.

My heart stops, but to my amazement, my life does not end. Overjoyed as I continue to breathe. Defiance in death, with the notion: *If I'm dead, no-one can persecute or try to kill me any longer!*

I excite many. Fascinate some, but others are sceptical and want to test me. To see how long I will live without my beating heart?

A challenge to run on a special treadmill in Bilston on a tour bus by Market Way excites me. Especially as BBC Radio 1 are there, with a roadshow just for me, and the disc jockeys are urging me on to run faster. But some wait for me to stop or fall, and die. It's great; I become the star attraction.

One side of the bus is open, where the treadmill is as my stage. Hamburgers and chips are being given away for free from open window counters, serving hatches in the other half of the bus.

There is a frenzied air of excitement. In celebration and awe of the macabre spectacle, the man who continues to live. Lives on after his heart has stopped.

I feel fantastic, strong and run faster and faster; thrilling, infinite power as I laugh with excitement. Such strange, unnatural prowess causes resentment, anger as the crowd jeer and taunt. Do they think my heart still beats as I continue to run?

Morbid curiosity attracts ever more attention and crowds, including the gang, watching every stride, waiting for me to either fall or continue.

One gang member is shaking their head. Two others, behind the crowds brandish and wave their knives. The metal blades glint in the sun.

I'm not worried; I want to keep on running, although the exhibition has to end eventually, and the evil gang are waiting, as the crowds abate, and the DJ becomes silent. I'm not tired, can run forever, but dart from the running machine, as swift as I can.

Must elude them by running. *They killed me. My heart has stopped. Why won't they leave me alone?* They still gloat as they capture me and put a large, heavy wooden collar around my neck to impede my continuing existence.

It's a symbol for an outcast, a freak of nature, following triumphant and euphoric feelings of success, a moment of fame. But for something not possible, then nothing.

The loneliness continues, but word of my fame has spread far and wide. Others of higher intelligence wish to test the endurance of the man whose heart stopped but lived on — in defiance. The next test is despicable and cruel.

How much more can I take? Mortal enemies want me to fail and die. Why couldn't I just die? Maybe I wanted to live and defy the gangs. See the angels once more. To keep on — going... driven by the hope of finding solace and love.

12.

ENDURANCE TEST

*M*y continued survival, despite gruelling tests that should have been fatal astonishes and instils curiosity in many. How can I still live?

Immense pride at my resilience. But tired, as my legendary endurance sets new benchmarks and attracts attention far beyond Earth to other galaxies. *I wanted solace, not fame!*

God had dealt with Iceman, his brother, and their race no longer had qualms with primitive humans. More advanced aliens had their sights on Earth, but first they had to assess human frailty and resilience.

There's cruel torture. An experiment devised by aliens. The purpose: how much radiation can humans withstand before they perish and die, lose their will to live?

Tentative as I approach a clearing near Bilston Library, anticipating the test, and ever anxious, hot and strange. I near a red-brick building. The door is open; I enter, but dread and overwhelming horror plague my mind as I look at an exposed white hot, glowing, pulsating reactor core.

Many are walking round the oblong-shaped reactor. Old, young, men, women, determined to survive. But bedraggled and lost, and oblivious to the task. The profoundness, the sheer cruelty as the radiation is intense and deadly.

Debilitating as mind-numbing dull, low-pitched sound and overpowering heat, saps energy, and hope. The will to live; fight death.

Signifying new extremes, as each step is like a marathon as I fight intense fatigue and nausea. Many collapse from intense radiation, dwindle away in confused despair. I keep on striving in sheer defiance, determined to prove my endurance even though my heart stopped long ago.

A while longer, an extra step. The resilience and fighting spirit of the whole human race on my shoulders. So somnolent, close to death, many had given up, succumbed and fallen. I am the only one that can muster the inner strength, energy from nowhere, in defiance to astound the aliens; I cannot fall.

I couldn't be like the masses of bedraggled people, poisoned by deadly radiation. Weak, finished, but still they continue to walk but will fall. They plod on, near standstill but chasing hope, defiantly drag themselves on with dreams of seeing the sun, daylight, loved ones. To survive, although lost.

Few can go on, continue. Even the strongest – most resolute drop to the floor and perish – not me. Fatigued, languid, my body's so heavy, legs like lead weights. I drag myself ever forward, centimetre by centimetre, and ever smaller increments before collapsing to my knees.

I try so hard to stand back up but cannot. So tired, I want to lie down, rest, accept the end and defeat.

I make it so far. Nearly the entire way round, but exhausted. The exit's in sight, but I'm too weak to even give a wry smile. My anticipated triumph, in escaping and enduring that cruellest of tests, meaningless.

Two metres from the exit, drained, but defiant, I continue to crawl; no more energy, totally sapped, so close, so hot — intense radiation. The Bee Gees, *You Win Again* plays as I rest and fade away, await imminent death.

I finally pass away and want to rest. So many attempts to kill me, relentless persecution and pain. Solace at last as I am placed in my coffin at my funeral. A vicar in a shiny, dark, silken, purple sash stands at the base of my coffin and says burial words seven times.

Or rather, attempts to, in unusual, difficult circumstances. He tries in vain to make himself heard above the shouting vandals. Evil, malicious vandals around the room shout abuse, jeer, as they spray multicoloured graffiti and slogans on the walls with aerosol paint.

So tired, but powerless and unable to express my extreme annoyance with the unruly, disrespectful vandals. How can they be so despicable? How can fellow humans be so cruel, disrespectful, so blatantly evil? What could their motives be?

Seven funerals, futile and pointless. I am so confused and tired. Why can't I just rest, go to sleep? I am in my coffin, so must have died. The vicar, holding his head in despair, adds to my despondence as I wonder if I can die, or even rest.

Was he mistaken, as they had somehow misinterpreted my wishes? Do they believe I am still alive? Clearly, the vicar represented the epitome of goodness, the vandals, the stark opposite, pure evil.

If I cannot die, maybe I must try to live and there's another purpose. To use my mind and utilise what I have, my enduring mind. I return to Welshpool and amazingly possess great intelligence, with a deep understanding of the universe and the knowledge of its secrets.

Such secrets, ingenious ideas, and complex concepts delight me, and intellectual capacity, beyond that of the cleverest humans, overwhelms. Most thrilling is, I instinctively know how to build a time machine; a spacecraft to leave the Earth.

Even transcend dimensions; I can finally reach other worlds, escape loneliness, and the confines of Earth; find love. Perhaps God gave me such knowledge and companions as a gift.

Yes, solace, admiration as I sit opposite two girls, that smile and I'm one of two boys in the time machine, as its proud creator. I am excited by the prospect of leaving Earth, traversing dimensions, and time; ability to teleport myself and romance.

Poised to liftoff in that incredible machine, we anticipate fresh adventures, but hear voices. More sounds, mechanised vehicles, heavy boots, and the loading of rifles we assume are pointing at us prompt us to pause.

And to look at each other, as a male, authoritarian, voice says: "We are the U.S. Navy. Surrender your time machine. Leave your craft immediately. Humans cannot understand such advanced technology, that is dangerous for humanity."

It's so unfair; I'd created that time machine to traverse time, visit other worlds without the help of angels.

The U.S. Navy were mere messengers, part of an elaborate ploy, the military want to test my legendary resilience. Why do I still exist? My continued existence, despite ever more determined and ruthless enemies. Enemies that had made me notorious.

They don't test my physical endurance; they test my mind with psychological methods. Well, it's an unconventional approach by the military. In a darkened room, I'm part of a packed audience. A film begins with the whir of a projector.

There's suspense and excitement until we realise it's an absolutely terrifying and realistic war film, bringing sheer mental pain! Many cry and scream. Clamber across the seated audience to the door; it's locked, so they bang on it while they say, "Let me out. I can't take any more."

Watching the film is an endurance test of nerve and character for joining the U.S. Marines. I became one of many recruits, lined up in a queue, joining one-by-one, having our hair shaved off, by barbers with clippers.

After joining, we lie in chromed steel framed hospital beds. The beds are our unusual vessels to ascend to heaven, and I have a belt with metal on to attract the lightning strike.

A fellow marine checks my belt. "OK, soldier. Get ready." Anxious, but excited, as I watch many ascend after a lightning strike and wait. I wait in earnest but with a brilliant, white, flash of power to my belt buckle and the bed, granted one more chance to enter heaven.

13.

STAIRCASE TO HEAVEN

*O*n an amazing flat, bright, white field that meets a pure, white sky, a line of shining gold ascends to heaven. The gold is part of a golden two-way conveyor belt. It gently whirs at the foot of heaven.

Babies wrapped in white cloths, and people dressed in white clothes are on the conveyor belt. Travelling upwards and downwards, to and from heaven as occupants, stationary passengers who do not speak, murmur, smile or cry.

The Alarm, *Rain In The Summertime,* plays. I'm dressed in white and sitting at the foot of the conveyor. In a quandary mixed with nonchalance as I sit watching and pondering, as I've experienced other parts of heaven, and always returned to Earth, or other realms.

Ever intrigued by the bright-red bus. People on there, smiling as they reach their hands to catch lost artefacts of theirs and precious gold coins that glint as they fall. There are shouts and screams of delight for material prizes.

It's obvious, the longer I stay off the bus, the bigger prize I will get once I get onto it. Still, I'm not tempted and focus on the smiling bus passengers, rather than the conveyor belt. *Those on the bus have given up, lost, although they think they're winning.* Were they the lucky ones? Were they happy?

Although it's raining hard, it's like stinging hail; determined to brave the elements, whilst I wonder if either the bus or conveyor belt will get me to heaven. I fail to realise it may be a test and cannot bear to contemplate or entertain the prospect of returning on my next and possibly last visit to heaven.

Thoughts of the angels versus material wealth sway my

decision, but as I decide to stand, there's a magnificent white flash, heat, and searing pain as lightning strikes me for being too greedy and wanting a material prize.

The lightning bolt transports me to another place, opposite and contrasting, pure brilliant white to black. It's dark, but in an instant I know where I am by the familiar sound of gently, rushing river water and the crunching sound of the loose stone beneath my feet.

I'm near Welshpool, by the railway bridge. Cold and lonely as I reminisce about walking over loose stones alongside the railway tracks leading to the woods, the other site and to the railway bridge, which had an iron shelf.

I climbed onto this and held the rail. The river was a wondrous sight, flanked by tall, majestic trees on either side.

I threw stones straight up into the air and watched them plummet into the river below the bridge. As the stone hit the water at impressive speed, it made an entertaining sound, like *'tunk'*, rather like a speargun being shot underwater.

From here, too, the sounds of children playing in the river downstream, and the occasional scream as the rumbling, black water gushed beneath me, between the two embankments.

Lapping and swirling waves with dynamic undulating watery curves, tinged with deep shades of dark-green topped with edges of white crescent flumes.

Foamy droplets of white-water, where waves frequently met, became more visible, illuminated and bought to life by summer rays of dazzling, glistening sunlight.

It is much less scenic now, dark and dank. This adds to the tension and my anxiety. *Is a train coming?*

But, I'm alarmed as jet engines roar under strain, before an explosive boom as the jumbo jet impacts onto the railway bridge. The screeching sound of metal on metal, as the twisted iron of the bridge and its stony platform, is lit up by yellow fire.

It is horrifying; the part-disintegrated plane explodes as it slides along and comes to rest precariously on the iron bridge spanning the river. Petrified as I run through the darkness, toward the yellow flames, and jump onto the bridge. I stand on the railings, and carefully climb onto the plane, teetering high above the river.

Sporadic, yellow, flickering fuel fires are the only lights in the blackness. Illuminating the plane as it creaks with the tranquil sound of the flowing river. In total contrast, I hear the dogs' shallow breathing as I approach, one growls, tentative as I walk by as stealthily as I can.

Terror-stricken, as I realise many sleeping Dobermann dogs are on the plane, in the aisle, and on the seats next to perished humans. There's nowhere to tread without disturbing them, and it's so dark.

People, passengers, dead in their seats. As another test of bravery, I have to creep past the dogs as they sleep, and the people who haven't survived. Then jump 14ft from the plane on the bridge to the railway below, onto the loose stones.

Saddened by the disaster as I land on the stony ground, but proud of completing those terrifying tasks, immense tests that subjected me to some of my greatest fears.

Success, though, becomes jaded, almost insignificant as I see a light in the distance. By the arch of the bridge, where I remember old, broken-down lorries, the smell of diesel and dirty engine oil.

I make out it's from the interior of a silhouetted, long, old-fashioned, black car, waiting. I run toward it; the stones make a crunching sound as I sink into them with each stride.

A car door opens as I approach, which I walk toward and see the smiling faces of a dapper dressed man and a classy lady.

The lady is stunning, a brunette hottie with long, wavy hair wearing black heels, a white partially unbuttoned blouse and a tight, grey skirt with hemline just above her knees. I cannot help focussing on her full lips, painted with bright-red lipstick.

Lips, that to my delight purse, and softly kiss my cheek as she gives me a half open brown briefcase packed with ornate golden and sparkling jewellery. "Well done. Here's your reward, £500 and jewellery."

The sight of such riches amazes me, exhibiting such bravery makes me ecstatically proud.

My briefcase of jewellery attracts an invitation to a prestigious social event. *What am I doing here*, as I sit, out of place, amongst smartly dressed strangers? To my dismay, they knock my briefcase out of my hand, and the contents scatter everywhere.

People gasp at such riches, scattered on the floor. They search round for it, but steal my jewellery, and or it's lost. No-one asks or wishes to know how I gained such riches.

Still, I have enough to buy a lavish, luxury house and am content there with an ex-girlfriend, Kate, and her friend Angela. A man is there, too. A suave and popular friend I didn't trust in the past world. Wary, he's only here because of my success and wealth. *Why are they here?*

The girls dress up to go out. In a rush to leave, but admire themselves in the mirror, "Bye Paul, bus to catch." They didn't want me, just my jewellery and stole my briefcase reward and went out on a bus.

There's the screech and whoosh of hydraulic brakes at each stop, and a loud manly voice confiscating jewellery from them. I'm deeply disappointed and frustrated, as I'm powerless as they return. They look at the floor. "We're sorry, Paul."

It's cruel; I had gained and lost wealth and experienced duplicitous false love. Was the purpose and moral to receive no reward for greed in a wonderful place, then earn my reward from genuine, unconditional bravery with no knowledge or expectation of reward?

I do wonder and am surprised as I expect to be despondent but am focused, in a sombre mood with plaguing, ominous thoughts.

It's all so different, squalid, damp, and dark, near the old mill, at Welshpool. *How did I get here?* On the driveway to the caravans, where I walked and ran as a child? Older now and my clothes are very different, worn and threadbare; rags. My trousers, ripped and ragged.

I am there to entertain, and proud of my talent. I remember being taught how to make whisky out of water. It's the only desperate thing I can do and beg. Entertain with magic whisky. I learn how to jig and dance, too. With moves that remind me of a tap-dancing class I attended once as a child.

Puzzled too, to be in a different era: the total opposite of the fineries of lavish wealth I had experienced earlier. I wonder if it could be during World War II as I hear old planes and distant explosions.

White flashes fade as light beams probe the black sky, like my torch did as a youngster when I ventured outdoors to explore on night walks. Looked for bats near the old mill, which as we neared, was a brick spectre that shrouded the stars.

I am a beggar now, and destitute. Close to where the assassin shot me, but many decades in the past. I have nothing, only the rags I wear. A few possessions and an old, ripped tarpaulin for shelter against the harsh elements.

In the pouring rain, I stand in my shoddy tarpaulin shack, in my old leaky worn boots with holes in them and an old, torn canvas jacket. It is at night and dark. The dim light of a yellow flame in a paraffin fuelled lantern flickers.

Illuminates a shanty shack, covered in khaki canvass, where I beg. Numerous artefacts, pots, and pans and tranklements suspended from the sides where poles extend upward, jangle and sway.

I experience strange contentment as I gain popularity as a beggar, but know I shall never make my fortune and that it's not my destiny.

I don't know why I didn't go to war. But am what I am. And can do what I do. Still glad within another era, different classes, although I am not part of any class, I'm a mere beggar with nothing but my rags, my trade, and ramshackle shack.

Many people come to watch. Most ignore me, turn up their noses in repugnance and revile, even looking at me. They watch with pity and throw me coins between air-raids and probing white search lights, piercing the black night skies.

As dawn breaks, and a gradual silhouette of colour springs to life, a woodland landscape before a cloudless sky, I'm glad. There are crowds walking past that I follow and walk toward an area of grass by the caravans.

I am with crowds of people. No inkling of what's instilling excitement in everyone, though, or what we're waiting for, or whom. Until they look up to the skies.

The only one who's anxious as I realise they're hoping for an alien spaceship to appear. I hope one doesn't appear. And become alarmed by the approach of a distant silver object that evokes frenzied excitement.

The silver object becomes distinguishable as it descends. It's a huge oval-shaped object that escalates the excitement to near hysteria. Brilliant red, green, blue, and white lights pulsate, and become larger as the craft enters the Earth's atmosphere and descends toward the grassed area by the caravans and facing the woods.

Beneath the spaceship, crowds congregate, a sea of raised arms reaching upwards. Excitement escalates as hundreds of balloons drop from the spaceship. The balloons have tickets attached to them, allowing access to heaven for a day. Many try to catch these, I don't.

There is sheer delight for those catching a ticketed balloon. Yet, heartache in deciding as many are reluctant to leave loved ones. The alien craft hovers above the sea of hands, above animated, excited faces.

I didn't raise my hands, dubious, as each of my visits to heaven bought frustration and false joy. Did the aliens have access to a real heaven, or a mini hell? I know it's an elaborate ploy to capture naive earthlings eager to eat a slice of supremely delicious cake.

It turns out to be more... My inquisitive mind passes the complex test set by aliens. Maybe my desire and motivation to get to heaven had rippled far. Such profound defining experiences made heaven seem further away. The next adventure is terrifying and sad.

14.

NORTHERN IRELAND TERROR

hy am I here, in a region I feared, never thought I would be, in Northern Ireland, especially at the assassin's funeral? The same who stalked and shot me, but failing to kill me infuriated the gang who focus their resolve on him.

Funeral attendees include some of my family, and I know my attendance will annoy the gang who failed. I also attend out of respect for the tricked victim assassin. Still, it's bizarre to be in a place I considered hostile.

And, dangerous, I'd seen TV news coverage of violence and Northern Ireland troubles as a youngster. I'm with my cousin, aunty, and a friend, mourning with everyone else.

Mourners as strangers, sobbing inside a large black, dimly lit marquee, men dressed in black suits and white shirts. The ladies in black dresses, others in dark-purple attire proper for that most sombre of events.

There's a table with various drinks, including a large bowl full of purple liquid. I taste the drink from the bowl; liquid that's unbelievably exquisite. Words cannot describe the taste.

It is utterly delicious, addictive, precious. So lovely, I want more. But cannot have any. Dava nonchalantly has two glasses. Envious, I wished I was as confident.

Although, I worried they may deploy him in a hostile region like we're in now; I am pleased he's with us. Especially when a flash of yellow flames flies past me before a petrol bomb lands and explodes near us.

There's panic and screams as many disperse and run. The table tips onto its side, acts as a flimsy barricade to hide behind as another petrol bomb hits the table and explodes. Igniting spilled alcohol on the floor.

Besieged by a rampaging maniac; there's no escape. I see my friend by the light of the flames. He's on the ground, severely injured, and dies from the attack. A sad occasion becomes even sadder.

There is another funeral for the friend at dawn, but I sit outside as the church bells ring. Nuns attend, mill around with heads bowed, as they enter the church via a huge, ornate, gothic archway of stone.

That same day, my aunty, Dava, and I begin a long journey across Ireland, by coach. As the journey begins and throughout, there's much tension and few words as Dava scouts the bus, walks along, scours the terrain as a trainee Royal Marine® with his rifle.

He looks for hidden snipers in the trees and forest areas beside the road, wary as we travel across Ireland; intrepidly venture on and become more anxious and alert as night descends.

As dawn breaks, we feel safer as we reach our unknown destination and meet up with my dad somewhere in Ireland. We exchange warm greetings, but other family members return to England, so Dad and I are alone. It all happened so quick. To our dismay, a notorious gang surrounds us.

They tie my dad's hands together, kick, punch, and torture him in front of me. I implore them, "Don't hurt my dad. He's done nothing to you. Have me instead!"

"You're no use to us, we know we can't kill you… We heard your dad helped ya to win a wager."

I rapidly realise I'm powerless and of the futility of reasoning. Even begging for mercy as we walk along a gentle slope to a stretch of secluded, still water. A strange, overwhelming calmness urges me not to run or even try to fight.

I wish Dava was here, though, to help, but I'm glad he's not. The gang would've eventually got to him. Even if my other cousin and aunt had been with us, still outnumbered, powerless, and they'd die.

As we reach the water's edge, Dad says, "Don't look, don't look, son, turn around," as he cries. A gunshot cracks and echoes after the silence, and there's a splash as Dad falls. Killed, blatantly, cruelly slaughtered, murdered before my eyes, and dumped in the shallow water. I scream with anger and with intense anguish and sorrow as I sob.

Enraged, as I stand at the water's edge, wanting to wail and scream as the terrorists walk back up the slope but feeling hopelessly inadequate. *This wouldn't avenge their cruelty.*

The water shimmering grey, reverently reflecting a moody sky I long to be in and wonder if my dad's there, or beneath the water I transfix upon, as waves ripple, entwined with clouds.

My friend and dad, murdered. They cannot physically hurt or kill me, so inflict hurt and another form of pain.

Deeply upset, inconsolable as I begin the melancholic and dangerous journey back home. *What can I do to avenge the cold-blooded murders? Train to fight, battle the terrorists one day, to make them suffer, to feel pain, to make them beg for mercy, on their knees as they pray to their God. What if I had the power, and they were weak?*

As I reflect and contemplate revenge, a hand firmly grips around my arm, and a sharp knife presses at my throat from behind me. A deep, rough man's voice says, "Gotcha. Walk and do not make a sound. "

Forcibly held, blindfolded, and thrown into the boot of a nearby car. I hear the doors close, the engine starts. But, no words as I sense the car's in motion, and as it stops; *where've they driven me to* as the handbrake applies, and the boot opens? We arrive and I am led up a flight of stairs into an apartment; I presume.

I squint as they remove the blindfold. My eyes focus on two, rough-looking, knife wielding men. They are tall with long hair and unshaven but smart in grey suits and open collared shirts.

Led to a balcony, through an open-plan lounge, past two attractive female accomplices. Sitting on a black leather sofa, silent, but they stare, as they uncross their bare legs.

Forced onto a hard-backed wooden chair, I sit, pensive and reflective, as they tie my hands to the chair and I stare in front at a cloudy sky from a platform balcony adjoining the lounge.

It's hopeless. Such anguish – *I despise and pity them – but I must win their trust. Befriend, beguile and charm the women, so they'll get to like me. Use my cunning and powers of persuasion to escape whilst convincing them it's pointless as I am hopelessly outnumbered, and that I'm no threat and more useful alive.*

It's a desperate and complex plan, involving difficult and dangerous tasks, but my only chance. *Stay calm, composed;* as one of the women approaches from behind. She stands facing me, reacting to my unaverted gaze.

"It's so hot... Do you like my outfit? You can look at me; I won't bite." *What a sexy temptress,* long, gingery-brown hair with fringe and long curved strands to the sides of her brown eyes. An incredible body, tanned flesh in a tight, skimpy, black bikini, and tremendous cleavage between large breasts.

She sprawls her long, shapely legs in my line-of-sight as she leans back with her hands against the balcony wall, and big, brown, seductive eyes staring at me.

"Ha, bet you wish your hands were free, don't you?... I'm Tonya." I stay silent. "You're shy? Come on, talk to me. Tell me about yourself. Don't be shy now?"

I glare as Tonya walks towards me and eases her legs, either side of mine, straddling me. "I know you're tempted," as her head arches back and forward.

Her cleavage nears my face, and she lowers her head to mine until her lips softly touch mine; then press more firmly. "You might as well kiss me. Kiss me, as you'll never leave here alive... Unless, if it is true, we cannot kill you."

Aroused, as her lips brush against mine as she speaks. My lips tingling as I smell sweet perfume, and the kiss deepens, lingering, sensuous.

My heart beats faster as the other woman laughs. "Hey, leave him alone. Don't tease him like that."

Tonya leans forward, whispers in my ear as she gets off me to walk into the lounge. "I'm not teasing, and you're cute."

The other woman glares at me. "Hey, don't get any ideas."

"Nor you, Rachel." Tonya replies.

A moment later, I hear a key turn in the door, footsteps. Tonya says, "So, what shall we do with him, Frank?"

"What do you mean? You know exactly what to do now." Frank replies in an Irish accent.

"Yes, but do I have to?"

Frank laughs. "I'll leave you two alone?"

"Go on then." As Tonya walks toward me, smiling.

I hear Frank's footsteps as he says, "All right." The door opens and shuts. Tonya faces me again, seductively waggling her hips from side to side and with her legs open, and pouting her sweet, full, oh so kissable lips.

She flicks her head and hair back, as if teasing me in anticipation, but brandishes a long, shiny curved knife. "Should I kill you?... I think so; what do you think?"

How could anyone so lovely be part of a poisonous evil mechanism? Silence and expressionless before a gentle smile, then sadness as I feel the hurt. Consider my dad's brutal killing, a kind gent to even strangers.

"I don't care. Do whatever you want!"

"Aww, why the sad face? Don't be sad, I still think you're cute!" in a demure tone as she crosses her legs, turns to face the balcony, exposing a pert bottom and long legs.

She walks toward the balcony and places the knife on the balcony ledge, followed by her hands and manicured nails tap and drum to the side of the knife, "Such a beautiful blue sky, shall we fly away together... above the clouds?" as she spins, faces me. "I don't have to kill you. I should, but don't have to."

"So." As I pull on the ropes binding my hands.

Tonya picks up the knife, approaches, still faces me as she stands, then edges forward, straddles me again.

Her legs are straight, and revealing part of her chest, as she bends her upper body to the side, flicks her hair, adopts a racy pose, looks into my eyes. "You have honest eyes. I think you're a good man. What will you do if I untie your hands?"

"I won't hurt you... I might say a prayer."

Tonya walks to the balcony, turns and looks at me, "Maybe

I'm not as bad as you think."

She walks behind the chair, unties the ropes, "I don't care either. We can do anything we want... Even escape."

My hands are free; I rub them together and touch the indentations from the rope marks on the back of my hands and wrists. Tonya drops the knife onto the floor and strolls to the balcony, leans her arms on the edge, "Ever wished you could fly?"

I stand up, approach, but stop as I near her.

She turns to face me. "I fancy the pants off you."

As we stare at each other. "You're not an angel. But you're not an evil woman. Thank you." I place a soft kiss on her lovely lips.

Tonya's arms rest on my shoulders. My skin tingles as the tips of her manicured nails stroke the back of my neck. Then move lower, her soft nimble fingers unfasten my top shirt button, then the next as her hands touch my chest and tantalisingly move lower, as she stares into my eyes.

Her arms move up again, drape across my shoulders and wrap around me as we kiss, ever deeper, passionate, whilst we embrace. Her lovely, silky legs against mine. "Who are you?" Tonya asks in a soft voice.

Unresponsive as I gaze at the sun, a brilliant orb, low in the sky, brushing distant hills on the horizon. The door opens, there's the gentle tap of heels on the wooden floor. I smell the waft of perfume and turn to see Rachel in a tight, black dress, matching stockings and black high heels.

A glimpse of tanned fleshy cleavage as I scan upwards to a perfect-painted face, pouting lips and wavy, shiny hair.

"Tut, hasn't Tonya killed you yet? She will, you know, but she might seduce you first."

Tonya turns to Rachel. "Ha, leave me alone." Then looks at me. "She's jealous; don't listen to her."

"Oh really, let's see." Rachel walks toward me and faces me as she stares. "Who do you prefer? One of us will kill you, one of us can save you, and fulfil your wildest dreams. Even make you happy."

Flattered by those luscious women, but confused by the choice. "So, you both like me?"

"You want both of us? Look, I can make you happy, but you need to decide who can make you truly happy, even take you to heaven?" Rachel's reply as she approaches the bedroom, "I'll wait for you."

Tonya says, "Well, decisions, decisions, hurry; Frank may return soon. I'll help you escape and come with you, make you happy." Tonya reaches and grasps my hands. "It's your choice, Paul. I'm here; she'll be waiting."

As I enter the bedroom, Tonya sighs. "Oh dear," as Rachel's lying on the bed with dress off, revealing her tanned legs, black bra, and toned stomach. A seductive pose, ravishing, and a sexy stare as she smiles, lifts her legs and arches her head back, then up as she turns toward me. "Aww, you chose."

Hmm, have I? As I lay on top of her, plant a kiss on her lips and her legs' grip me. "Ha, no escape."

I glance across to Tonya in the bedroom doorway, tears glisten in her eyes.

"Give me the bedsheets," as I pull the bedsheets from the bed and turn to Tonya.

She's not in the doorway. So, I rush out as she approaches the balcony and climbs over the edge. "Wait, I chose you." Tonya beams as she turns to me and her eyes widen.

She insists I go first as we franticly knot the sheets together by the balcony.

"No, you first, Tonya."

"Look, I can stall Frank; and handle Rachel." As she touches my face and kisses me.

So I begin my reluctant descent, climb downward from the balcony first. Along the cool white sheets as quick as possible, and jump from the last sheet as they're not long enough to reach the ground and Tonya begins her descent.

"Hey, wait for me, Paul." But, shortly after, Rachel laughs as she leans over the balcony, holding the knife. It shines and glistens, reflects the sun.

Tonya screams as she falls to the ground, followed by the knotted, severed white sheets.

Rachel said from above, "You chose her; wrong choice!"

I rush over to Tonya, hold her in my arms as I look into her loving eyes. "You're almost an angel."

Tonya smiles. "I couldn't have killed you." Her eyes close.

Distraught because of the tragic, fast-paced events, but ever wiser, and although things begin to make sense, I cannot help wonder what would have happened if I hadn't chosen Tonya? She'd have lived on; I'd be with Rachel. Why did Tonya cry? Had she grown to love me, or did she think I'd made the wrong choice?

I still plan to return to England, glad to evade the terrorists, but sad about my dad, my friend, and Tonya. Seated on a packed commercial jet, eagerly waiting to takeoff, leave Ireland, I think nothing of a man in a smart, grey suit, and white shirt, who springs up from his seat and opens the overhead compartments.

Fellow passengers gasp and shout as they see a flaming, petrol-soaked rag immersed in a glass bottle of liquid brandished by the man, setting fire to the luggage. Molten-ignited plastic falls on the passengers, who scream in terror.

Blobs of molten plastic burn on the floor as the fanatical terrorist glares at me. He is holding the glass bottle, a petrol bomb, walks along the aisle, towards me and ignites more overhead cargo.

He returns to the front of the plane, wide maniacal, hatred filled eyes, "Anyone can leave the plane if they walk in bare feet." Metal trays are on the burning-hot plane floor, hotter by the second, as he sets more of the plane ablaze. Thick, black, acrid, choking smoke rapidly fills the plane.

The terrorist glares straight at me, walks closer, singles me out for personal attention and torture. His leering face amid curling wispy smoke as he lunges the flaming petrol bomb toward me, uses it for me to obey. "Stand up,... stand on the trays." He said. The metal's so hot.

Trapped with no escape as the terrorist approaches the plane door. I follow and escape as soldiers dressed in camouflage and armed with rifles storm the plane, rescuing me from that burning plane. I return to England with a plan to come back to Ireland one day.

15.

MERCENARY

*M*y uncle Albert heard the dreadful news about my dad and of the terror in Ireland and knows of the gang's relentless persecution. He takes me under his wing: looks after me, protects and trains me as a stealthy sniper — knowing one day, I will avenge my father's cruel fate.

I know I'm safer with him and become less fearful of the gangs; he is an ex-night watchman and a time traveller.

He is 6ft tall with a long warm face, a flat long nose and wild grey receding hair. A kind, comedian, and joker is how I remember him in the old world. Now, he is wearing a black police coat, faded to grey at the shoulders and with three white sergeant chevron shaped stripes on both sleeves.

I accompany him on several jobs, the most secret of missions, and become spellbound, in awe of his stature and skill. I aspire to become a mercenary.

Like my uncle, who has the world's most powerful rifle. With a powerful, highly accurate telescopic sight, that makes him supreme. With such skills, I'd be more able to defend myself against evil enemies.

We intrepidly walk toward the leery silhouette of trees, facing the blackness of night and ever dense trees of nearby Peascroft Wood, known as the Fozza in the old world.

It was a great place for kids to play, which attracted many visitors: older kids and in their early teens from various estates. I tagged along when I was about 10, accompanying my friend Ian and others.

Scary though, as many tall trees provided darkness and a dense canopy of shade onto rough walkways, steep embankments, and brighter, sunlit grassy areas. An eerie realm which at first glance opened up a leafy archway, like a dragon's mouth opening. Once inside the woods, there was no escape.

Some peddled horrific stories about this place, sinister tales, ghouls, and macabre fates of past nightly visitors, compelled not to enter the Fozza at night. It was scary even in daylight. Sometimes even with others, as I sensed evil and knew I was being watched.

Perhaps within the wood, within and amongst the trees and bushes, many captured secrets. Secrets held forever and understood only by nature, the howling, moaning wind whistling through the trees. Curiously, you rarely heard birdsong either. Were they even afraid?

This evoked suspense and instilled excitement as I loved the atmosphere, trees, and fantasised about living in a treehouse despite jumping from the apple tree in our garden and being covered in blood as a branch brushed my head!

That secluded Fozza was a haven for older kids and ever-exciting, daring adventures; increased dangers; you never knew what to expect. And hoped to encounter friendly folk.

One summer, a particularly crazy kid, set to shoot everybody with his gat-gun. A sick initiation ritual, only for the sake of being assigned to a fictitious elite class. Hard and able to take pain.

I watched each kid squirm; their faces screw up in agony, then euphoric joy the moment of realising they had endured the sadistic punishment and on realising they had joined the elite class. "Who haven't I done?" He said with a lisp. As he looked straight at me, knowing I was the last.

Crazed, determined eyes trained on me — the hunted as I struggled to evade the punishment by running, but in vain. Caught and held tightly by my arm, the gun pressed firmly on my upper thigh. "Don't!" I said.

Too late, they had pulled the trigger. Shot at point-blank range with the air gat-gun. The pellet's impact stung like hell as I hopped around, holding my leg. I wanted to get him back, shout and fight. But I couldn't, as he ran off like a lunatic.

If only I could have hidden. Hid in the long yellow grass.

Faded by the sun, among the jumping grasshoppers. No-one would've found me in that version of hide-and-seek on a much grander scale.

We entertained ourselves with a rope swing. A downtrodden, wide, dark-grey, dried and black, muddy soil, platform along the embankment where we swung out.

The rope was long, suspended from a high branch of a large tree. We swung the rope swing for us to catch it, jumped on, and swung off from the platform, before shouting, "Pilon," and jumped onto the wooden branched seat one-by-one.

Others jumped onto everyone else, doing our utmost to cling on and hold on to nothingness. The rope strained; the branch bowed and 'creaked'.

Until five or six kids were on at once, holding on, onlookers in suspense, envious, awaiting their turn as the rope snapped. So we ended up in a massive, bruised, tangled heap on the muddy ground, groaning and laughing.

When bored with those games, we sat on a high wall overlooking the large grassy field and next to a high, galvanised metal, mesh fence, industrial units beyond in the distance.

I sat facing the expanse of grass and focussed on the high woodland trees beyond and fought curiosity to turn round and look. An elder friend had told me: in the distant factory units there're nuclear warheads.

The sinister secret freaked me out with ominous emotions. Made me feel more grown up, but I wished the friend hadn't told me. That fantastic, fun place became tinged with a funereal flavour.

It's strange, but exciting to return to that place at night. A place I feared, even in the daytime.

My uncle has the gun now, too. Still, as we stealthily approach the distant forest, into the sinister dark, my heart beats so fast in anticipative awe at what we may soon encounter.

I walk close behind and edge closer as uncle Albert stops, stands poised, holding his rifle so still, carefully aiming, scanning the terrain with his telescopic sight.

I'd seen him do this frequently, and he always lowered the rifle but never spoke. Tonight, is different as he aims. More suspense and tension, as he's more tentative, somewhat agitated.

Ever more focussed, perhaps because of the cold, lingering, watery mist in the air as a sudden almighty bang echoes shortly before the faint movement in distant trees and a distant thud.

Albert says, "Got him!" In a quiet, non-triumphant tone, adding to the drama.

We continue to walk toward the Fozza, a silent trek; the mission is not over. Other dangers lurk. One hooligan eliminated from afar; more lurked. As we approach a derelict house by the gates of my old school, my heart pounds as I remember the gang and wonder who the next target might be.

How can Albert be so cool? Is he the same man who brought us fabulous gifts, boxes of chocolate bars with delicious fondant-fillings from the boot of his car? We were always excited to see him, and his unusual gifts; kindness in the other world.

My uncle was not that man anymore, and I had changed, too. Memories of my dad filled my mind, though, and disturbing emotions about the nature of his cruel demise, but I'm glad with my uncle.

We are at the derelict house; a dirty door with flaked paint is ajar and creaks as Albert pushes it and we enter. He leads the way, carefully treads past the doorway.

Careful as I follow, tread in the same place. Both into a dank, dark, squalid house, and the pungent smell of damp combined with rain. Dirt-daubed, mouldy walls, and torn strips of wallpaper hang from the walls.

Water droplets and mini-streams on the ceiling from leaky pipes add to the slow, steady drip of water, soothing and complimenting the sound of creaking floorboards.

"Come on, get me, I'm up here." I recognise the voice, the whispers before the piercing knives. Albert coolly poises himself, ultra-calm, totally focused and as still as a statue as he shoots up into the ceiling and there's a loud thud on the floorboards upstairs.

Albert beckons me nearer with his index finger and whispers in my ear, "Got him, too. That's how you do it."

Stealthy and wily, silence allows him to hone in for the incisive kill. Albert's ability to travel through space and time makes him ever more formidable; no escape or refuge for any of the designated targets.

The acquisition of such a skill instils confidence as I become wiser and wilier, another string to my non-existent bow. However, other quests are more pressing and I doubt I could kill anyone. I have greater skills, though, and tasks associated with a wider purpose.

16.

MODEL MURDERS

*T*he gangs learn of my newly gained skills and know they cannot kill me. So, in an effort to demoralise me, they ask me to take part in another motorbike race, and think I will lose without my dad.

And, I'd never ridden a motorbike. Had only been a pillion passenger. So it's quite a challenge. Especially as I dislike motorbikes and considered them too dangerous.

The gang take me to Welshpool and try to befriend me by buying me drinks in The Square and Compass Pub. An old, white bricked pub, I'm so hot and thirsty. The pub is full of drinkers. We're shoulder to shoulder with revelry and aromas of beer fill the air.

The bar-lady pulls a pint for me, but the glass glows and spews fumes. Renowned for drinking fast and not refusing drinks, especially gifts, in the other world, I know I must drink the brew.

Still, I am wary as the drink nears my lips, my nostrils tasting the fumes. Unaware the glass contains liquid plutonium, a noxious potent and hot liquid.

The drink is unpleasant, but I am determined to empty the glass and its effects amaze and excite me; makes me so alert, powerful and brave, with heightened perceptions and reflexes that make me supreme.

And, my black motorbike is fantastic as I rev up, poised to race. Competitors fear me and enter the race in which I am unbeatable! Others are not as brave as me. Some skid, lose control. But I knew that stretch of road well and remembered a sultry summer's day.

The welcome refreshing breeze from my open car window as I cruise along a gradual descent. Excited by the heat and increasing speed toward the pale-blue sky, the mill, and tall trees of the woods.

Downhill from Montgomery, away from its ruined castle on high, ravaged by history and time. The roadside greenery looked like a time warp in my peripheral vision as I reached 50 miles per hour (mph). Nostalgic, as I reminisced, envisaged the bridge over the railway tracks and the River Severn.

I go much faster now. Although I know, like then, the "SLOW DOWN" road markings will soon become a distant white blur before the turn and the bridge. Some had gone too fast. When will I dare to brake? Not when my rivals think I will!

A brilliant driver, not a biker, but still my determination to defy the gangs and win, boundless as I uncannily pass beneath the region of sky, I saw the moon move in front of the sun as my brother and I gazed below us from the road bridge at the darkening, rushing, river water, years earlier.

So excited and surprised; spellbound by the celestial show, an encroaching shadow on the Earth as part of the sun disappeared. We ran to the caravan to tell Mom and Dad. Melancholy, as I approach the turn. *Will I see my brother again?*

Even so, I'm elated about my great triumph; defying the gang again. After the race, though, an American secret agent dressed in a smart suit approaches. "Hey, as you drank the plutonium, you're responsible for a recent land-shift in California." A stern expression as he opens a large map and points to California, "See?"

He continues, "We'll ignore the liquid plutonium and the continental land-shift if you solve a mystery that's baffled our agents, and the best minds. A sadistic murderer has killed several top models, women. They are cunning, clever. The clues are jewels, 13 emeralds, one dove of peace, and other precious stones."

Peculiarly, I am asked to recite a long list of precious stones that I had won for bravery. Snow covers the ground, but I see half a dove of peace, partially buried in the snow by the old mill.

It's a complex and perplexing task that seems unsolvable. I suspect a mysterious doctor is responsible, but he has friends in high and low places.

An old friend says I can stay at his house and that he thinks he knows who the murderer is. Unbeknown to me, a ploy as a powerful madman instructs him to capture me and try to frighten and silence me.

With mixed emotions, I accept the invite to stay with the friend, but am surprised by the drab living conditions. At a dark, dismal house on high, but I soon realise it's part of a shrewd plan to keep me captive.

I am in a squalid room with white walls daubed with black, dirty marks. Two single beds are side by side, no mattresses, only bare, dull metal springs. My old friend is in a grubby, white vest, unshaven with scruffy, wild, dark hair.

Uneasy, uncomfortable as my friend acts strangely, but assume because I suspect the evil doctor and that very notion conflicts with his ideals. We sit at the ends of the beds and chat.

"P, why do you think the doctor is the murderer?" Asks Peter.

"You mean the evil doctor?"

Peter frowns. "Evil, no. Why is he evil?" His vehemence seems defensive. *The evil doctor has brainwashed my friend.*

"He's very clever. What makes you think he's not evil?"

"He's not evil, you're wrong."

I realise the house is next door to my aunt, afraid, but hope to outwit my captor. It's obvious the purpose of detainment is to delay, and try to dissuade, change my mind about the evil doctor.

Even more uncomfortable as I'm forced to partake in what seems religious rituals. Made to put my hand in a dish of salt and throw a handful of salt over my shoulder three times before lying on my uncomfortable bed of grey steel springs with no mattress or pillow.

I hate the ritualistic ordeal, the captivity, but have to fight the resentment and play along, comply to allay antagonism.

After trying to assure my captor that I won't escape, I wait for my chance. Throw the salt over my shoulder, place the palms of my hands together and pretend to pray in silence before I lie on the steel springs, and wait until Peter is asleep before attempting to escape.

Wary, as I sit up, get up from the bed. As I do, a firm arm grips around my neck and I hear, "Don't try. You can't escape."

My non-compliance angers my captor, rebelling and attempting to leave, apoplectic as he releases his hold. He stamps his feet and shoots his brother with an airgun as he enters the room. "Stay there."

A sudden, loud crashing sound prompts me to turn to see the wall crumbling and part of a lorry cab. Alarmed, but smug, at the distraction. Then delighted as I see my uncle John in his lorry cab and that he rescues me. He jumps out from his cab. "Quick, Paul."

I rush over, clamber across the brick debris. Through the thick choking dust that lingers in the air. It's great as I climb into the cab, proud as I remember I accompanied him. In his lorry to a distant destination, I helped for a day. When I was about 14.

It's so different now. "Don't worry. I'll take you somewhere safe, Paul." Great, but I wonder if they have tricked him as the journey begins onto open roads before an overcast sky.

We arrive at an extensive building. "Someone here has said they'll look after you, Paul." I know he believed that, but I suspected otherwise. Even more daunted as I am taken to a large white room, with white walls and white lavish couches.

A man in a suit and a white doctor's coat greets us and shakes mine and my uncle's hands. "Hello. Welcome, relax; make yourselves comfortable."

But he is trying to charm pretty ladies in the room, as he sits by them on the couches. Others are standing, chatting with each other. Dressed in smart clothes, slinky figure-hugging dresses above the knee, and wearing makeup on their faces, I assume they have been to a nightclub or party.

I want to talk to them as it had been so long since seeing any women, but I watch in awe as he injects sedatives into those who succumb to his charms. They slouch on the couches as they become drowsy.

Proving my suspicion, the man is an evil doctor, and he doesn't approve of me seeing his deeds. He approaches and tries to cajole me. "I only help people get better. You will find these eye pads soothing." As he places them over my eyes.

My reluctance to comply evokes hostility as he forces the foam sponge pads onto my eyes. "Come on. You'll find these soothing" and with increasing vehemence, but the pads smell of ethanol, I know, is inflammable.

I'm horrified by the crackling sound of a match as it strikes, the brimstone smell and glimpse at a faint glow of yellow flame through the side of the eye pad. *He wants to burn my eyes by igniting the ethanol doused eye pads.*

No — in desperation, I try to blow out the flaming matches and dismiss the instilled sheer terror whilst trying to remove the eye pads.

The doctor is too strong and holds my arms. He persists; becomes even more vocal as he continues trying to blind me. "Relax. Let me cover your eyes. Don't blow out the matches," as Erasure, *The Circus* plays.

Alas, I had witnessed his deeds. The injections of sedatives into the girls to seduce them, and deducing he is the murderer, makes him ever more determined to not only blind me, but kill me, after torturing me to prolong the ordeal of terror.

There is no escape or defence. It's futile to reason. *Does he know he cannot kill me?* I wonder as he tries to prevent me from seeing his further evil actions and inflicts torture for pleasure, and demoralising me, gives him feelings of power and dominance. Stalling to enable, prolong the depraved evil is his actual goal...

A lovely, drugged female waking from her slumber distracts the evil doctor. "Hey, what have you done to me?"

"There, there, don't worry, my sweet." He replies as he injects her again.

He places me on a bed of nails, too, making it much more difficult for me to resist or even flinch. I am in intense pain, locked in a bare white room, lying on that cruel bed of nails; confused and terrified. *The evil doctor may return at any moment.*

But, I become intrigued. There is a TV on the wall. The volume is too low for me to hear. I just see the moving pictures and colours in my periphery vision. In too much pain, I dare not turn my head for a better view.

Overwhelmed by angst as a quiet, hardly audible whisper comes from the door, "You're Micro Man, and I'm a Micro Man, too, and I'm inside the keyhole. I'll help you escape."

This is comforting, but puzzling. *How can he help or rescue me from this room of torture and terror?*

Such excruciating, inescapable pain as I try to keep still, not even flinch; keeping completely still is impossible. I'm scared, lonely, but nothing I can do, just wait, hope. Endure the pain. Suffer the extra torture, knowing the pain will intensify if I'm eventually removed.

I only hope Micro Man climbs through the keyhole, but how can he help me, anyway? I become confused: *If I can shrink, become so small that I fall through the gaps in the nails, the evil doctor won't find me; I can escape through the keyhole. Is that possible? It's hopeless.*

I turn my head to face the TV, interested in images of sports cars, airplanes, luxury items, such as jewellery, all stolen. They appear on the TV. I am even more surprised to learn the items are projections via the psychic powers of a distant relative.

Unbeknown to me, the relative had become a celebrity! I'm amazed as I watch him demonstrate his psychic powers on TV. He holds his head, enters a trance and locates missing items. He is a sensation and superstar, but such demonstrations anger and delight; make enemies of those with criminal minds.

His psychic powers also expose the evil doctor and the plight of the women he has kept captive, both physically and mentally. It's great for all to be awake and free. Rescued from the pain.

I want to chat to the ladies, but only see them fleetingly. They disperse and weren't angels. Still, I would have liked them to thank, or at least acknowledge, me.

As a reward, I may travel to another place. A special place on Earth, but wars beckon and other adventures.

17.

ARMY TENT

*T*he sun's long since left the horizon, on its own as a fiery ball, ascended into the pale-blue sky. A part of an idyllic scene at a beauty spot near Llanrhaeadr, Mid Wales, where there's a carnival.

Many attractions are there, stalls and tents, including a huge high, khaki-coloured canvas tent on a grassy field against lush green mountains tinged with grey stone and white quartz.

People queue to enter one tent as the base of the tent inflates with air and becomes bouncy and I see the smiling, joyous expressions of those who leave the tent. Fond memories as I reminisce about being inside the bouncy castle at Bilston Carnival at Hickman Park as a youngster in the past world.

Excited by the prospect of a similar fun experience. I queue with others and enter with them; they seal the front door flaps shut, but my expectations of fun – quashed – as there's a hissing sound, before the smell of a pungent gas, like stale air being pumped into the tent.

The experience is frightening, but necessary. Inhaling the gas makes me immune to the effects of poison gas in a future war.

None are told this; the truth would cause widespread panic. It's brilliant fun in the tent as I bounce around and rebound from the walls, but I walk to another tent near a lake where I swam and paddled a canoe in the other world.

From behind, there's distant chatter. I turn around, pleased that two women are approaching, both pretty, tall and slim, with well-fitting, but shimmering garments.

One with long straight blonde hair and dressed in a black silk dress with tassels on the hemline. The other is in a similar styled pink, silk dress and has long, brown wavy hair.

I face them, stand up in anticipation of greeting them, and cannot help but smile at their good-looks, even from afar. Elated at the prospect of human company.

Increasingly excited, as they approach, smile and stare at me for a moment with lovely, captivating eyes of deep blue and brown. They stop, chat with each other. Look at each other as they walk.

Their heads face forwards again, smiling as they turn and become ever nearer. Excited as they reach me, and as the one dressed in black says, in a quiet and seductive voice, "Hello, lovely day!"

"Yes, it is… where are you going?" As I smile, too. She is silent as she stares, scans my face. Tantalisingly grins as the strands of her blonde hair part momentarily, then fall back in place, and her silk, loose-fitting garment shimmers in a gentle breeze.

The brown-haired woman steps forward; I watch as her perfect, painted lips open. A sweet voice says, "Walk to our tent with us?" Their beaming, enticing smiles arouse intense emotion and desire.

"OK, let's go." *What an invitation!*

We soon arrive at a large tent. The flaps open as we enter. To my glee and disbelief, packed with women dressed in lingerie, so sexy, alluring. One of them with wavy brown hair, brown seductive eyes and long, tanned, shapely legs approaches and wraps her arms around me in an embrace.

She looks into my eyes as her soft hand strokes my face and her luscious lips touch mine. What a greeting, incredible, I want to stay with her, and those gorgeous women, get to know them, kiss them.

Romantic walks, oh the bliss, but I hear a sterner voice, from the open door flaps, "Come on, Paul. It's time to leave. Youths have hijacked a coach!"

"Aww, can't I stay?"

My attractive partner comes closer, her soft warm lips brush my ear as she whispers, "You'll see me in your dreams." Dismayed at having to leave that amazing place.

"I'll be back, don't worry" as I hold her hand. *I can't bear not to return!* But, my presence fades from that time as I'm teleported into the future.

18.

EARTH INVASION

*A*nnoyed to leave that idyllic, intriguing place of tantalising beauty and fun. Now in another time. A place I know cannot be as much fun, although familiar. I am lying on my front in a building opposite a school in Bilston.

It is strange to be overlooking it, holding a rifle, pointed above the school at a blue sky entirely blotted out by a mass of black. Black, because countless aliens parachute from their ships, descending to Earth to fight, to wipeout humankind.

As part of one of the last pockets of resistance as a soldier, I've won medals for heroism. Lying on my front on the deck of a motorboat speeding toward a hostile enemy shore, I was unfazed as I aimed my rifle. I captured a beach.

Now I'm one of a few fighting to defend the school. We cannot defend the world. The streets, deserted. But those lucky enough to still live are in sheer panic as they run along the corridors in fear, hoping to find non-existent refuge.

Some are braver and cooler than others. Many look out of the windows. Transfixed in awe and despairing disbelief at the enormous mass of invaders; none pray.

The few soldiers train their guns on the aliens, follow them to the ground. There are so many, and not enough guns. It's inevitable the corridors become invaded, and I engage a hostile alien in hand-to-hand combat; fierce expressions and dressed in black. A daunting foe, although it looked human.

Fast and wily, with immense fighting skills that make me think I will lose the fight. Kicked to the floor, but I kick the alien over my head, stand up and keep punching, although drained.

I win that fight, but it's merely a matter of time. There's no hope. The invasion will wipe civilisation out. It's an inevitable phase in annihilation and extinction of the human race. Yet, I fight valiantly, but not to be a hero, or any prize.

Medals and such acclaim, though, symbols of meaningless triumph, mere tokens of futile defiance against a relentless enemy, the most formidable and merciless enemy ever faced.

I flee, with others, running through the streets in panic, repelling and try desperately to defend, protect and survive amid the mayhem and anarchy. We find a house that seems an ideal refuge. It's a lovely, enormous house, as I sit in a nice open-plan room, with various ground floor levels.

Lavish and luxurious rooms with leopardskin blankets on the several black leather sofas, and lush, thick rugs and dark polished wooden floors extend to the rear of the house. There are huge glass patio doors to the right, leading to a large slabbed garden area.

Excited by the opulence of that dwelling, but concerned and curious. I hear a helicopter; intuitively, I walk toward the back of the room. Dazzled by a glint of sunshine on the glass of a round-fronted helicopter, hovering outside the patio doors of the house, just above the patio slabs.

Most intriguing is the object. It's an enormous orange ball, suspended from the helicopter via a cable, and resembles a large, round orange fruit. It reminds me of the oranges my aunt gave my cousins in the other world.

Shouts from behind are faint, barely audible above the helicopter engine noise, and prompt me to turn around to see several bedraggled, scruffy men behind a smooth-talking, and clean-shaven, smartly dressed man who holds my arm and says, "These people are Mombasan refugees. Let them stay here, and I will pay you."

Bizarre in another world, one of my T-shirts had "team Mombasa" written on the front.

More refugees appear as the man adds, "If you refuse, the helicopter pilot will release his cargo. The orange ball is an atomic bomb."

Before I even answer, a 10 second countdown begins. No

time to run. Sheer terror and horror. No escape as the bomb drops and detonates. Such intense white-fiery heat for a millisecond, and dread as I am instantaneously atomised by the nuclear fission.

Of all the crude methods, the atomic bomb is the most evil, terrifying and excruciating, but the fastest fate. I had experienced the first of hundreds of atomic, nuclear bombs. Bombs so powerful — they would obliterate life on Earth.

No living, mortal-being, could survive against such destructive power. Am I now immortal? Where had I gone, my soul, my thoughts, me? A mortal in a mysterious, unbounded realm; not a god. Will ingenuity and defiance deliver any hope for humanity?

How could I possibly materialise anywhere else after being atomised?

Some of my biggest fears were an alien invasion, nuclear war, and the aftermath. I wanted a bombproof bunker in the early 1980s and had played in a zigzag complex air-raid shelter on Green Lanes in Bilston as a child, but there was a filled in shelter next door.

19.

WAR ON HIGH

I emerge in a strange place, an open-plan bedroom high in the sky. The room's walls are white, and I lie on white bed sheets, on a bed. A white floor leads to a long open balcony below a pale-blue sky with white clouds. Cool and fresh air blows upon my face from a steel-grilled fan by the side of my bed.

Comfortable, but unwell. *Is this a hospital room? No-one else is here.* I must have survived, although I have no recollection of being atomised. I just remember the pain deep within, the invasion, and many battles. *Am I here because of my experiences in other realms?*

Many millennia have passed, and I am in the realm of Earth, but high above, not heaven. Even sadder, I cannot see any angels, or any beauty. I just hear explosions, plane engines, and strange sounding guns evoking angst and bewilderment, sorrow as I realise the Earth I knew no longer exists.

It's barren, ravaged and ruined by the spectre of war; spoiled for all-dwellers, its surface inhabitable. No life or shadows, atomic ash, and decay; poison from the aftermath of nuclear war that still rages.

Alas, centuries of conflict have led to the wipeout of humanity. The destruction of humankind brings despair, wanton hopelessness, with a perplexing paradox. Fight, or perish, and still to perish if you fight.

Alien attraction to Earth has led to its demise. Aeons of achievements and triumphs, meaningless. Such a travesty that the least of misdemeanours, personal escalating battles and quests for love and solace may have caused our Earth to suffer the cruel ravages of war.

The clever and superior aliens had won and claimed their world. A spoiled inhabitable prize and left the last remnants of humankind, knowing they'd perish. Or fight among themselves, wage their own war for the only remaining territory in the skies.

Survival in the air becomes the goal. The struggles to survive and battles, though, were petty compared to grander scales. Humans had become feeble, insignificant slaves, the aliens, masters.

And, as human slaves squabble in their petty wars, the aliens knew the last few humans will cancel themselves out. The eradication of humanity is imminent.

The distant sound of a plane intrigues me, but I'm too weak to get out of bed. Its engines become louder, a deafening roar that alarms me as I see the spinning propellers of a twin-engine, khaki-green war plane with crimson, deep-red circles on the fuselage fly past the balcony.

The engines slow and quieten as unfamiliar and familiar voices become audible and progressively louder.

Noises, frightening and perturbing, but my instincts encourage me to leave the room via a door in the room's corner. I tentatively turn the door handle, open the door into an unlit corridor. It is sheer mayhem, shouting and chaos as I realise I am in a warzone.

A war against Japan, fought high above the Earth in enormous floating fortresses. Some of my closest friends are with me, fellow soldiers fighting with much more advanced weaponry than any I had ever seen.

So, it's puzzling to hear old aircraft engines and propellers of aircraft that must have taken off from air bases on high.

I am a soldier wearing camouflage like the others, but am ill and immobile as I sit outside the strange bedroom on one of the long settee benches that resemble train seats within these bases, high in the sky.

The floating bases are like long, dark train corridors, only wider, with glassless window openings open to the elements and give little protection, but some refuge from the ravages of war.

Respite from the madness, in the sky, above the clouds,

it's a little less fierce. Tamer than Earth's surface, the ferocious firestorms, and radiation. It's inhospitable, ominous, depressing, more so as brilliant bright white light lit up the corridor.

It is frightening. More so, as there's no escape or chance to repel a formidable enemy, as soldiers in camouflage and round, green helmets land on the fortresses in their planes and constantly storm. There's no limit to their aggression, an unrelenting and merciless enemy; ruthless.

Gun battles, hand-to-hand combat, poisonous gas; so much noise accompanies the anarchy and chaos. Despair, as ever brilliant nuclear flashes brighter than the lightning from the heavens, adds to the drama.

Are the bombs ever closer, ever powerful? What if they become so powerful, they reach the floating fortresses, to bring them crashing to Earth? It is only a matter of time in a pandemonium hour glass.

We are being overrun, enemy soldiers heading towards us for an imminent confrontation. There are shouts and panic as an enemy soldier throws an object to the fortress floor. It lands by my friend, a war colleague.

Gyrates and hisses on impact as it releases poison gas. Death is instant as he falls, perishes, his eyes widen, then close.

We are losing the war. It's hopeless, our efforts futile and inane as we're swarmed and overpowered by soldiers and bombs. The situation worsens. Becomes desperate as the sounds of unfamiliar plane engines, and soldiers running in boots, gunfire, and American accents become distinct.

We are delighted to see non-hostile allies and that they join us, help us fight. A refreshing novelty, too, as men and women fight side by side.

The Americans bring us up-to-date weaponry, special guns, an antidote for poison gas and flash blankets to shield us from the nuclear flashes of bombs detonating far below us on the Earth's surface.

An American soldier briefs me. She's a stunning, attractive woman, with short bobbed black hair and in camouflage attire.

Ultra-professional, impressive, quick, cool and efficient, I admire and revere her at once as she briefs me and demonstrates those counter weapons of war; throws a small shiny metallic oval-shaped capsule to the floor in front of us that breaks on impact.

Its contents fizz, melt the floor. Diffuse upward as an enemy soldier, enters through the window. Impeccable timing for a lethal demonstration. He perishes as grey-green-gas rapidly diffuses and envelops him.

She shows no remorse. The gas's potency is alarming as the bright white light flashes I can see from the windows become more frequent.

The entire section is lit up by a light so intense, it's frightening and more intense than the brightest lightning. It's pointless to shelter from the nuclear flashes, but I feel safer shielding myself by holding one of the shiny, silver-coated flash blankets over me.

The hiding provides little solace from the inner fear. It's just a matter of time. But I hope to survive against the odds, although vastly outnumbered.

We fight on, against the tyranny, in defiance of the destruction of the Earth, humanity, and life. We don't have to, but it's right to fight. The flame of humanity extinguished, but not the human spirit.

Still, it's incomprehensible, and where next, higher in the skies to an elusive heaven?

The angels, the gangs seem so far away and so long ago; estranged, alone, as one of the last humans. Yet, I am privileged. To be among the few in the skies, although there's no refuge, comfort, or solace, only destruction and chaotic, wanton despair whilst searching for the faintest glimmers of hope, although hopeless.

20.

SPACE WAR

The war on high, a consequence of Iceman's wrath and his intention to decimate Earth. The invasion and nuclear annihilation of planet Earth many years later represented the last and inevitable phase for humanity. Life on Earth is no more. There's cold blackness, no solace. Where are the angels, the sweet voice?

There was no respite or lull. The onslaught of the human race continues, as the battles in the fortresses transcended into space, against an ever more formidable foe, a sister race so powerful they dominate space.

They wage an unyielding vendetta, deep in space that seems so very far from heaven, and even further from the desolate, spoilt Earth. A few remaining humans live to fight on, or rather, exist. Is this a privilege or curse, knowing billions have perished?

Are the aliens so powerful, they have destroyed heaven? Have they decimated all-beings mortal and immortal, the angels — God himself with overpowering darkness as I dream of seeing the stars?

Such dreadful contemplations amplified by the ominous, black, empty, void add to the sense of despair. My skin tingles as I shiver with the cold. It's so different to heaven.

A vast wilderness, trying to consume and swallow all with no mercy or purpose, other than to provide a daunting, but glorious stage. An amphitheatre stage for a futile war in the vacuum of space.

It's a magnificent arena for the battles to rage midst an awe-inspiring backdrop of magnificent stars, galaxies, and distant multicoloured nebulae.

The fighting is fierce, and against alien beings whose strength depends on temperature. The colder the temperature, the stronger and more hostile they became. This makes them the most formidable enemy I had faced! But, I don't fear them as I watch them through a space window.

They had sinister, expressionless, menacing faces with deep tanned perfect skin. Some males of the species could only make one sound. A grunt, but they didn't need to communicate.

Thousands of years in battle, destroying many worlds, and civilisations have made them highly advanced, honed their innate combat skills and instincts to destroy. To kill, wreak havoc, and ruin.

Their sole purpose, and motivation is to conquer. Yet, the aliens take great pride in their appearance. Particularly their meticulously shaped hair, sculpted with jets of icy air blown from hair dryers.

The more flamboyant male styles represent a mark of prowess, a sign of their bravery, complementing muscular size.

Good-looking alien women with similarly sculpted hair craft and set an extensive variety of sleek, smart styles into place with snow-like ice spray.

In a section of the spaceship that resembles a busy hairdresser's salon, they mill around a row of four white chairs that are seldom empty. As someone stands up to return to the fighting outside, another sits on the vacant chairs.

I much prefer the warmth of the spaceship and never ventured outside, but know the main brunt of the fighting takes place outside the stationary spacecraft. I heard unusual '*zoing*' noises shortly before seeing dazed alien expressions as they entered the spaceship through a space-hatch.

An alien being knocked out causes the strange noise? The energy-sapping effects of being inside the warm spaceship also become clear and make them less menacing.

This is the only momentary respite to the relentless fighting. The frosty air jets and ice spray partially re-energises them. Only a few minutes in the extreme coldness outside the spaceship replenishes their strength.

Content in the warm spaceship, fascinated and sometimes entertained by the peculiar noises, but I know I cannot stay. And will have to venture into the dark cold of space. I will confront one alien. *How can I fight those inexorable automatons?* It's hopeless. I have no chance against such formidable adversaries. I am so feeble. To knockout even the weakest requires enormous force.

If I was strong enough, I would need to be agile, fast, and precise. To deliver such a punch is exceptionally difficult. Virtually impossible, as the deep cold of space makes them invincible.

Even so, I want to calm the turmoil within my mind. Prepare to face and defend myself from a lethal enemy, and go outside despite ever-foreboding, ominous thoughts filling my mind as the *zoing* noises become less frequent; as fellow humans perish. I know it's because of fewer knockouts.

It will soon be my turn and I cannot imagine, or anticipate, the challenge; the magnitude of the task I will encounter.

I enter the space-hatch, realising I am the last; the sole surviving human of an entire race adds to the solemn scale of expectation. I become mesmerised in humbled awe at the strange serenity.

Beauty as I emerge onto a dark, grey hull, stretching into the distance and meeting a pristine black panorama speckled with stars.

Immensely cold, and I am fearful but accepting; thankful I can breathe in a thin atmosphere held by artificial gravity. I wonder if the aliens believe in gods or our same God? There's no hope. But is there salvation without perpetuity? Solace, as the last human?

My adversary approaches immediately, stands in front of me. A tall stature and styled hair, glistening from the dim light from the spaceship and distant suns; a white, styled curve in front of an infinite black cosmos.

Before an alien silhouette, I stand and bravely punch, aim just below the white hairline. With all my effort, I deliver two punches without success, and hardly touch his resolute, expressionless face. Sanguine, soulless, but raging brown eyes calculate and evaluate where to strike back at me.

White frost-like flecks, glow like faint stars in the distance and spin around black wide pupils, trained on me. Their muscular arms rapidly retract, then lunge forward towards me. Rocked, but I still stand. I punch again without success, despite all-my-might.

Anguish from such a desperate situation, Iceman, the champion boxer, the gangs, all less powerful than the alien adversary I now face. Those former enemies, I had no power to fight back, like a butterfly against 1,000 stampeding elephants.

How can I fight back? Even though it's hopeless and futile. Still, could they do what earlier adversaries didn't achieve?

I have already given my all to no avail. I have to knock him out for my sake. What will become of me if I fail? Will they spare me, or knock me out to drift into space and eventually perish? What prize if I succeed?

Are the stakes higher than I can imagine, the entire lasting legacy of a beaten human race? Human spirit of defiance entwined with compassion from all hearts that no longer exist? The whole of humankind depending on me, the last human, in the final conflict; the sole defining moment.

Can I do it, accomplish the impossible, succeed? I remember the gasps of shock preceding silence as my school friends in the other world watched me deliver an exceptional karate punch to my instructor.

It is more silent now, colder, picturesque, as I focus on a blurry backdrop of distant twinkling stars and then on my adversary. I summon up every bit of strength from my body, everything I have, absolutely all I can give, and lash out with all-my-might.

The alien's head rocks back, his eyes close. A few attempts, but I did it, eventually; knock the alien out. They don't stay unconscious for long.

Wild, brown eyes spring open and immediately fix on me, filling me with dread, escalating to horror as I see the rage of a determined alien soul. Mean with insatiable hunger for revenge; to never lose again, or allow one blow to penetrate.

I hear the space-hatch door open behind me and beckoning sweet voices. I step backwards but stay transfixed on the alien's eyes amid the stars as I am taken into refuge by alien ladies; delighted and such cute faces and exquisitely sculpted white frosty hair. Beautiful, although not resembling angels I had previously encountered.

Still, I am grateful for being saved. For the warmth, particularly after the frigidness of space. Contented and safe in their presence, my prize for a special victory in becoming the only surviving human in that ungodly war in the bitter, forsaken depths of space.

Will I live on to represent the last shred of humanity in the universe? In contempt of the cosmic might of a superior race?

I had reached a place midst and amongst the stars themselves, stars I had won and given to angels. So many long, arduous battles in other worlds, outer space, and heaven, adventures, all different, so real, all I believed in the physical world. My deepest fears, desires, all I ever wanted, but more intense and more frightening.

Did I make a choice to live on in defiance? Or was I a proactive observer of subconscious projections of memories and entwined emotions?

Angels, aliens, good and evil, wars, phantoms fighting phantoms, sinister versus divine characters created by my mind or conjured for the purpose of providing fear, comfort, and pleasure?

What defined an angel? A pure, divine heart unconditionally loving, rescuing the lost, those suffering or in need? Were the aliens, the gangs, all angels in disguise, angels of a different type? Actually allies with a sole aim and purpose to test my core, my mind, body, and soul to establish if I had the desire, strength, and the will to continue to fight?

My success in knocking out that immensely powerful alien stood as a testament to conquering fear in a new reality. Soon I would emerge from coma. Begin the transcendental journey through subconscious realms and states, reborn as a sentient being.

But, into what world? What dimension?

Had I escaped the other realms? The endless pain, and fleeting joy, light and dark, fear, and enlightenment? The all-knowing and wise, cosmic harmony and raging woe with the all engulfing cosmic tide absorbing time; reflecting, mirroring, surfacing emotions and fears? Were the experiences lessons? Cryptic and gruelling tests of human spirit — bespoke ubiquitous gifts from angels to decide worthiness; and my right to dwell in wondrous celestial places with the angels and amid the stars: heaven?

Maybe the angels knew people loved me on Earth. I would have stayed or been free to roam, wander in my desperate plight for love and solace. If there had not have been distractions. Alas, wrenched from my joy and misery of the epic journey when music played or someone spoke.

What or who orchestrated the events? Was it God himself, another supreme being, or alien beings from other dimensions in tune with a part of me no human could comprehend or ever understand?

Or were such events randomly conjured phantasms of a physical-biochemical nature as my mind tried to grapple with memories and emotions and construct order, logic, and sense from the trauma?

Maybe the experiences, adventures, and challenges constituted part of the recovery of my subconscious mind and an innate survival mechanism.

A being emerges from the infinitely complex labyrinth, akin to a cocooned chrysalis.

Was I actually returning to the Earth I had departed?

Section III

AFTERMATH

21.

AWAKENING

*D*id I survive or was I spared? I am now in-between states. In an epic limbo, on the edge of a preliminary stage of a slow awakening, suffused with intensifying confusion and curious magic.

It's akin to being tugged between two different realms. One in the material world of Earth, the other in the intangible, astral-like world of coma.

A realm of wistful amour, pain, and persecution where my emotions and sensations entwined with musical melody, as some events occurred. And, as I met angels, and evil gangs.

Oblivious to the softest whisper, and faintest glimmer. Time had little meaning; unquantifiable and immeasurable apart from when I stared at Dad's watch; willed my heart to keep beating in spite of the gangs.

Real pain, but no sensation of the external physical world that had inexorably moved on its cosmic path.

Still, it seemed two years had passed, with moments where pain lasted. Wondrous, tantalising moments of pleasure and happiness were ever fleeting, never quite graspable, despite diligent efforts. Just 12 days had elapsed in the physical world. This was the duration of my coma.

As I gradually approached a waking state, the sensations I experienced enhanced shock as the distinction between those two separate worlds became stark. And, I couldn't define or associate a route or channels of awareness of the two worlds.

Dulled and vague sensations of stimulus slowly intensified, surreptitiously transforming into a state of stunned bewilderment, pain, and escalating confusion as music played, and memories of other realms returned at once.

And, I remembered what seemed to be my previous life. Those memories, though, mere dreams belonging to a far gone and distant world; another universe, and dimension beyond return and where time warped.

I was in transit from mysterious subconscious realms, and accelerating toward a waking state of limited awareness.

As I began to perceive, I became a passenger in time. These new perceptions presented partial sentience, as I steadily transcended to a more conscious state of awareness.

It was an intermittent awareness that brought new sensations; a jaded, dreary realisation. A beautiful and sombre dawn as I woke to a new terrifying and painful reality. It was only the first step.

I was re-entering a physical, fake world: being reborn. Like a baby, much to learn. Some of me would never return.

My body is rigid, heavy, and my muscles hurt. *Why can't I move or make a sound? What is this sharp tube up my nose?* So uncomfortable. *Is it a piece of wire running from my throat into my stomach, the cool refreshing, vanilla flavoured thick liquid?*

Sometimes the tube came out. And, I felt pain at the top of my nose. Again, when the tube was reinserted, threaded up my nostril and downward to my stomach. All part of needless torture by strange, cruel alien life-forms, I was unaware the tube was feeding me with nutrients.

Alas, the pain, the persecution continued in that alien world. White-coloured, bland tasting liquid in small, circular shaped plastic pouches, squeezed into my mouth to poison me. And a doctor trying to rot my teeth with those chemical-laced brushes.

They tried to persuade me to release my grip with their soothing voice — no way. I bit the bristles so hard, and wouldn't loose! I didn't want my teeth rotted away!

Even more uncomfortable and frightening was the metal wire in my penis. It hurt, was sore, but bearable. The actual terror: that wire into me is a fuse for an intricate bomb mechanism made from thick white wires on a white wire frame.

My fake dad was a secret agent and an expert bomb diffuser.

But overwhelming despair quashed all hope. He could not help as that bomb is so complex, any attempt to defuse it would cause ever more intense pain as it would explode inside me.

So, no option. Just endure, wait, hoping this has to be a nightmare. I didn't know the wire was actually a catheter tube, the white frame a catheter bag stand.

I struggled to grasp that cruel new emergent reality. Tussled with turmoil and confusion, entwined with intense physical and mental pain. Mental pain that was greater because of fear entwined with frustration.

Ominous anguish because of a plethora of unanswered questions: *How can this be? Why am I here in this fake world, a nightmare reality?*

Yearning to return to the other realms. My only hope came at night. The times I lay in bed, and focussed on the orange light above my bed as that light is a direct channel to God and only link to heaven, other worlds, and the angels.

I relived the suspense, too, as I remembered my mom's aunt Mary's old caravan at Welshpool. Captivated as my great aunt told me about the orange, glowing, spinning orb she saw in the sky, hovering above the trees, then disappearing at great speed.

Her caravan was always homely, warm with a roaring or glowing gas fire, with a special atmosphere of suspense and intrigue. Perfect for the fortune-telling, she was renowned. She turned the ornate teacups upside down on their saucer.

Puffed on a cigarette, and flicked a long pile of cylindrical ash into the ashtray before it fell. Grey ash and cigarette butts soon filled the ashtray. The aromas churned with the atmosphere as she meticulously studied the tea-leaf patterns.

Her elaborate, pointed spectacles, halfway along her nose as she searched for patterns and experienced the vibes, became in tune. She called everyone "Cock." "Well, Cock, there's a letter T there." She brought the cup closer and scrutinised it before speaking again. "See there, birds, a flock of birds."

Engrossed and fascinated at mystical gifts to tell the future. None of us could leave. Or even make the slightest murmur, in that cosy mystical place of suspense and compelling fortune-telling during a reading.

So different now, but as intrigued. That light above my bed, special and brought slight solace. As did my brother's muffled quiet, sometimes echoed voice, trapped inside the wall, behind my bed, in-between mine and the next room.

The echoes, like we heard from a well my brother and I often visited in a field, between a wooden stile and the river in Welshpool.

It was a large, cylindrical grey concrete structure amid the grass. At first glance, it spoiled the green, scenic beauty, looking obtrusive and odd. We jumped up and perched on our arms. Leered through a square opening on top of the well at the dark, dank, motionless water deep below us. Then shouted into the void.

Eerie, echoed, sounds of distorted voices reverberated off the walls, and returned to us from the waters' surface. We dropped small stones into the well; watched them fall and heard *plop* as they hit the water, causing an upward splash and ripples, much to our satisfaction.

Such strange memories and sounds, but where was my brother now? I heard him talking, sometimes tapping on the wall and shouting for help.

No-one else could hear him. I heard peculiar voices from the corridor, footsteps, squeaky wheels, banging and intermittent low pitch tones; the chinking and rattling of teacups becoming louder, then fainter.

Sadly, there's no yielding from the pain or fear. Relentlessly, haunted, disturbed and plagued day and night by terrifying hallucinations. I saw blood on my hands and black tiny creatures moving over my skin. Multicoloured stars, in front of my eyes and everywhere I looked.

And babies falling out of the sky through the ceiling onto my lap as ghostly apparitions in grey ragged robes and large semi-opaque hands ominously appeared out of the walls and the air reaching for me. Shadowy faces and frightening spectres lunging toward me and passing through me.

These visions evoked sinister feelings, fear, and desperate confusion. *If these visions aren't real? Who is behind the expert illusions? The conjuring, and why? The cruel magic intensifying pain?* Pain in my arms and legs, from burning pressure sores because of being in bed so long, unable to move, turn over or walk.

The days were sometimes more frightening than the nights. One day in bed, I was in such pain from my legs and absolutely petrified that Satan's burning my bottom.

I shouted and screamed, but no-one came. Then shrieked with terror as I saw maggots crawling in my wrists and believed I was Rambo. I had to withstand the pain, meet the fear.

A magnificent beam of intense, brilliant bright white light shone across me and in my mind, a voice tells me the presence in my room and the light beam above my bed was Saint Andrew.

I reached up to shield myself. Touched the light, astonished it's a solid light beam. So afraid, helpless. No human or fake robot came. That encounter seemed endless.

Equally disturbing: a picture of a favourite film star attached to the mirror on the wall facing my bed made me scream in terror.

The image changed to an image of the devil, as they said, "Ready, one, two, three, look," and the image changed again to an animated picture video, my petrified dad covered in maggots. Wriggling over him, eating him alive; my actual dad being tortured by the devil.

Dad said, "Don't look, son." I knew he was suffering, though, and in pain. *If I look away or close my eyes, Dad might disappear. And the devil will reappear.*

I forgave Dad for making me sit on the stairs, in darkness, as a child. Absolutely scared stiff of the dark, and there were ghosts up those stairs. I screamed and sobbed.

And missing my favourite thing on television, the circus, I liked the clowns, the animals, the high-wire acts, and trapeze suspense. I never forgot that night near Christmas.

I had had dreams about Dracula, on the toilet downstairs, behind the hallway door. So, frightened, I curled up in a ball and closed my eyes tight. It was much worse now. There's no escape. I can only sit and lie in bed — unable to curl up for protection.

When not in my bed, I sat in my large, yellow Parker Knoll® armchair all day and sometimes all night. One-night, though, a nurse pushed me along corridors in my armchair.

I looked out from a high glass windowed corridor. Gazed upon the array of multicoloured fireworks. Ignited sparks in blackness, then whizzing, soaring upward into the black sky before exploding with an accompanying burst of sound.

I reminisced about cosmic scenes, beautiful twinkling stars, and the faces of angels in the other realms I longed to return. I tried to enjoy the pyrotechnic display but yearned to see the moon. It was November 5th, 1987, and a distinct memory after waking in that strange, alien world.

Soon after, on another day, a nurse pushed me from my private side room into the men's bay and placed me by a crimson, red, triangular shaped window. I looked through the open, red, velvety curtains at outside, at the panoramic dynamic tapestry before me and saw people, buses, cars.

Interesting, but they weren't people. They were clever robots that walked too fast and mechanically to be human. The cars didn't have wheels, they floated, were not real. An elaborate toytown hoax. Clever ploys trying to fool me into thinking that was Earth!

That day was strange, historic and special. I discovered I had telekinetic powers: everywhere I looked, the ability to move objects. And had hours of fun, using these powers and made intricate patterns with random objects.

This new skill became more defined and helped-endure the inescapable pain. I realised I had psychic powers and knew of a secret war.

A war in the sky that intrigued and entertained — the green lightning spears thrown by omnipotent warring gods, on high. Probably from Mount Olympus, battling against aliens from other worlds in a war no other mortal knew about.

But, I could tell no-one. If I physically could have, ordinary humans wouldn't have listened, and no point telling the strange robot clones.

Fake parents, fake family, and my impostor aunt visited daily, too, helped and often annoyed me, but sometimes told the nurses I was clever and my shouting was for a reason. That strange lady, who often arrived with wild, windswept hair, pushed me, but sometimes I thought, *Oh no, not again!*

I didn't realise that the impostor aunt had ridden her bike from Bilston to the hospital to see me. She got to know the alien nurses. One day a nurse greeted her as she arrived, said I had been screaming, shouting and they couldn't fathom out why.

That strange robot aunt painstakingly asked me questions to find out why I was shouting and counted my eyeblinks. Two for Yes, once for a No.

"Is your head hurting,... any pain in your head, Paul?... Your chest,... arms,... hands? Do your legs hurt?"

I blinked twice; relieved and overjoyed my aunt told my consultant about pains in my legs. The consultant asked me and I blinked twice. They increased my medication, so less pain, less screaming, and I endured the visions of phantoms and only occasionally shouted.

On another occasion, shouting as I wanted a proper bath, although being hoisted into the air was frightening. The bath seat hurt, too, as I'd become so thin. My bottom, so sore, hot, welded to the hard-plastic seat.

Relief as I and the seat entered the bathwater, even though it was often cold by the time they'd hoisted me in, and I became immersed.

Progress, and more so when my impostor aunt made me an alphabet board. She pointed to each letter. Again, I blinked for yes or no. Glad for that rudimentary form of communication, but still frustrated, I cannot speak!

Pleased though, as I gradually became able to move my right hand and arm with a lot of effort, but could not open my hand or stretch out my fingers. Yet, I progressed from that slow binary code of blinking.

The suspense: Was I still there? The me, in my mind, and the human I used to be? Oh, the excitement, as my impostor aunt got a piece of paper and pen to jot down my first communication with that robot alien race.

With determination and massive effort, I embraced and revelled the power as I began to spell. My impostor aunt wrote and only stopped to read when I had completed what I had to say. "F U C K O F F Y O U A R E N O T M Y A U N T Y." Wow, the power of communication!

So smug, and a bonus: The alien nurses, doctors, and health professionals know I can spell and as I can spell, I can think, construct language, show intelligence, and answer back. Just cannot speak. Besides a plethora of inabilities. I chose those first words, but wished I had a wider audience!

Freaky to think I used a similar crude method of communication, a few months earlier, on the Ouija board. I made one from an old, thick, varnished piece of plywood.

I wrote the letters of the alphabet in capitals in an arch shape on the upper half of the board. Numbers at the top from nought to 10. The words 'Yes' and 'No', in the middle with a silver marker pen.

And, intended to alleviate boredom; at best, find answers to profound queries that had puzzled and fascinated me. It's unbelievable I'm now in a hospital. Had dabbling with the unknown somehow led to an inextricable and cruel trick: role reversal?

How scary it may have been for my aunt in those new, early days of communication. Those unspoken words conveyed a deeper insight into a mind. A mind closed for so long. In that realm, yet trapped in another.

That night, memories of the past world plagued my mind. Memories from a year earlier, pastimes and interests I had.

Space, the unexplained, the paranormal, the supernatural, UFOs, tantalised my mind. A mind hungry for knowledge, answers to profound questions, few may think of, not mundane, but mystical.

Mom and Dad would be away for the weekend. So I asked

friends over for a drink, and a laugh, Andy, Dava, Sam and me. The beer flowed, we chatted, laughed, then talked about ghosts, and I described and relived an event, in that same room. I was about eight.

The sudden sound of the heavy solid wooden planked, downstairs toilet door slamming shut as we watched TV, startled my brother, mom, and I. It started banging, opening and shutting, and made a loud noise.

Frightening, but more so as we heard similar loud noises from upstairs. Huddled in the living room; Mom cried after trying to stay calm and composed.

We fled, entered the kitchen, and pulled the cupboard drawer out to wedge the living room door shut so no-one could follow. Rushed out the backdoor to fetch Dad from the Villiers Arms, the pub, nearby.

His bemused, alarmed expression when he saw our faces changed to stern anger as he rushed home with us, brandishing a beer bottle. "Come out, come out... come on." He said, as he searched the house but found no-one. It was an unforgettable and disturbing experience.

My friends listened intently. A brief discussion followed with boyish banter as Dava returned from the kitchen with a can of beer. "What you talking about?"

"Ghosts and stuff," I reply.

"Oh, right? Ooh... ooh, let's get pissed, man," as Dava lunges forward.

"I went on a Ouija board once. Me and a few others, nothing happened, boring." Andy said.

I resisted the temptation to tell anyone what I'd made as I waited for the reaction to the topic. Perturbed by Sam's unusual silence, and the conflicting views as I fetch myself a can of beer, and get the Ouija board from the kitchen.

Apprehensive as I wonder how my friends might react as I place it on the living room floor. Beside the gas fire, "I made this!" and open my beer.

"Nice one. Do you know how to use it, P?" Sam asked.

"I've heard how to."

"You get a small glass, turn it upside on the board, then break it afterwards," Andy said, followed by, "Got any candles, P?"

"The Young Ones had a seance… Neil, Rick, oh man," Dava said, lifting the mood as we laugh apart from Sam, who looks ever serious.

"I think so, Andy," as I stand and walk to the kitchen to look for one. I find a long white candle, a box of matches, and a small sherry glass from the glass cabinet.

And returned to the living room. Dava and Sam were still at the far ends of the sofa opposite the fire and Ouija board. Sam coolly sucked on his cigarette, flicking ash into an ashtray on his lap. Andy was already sitting on the floor next to the Ouija board.

I sit opposite, as Andy places the glass on the board. Get a match out of the box. My fingers are clammy against the wood, the pink brimstone head lights against the sandpaper edge of the box.

"Come on." I said to Dava and Sam on the sofa. Sam sucks harder on his cigarette and exhales blue smoke more rapidly than usual.

"I'll watch." Dava said as Sam stubs his cigarette out and sits between Andy and me. I ignite the candle and tilt it. Hot, molten wax drips, forming a liquid wax pool that fixes the candle to the board. "OK, Dava, turn the light off," Andy said.

Plunging the room into darkness, our eyes adjust as we try to focus on eerie outlines and shadows. The bright light from the flickering candle illuminates its body and our faces with a faint yellow glow. The board letters, distinct, and the shiny varnish of the board reflects like a dull mirror. "Put your fingertips on the glass. Don't push," Andy said.

Wondering, *Will this work?* "Is anybody there?" I ask.

"Ah, me," as Dava grins.

We laugh before settling. I ask again, "Is anybody there?… If anyone is there, give us a sign." My heart pounding as the upturned glass moves, stops at the YES. "What's your name?"

We stare at the motionless glass in anticipation and suspense.

"Will I get a nice girlfriend soon?" I ask. Still no movement. *Time for a much bolder question.* *"When* will I die?" Anxious to feel and see the glass move to 4, then 7. "47." *Why did I ask that?* I then ask, "How will I die?" The glass moves again. "B U R N." Scared, but I cannot show any fear.

There's universal silence as, to our amazement, the glass moves much faster than earlier. We keep our fingers on the rim of the upturned glass as it moves ever faster. "B U R N Y O U B A S T A R D."

The sudden mood change, unnerving as we watched so intently. Focussed on the glass, the letters, the shapes and faces in that transcended room of shadows. It's good to relieve boredom. But the trade, surreal, and unexpected with a sinister flavour: phantoms, whether fictitious and imagined or real, instilled fear.

The lights went on; we blew the candle flame out, bringing us into the light, like a dark, heavy cloak being lifted.

We drank more beer, and didn't worry or dwell on esoteric themes, or the messages and their origins. *Could we, or anyone of this Earth, invoke spirits and communicate with them?*

Naive curiosity, dabbling in things we shouldn't and couldn't understand, was compelling with the mystery. Had a trapdoor opened in my mind, or an esoteric one; all that's sinister. That shouldn't be in the world. Allowed to ascend, invade and menace?

We continued to drink, as we reflected on a night of twisted, strange fun, before becoming tired. I missed Mom and Dad and wished they weren't away.

As I lay in bed, tried to sleep, I was glad to be in an unfamiliar room, not my old bedroom. More ominously, I visualised the flames. Flickering flames in the room, and the mysterious fellow in my mind sat at his table.

The one who told me I had to count. Repeat everything to equate to the count of five, or multiples of five. Any interruption during the sequential procedure meant the repetition wouldn't count.

I recall shouting, "Goodnight," to my parents downstairs, and straight away, they had to answer. If they didn't, I could not set my mind at ease or sleep until I had performed the set procedure with impeccable precision.

Some nights, they only replied 24 times. I had to begin again and reach 125. *Please, please answer, I can't bear to lose you Dad. Answer fast, I don't want to cry again, like when I became lost at Rhyl. I must count, and you must answer. I dare not doubt that fellow in my mind, or think badly of him. He knows my thoughts, so no other way.*

He is so important in his strange room, surrounded by fire. Sometimes, his presence and instruction annoyed me and seemed silly. More so when I was tired. A special secret friend, comforting, but who was he? Why did he appear?

Never mind, I had real friends now, but why such ominous thoughts of flames? Were they significant, linked to that strange man… visions in my mind?

I slept eventually, and as I woke, I felt grateful I'd made it to morning, and for natural sunlight. I struggled to explain the previous night, though. And just hoped the messages were wrong.

I didn't think of future fate as I climbed out of my bed. Got dressed, walked downstairs, entered the living room but shriek. Petrified as the terrible message from a night earlier returns. I shout upstairs, "Wake up, wake up!"

"Why, P? It's early." A sleepy, nonchalant Andy answers from the landing. I'd already opened the front door in a sheer panic.

"We have to get out!" Frantic, there're matchsticks strewn by the gas fire. I ran to my aunt's house for refuge; did not stop, as so many dreadful thoughts wracked my brain.

The events caused unease. For quite a while, I stayed away from home. Despite admittance, my friends placed the matchsticks there. To me, there was no logical explanation. It was realer than imagination.

And, like now, I'm subjected to the mysterious unknown, but with the elusive distinction between reality and imagination, increasing the power, confusion, and torment.

I woke and remembered the response from the previous day, curious. *Is the robot imposter aunt the one I ran to in the other world? What would it do next, keep visiting?* Of course she would, but it seemed bizarre, more confused by its emotionless, simplistic reply; "Paul, that's not nice. Who am I then?"

"A robot."

My robot aunt laughed, making me even angrier. How could a robot have few emotions?

Blind faith, perhaps hiding discomfort. As time passed, I was grateful to my aunt. Even though she was a robot. A robot intelligent enough to know it was not me saying that. The truth, though, I was not the person I used to be, and to me, my robot aunt was not my real aunt. I did not know that purposeless alien world of cruel pain and frustration.

My first communication was part of the slow, sure, but uncertain transition to the waking state. And part of a long gruelling process, where I endured pain and terrifying, strange visceral perceptions, while confusion and sorrow filled my thoughts.

Sorrow at emerging from the new existence in other realms, I grew to love and revile as I embraced the continual journey of wonder and fear, experiences as reality. As I remembered what must have been dreams of my former life. The, me, now lost, but how could it be me?

Where was the world I basked in the sun, embraced and braved the wind? Saw the moon, trees, and birds and rivers, swam and ran. The world of before, I longed, although unable to move, let alone swim.

Where was I? Such a cruel joke; as if I'd been to heaven and returned to Earth. An earth I'd not previously been part of, not the same, I knew, but a dystopian reality.

An elaborate, painfully cruel version of a strange world, mimicking a world I did not belong. Yet being trapped as a reluctant part of that clockwork fake world I did not recognise or accept any part of evoked feelings of immense sadness. My new existence, pain, torment, frustration, fear: hell!

I endured, yearned and wished, then one day I fell asleep in my Parker Knoll® chair and feel tremendous peace as I floated up high above the hospital, into a blue sky. Excited and elated, the good witch I loved might have wanted me back.

As I hoped to hear a sweet, beckoning voice, I hear another voice that transports me from the sky, woken up by a worried nurse. Annoyed and sad to be back in my body. I may not have returned if I went a little higher. Sadly, no escape. Or route back to the other realms, or the distant world of the past, I longed.

Even more upsetting, *has my mom and dad passed away years earlier?* I'm convinced an ill man in the men's bay is my Welsh uncle, now in a wheelchair and unable to walk. And become upset and confused, too. Had I jumped forward in time?

The alien cleaners with fantastic, space-age haircuts and ornate, dangling, prismatic, pyramid shaped earrings further convinced me of the vast advancement in time. One chewed gum; she smiled and sometimes winked at me as she placed a plastic water jug and beaker on my yellow cupboard at the side of my bed.

They were in disguise, cleverer, empathic and kinder than the robot nurses who came to me with the squeaky wheeled medicine trolley. One said the number on the white strip of paper inserted into my semi-opaque, plastic wristband. I soon learned that number, D24734, ascribed to a person in a world of robots.

The robot nurses sometimes followed stern, serious groups of doctors in polished shoes, most of them in white gowns stood with their arms folded as they intently listened to the eloquent, confident words of the one in a suit.

Such glum expressions as they looked at me, fascinated, curious. Perhaps wondering how much of me was still there, mentally? How did I survive and emerge from a coma?

The problem patient that defied the odds, that can hardly move, cannot walk, speak, feed or wash himself, only writhe, fidget, nod his head, think, shout, scream and grunt in futile despair hoping that world wasn't lasting or real.

Exhibiting no intelligence or logic. Nobody took any notice of my screams. Frenzied, annoying, screams, absorbed via dimensions. Distinct realities as I sought to rebel against the futility of not wanting to be in or a part of that fake, alien world.

They ignored me the more I screamed. No escape or defence, no-one to shout or call.

Like the boy who cried wolf. But the wolves were 10ft tall, in packs throughout day and night. Perpetual terror, as if a sinister, evil presence had come for me, instead of angels. I had no more tears. Or right to murmur, let alone shout; who cared? I did not know what had happened. *What is this place? How have I got here?* And could ask no-one.

Such extreme anger, despair, confusion, together with intense pain, is unnatural, my legs and arms rigid and stiff, pain in my muscles and my bottom burning from pressure sores. So, wanting a nurse to turn me, to change my position.

But some said, "you're very naughty. This will keep you quiet." Their caring, determined stares preceding kindness; swiftly and professionally jabbed with needles, "now shut up." Injected drugs and instant sleep but grateful, just wished I could speak to ask for more potent, longer lasting drugs as their effects did not last long enough.

To tell them, the knives in the other realms were sharper, scarier. They hurt. Those needles did not. If they were trying to punish me for being noisy, they were not succeeding! They didn't know me. Who I once was and could do. In another life and dimension, they may well be sharing a beer or wine with me, even dancing.

To them sometimes I was the worst, noisiest nuisance ever a mere life-form above a stupid cabbage. Had they forgotten, or did they not know I had a brain? A tortured mind and a heart? Top in almost every class at school, all so irrelevant. The past world, beyond return.

Such a different era. All I had to do, be quiet. Not shout, so why couldn't I listen, understand, learn and just be quiet! I dreaded the nights more than the days. Worse, as I needed more help to ease the pain, but cannot be comfortable.

I spent many nights sleeping in my chunky Parker Knoll® chair, by the ward desk. Only trouble was I couldn't ever sleep, although used to the hallucinations. Strange people looked at me, spoke.

Strangers I didn't recognise. Were they mere figments of a past life? No escape or solace from that cruel living nightmare, the only brief respite, sleep, but always waking to pain and fear.

Then one-night, the drudgery of a miserable existence I am so reluctantly enduring makes sense. By the nursing station, I am writhing and screaming in pain, shouting as loud as I can and keeping the whole ward awake.

The shadow of a nurse approaches by the silhouette of bright light of the desk lamp. A firm, clammy hand holds my forearm, that startles and makes me uncomfortable. An angry, leering face stares down at me, ever closer.

She looks straight at me, eyes with menacing fire amid darkness. Comes closer to my face, leans on my chair and her warm, rapid breath on my face. "Shut up! You want to know why you're here? You put a vacuum cleaner pipe on your car exhaust, sat in your car and tried to kill yourself. Now will you shut up?"

Her words stun me, tears well up and stream from my eyes, wet my cheeks. That answer is so terrible and incomprehensible. I just want to die. The nurse silenced me, but many more unanswered questions spun round in my head.

For the rest of that night, I suppressed the pain. Tried not to whimper, or even murmur. Just endured the pain and added torment of a mental flavour. I had no right to keep a whole ward of ill people awake. How selfish and inconsiderate of me to shout out in pain, even murmur a sound at ghostlike terrifying visions.

The nurse must have told a blatant, cruel lie to quieten me, though? I did not believe her. Why was she saying such lies? What she said could not be true. If so, why hadn't my fake parents told me? And about who did this to me?

Why? Why? No! Me, the level-headed, always sensible one! What the nurse said explained why I was in the hospital. I shouldn't be in this place! Such profound, disturbing, heart-wrenching words. My life could have ended — I wouldn't have existed anymore. What would be the motives? Why should I do such a thing? Trying to kill myself?

By the morning, I am seething with anger. I eagerly await

whoever visits me first so I can ask them if what I was told the previous night is true.

My parents arrive and give me my alphabet board. I painstakingly spell out words, pointing with my knuckles as I'm unable to open my hands or stretch out my fingers.

I ask what happened, but cannot accept the explanation, and keep saying over and over, why don't they phone the police? A gang put me in the car! Why didn't they understand that was the only logical explanation?

They just look at me with blank expressions: How could I ever accept anything I didn't remember? The last thing I remembered. Going to work, I came home for lunch, made myself a sandwich. The next thing I'm aware of is being in other realms.

All this exacerbated emotions. Ever confused, angry. There was nothing I could do, apart from procrastinate. And hope it was all a dream.

As the days passed. The nurses didn't shout as much. I looked forward to speech therapy, and the challenges, respite from the nightmare. A lovely speech therapist visited my room as I sat in my Parker Knoll® sofa-type armchair.

She cheered me up and often praised me with her soft, kind voice. I wondered what the point was of copying mouth movements and trying to make basic sounds, and why that lady had faith in me.

Delighted, she even bought me a remote-control pad that enabled me to turn my stereo on and off by only a slight movement of my knee. Marvellous, although frustrated at so much and being unable to speak. I enjoyed the company, those sessions, and the immense challenges, even though pointless.

At least speech therapists didn't inflict torture and force me to do things I knew I couldn't. Yet, the psychological pain of remembering my former life of prowess and eloquence is the most difficult. Those sessions weren't ever long enough, but I detested physiotherapy.

If I was in my Parker Knoll® chair, I couldn't grip the shiny, yellow vinyl arms. So when they arrived, I grunted for my alphabet board. Sometimes they said, "Paul wants to tell us something." *Yes,* and as soon as I got my board on my lap, I engaged them in conversation as a delaying tactic.

After delaying as much as I could, I spelled. "G O A W A Y. P I S S O F F." It was no use; they'd soon lift me onto the torture table, strapped on with strong white Velcro, across my chest, hips, legs, and feet.

The bed tilted until I was in a near standing position; I felt intense pain through my arched feet and didn't know why. It was because my Achilles tendons had shrunk as I'd lain in bed so long, in my coma. So cruel, hated all that. I could not see the point. Or what good that torture did.

News of a potential solution to torture bed pain brought hope. Surgery to extend my Achilles tendons would allow me to place my feet on the floor again, without experiencing pain and maybe I'd even walk. I remember the sharp scratch on the rear of my hand, counting to four, then waking from the anaesthetic in intense pain.

A stout, black man, sweat on his brow, was pressing my foot against his chest with all his might, against my rebelling, spasming muscles. So strong: *Is he an Olympic wrestler?*

"Relax. You want to walk again, don't you?" he said with a determined expression.

I tried to relax my muscles, so wanting to walk again, with my newly cut tendons extended, then set in plaster. After that, the torture bed didn't hurt so much; I could bear weight, almost without pain, and lift my arms. Just couldn't balance and I needed a few physiotherapists to support me. Their determination inspired me to do my best, too.

So I tolerated the physiotherapy. Occupational therapy and the speech therapy stimulated me more. And, I relished the insurmountable challenges; even pushed the boundaries. Although immense challenges, just to sit and roll on the smooth blue cushioned floor mats, but I enjoyed the activities.

It was such an effort to roll onto my front, and then blow into a spirometer to measure my lung capacity with the pressure of the floor against my lungs, as the physio sat on the mat next to me, looking at the meter reading, I blew as hard as I could.

"Pathetic, come on. I think Ratbag is a good name for you. Come on, Ratbag." she said.

I blew again. Angry, but not at the physio, or being called Ratbag. It was frustration at being pathetic, weak compared to my former self.

Oh, how could everything be so different? She was like a sergeant major, but calmer.

A few months ago, I would have gloated and grinned at a real sergeant major's order, "Drop and give me 20," they would have got 200 — *too easy!*

Also, I pumped iron, arm-curled with my set of weights, proudly bought with my paper round money. Four blue plastic discs filled with sand and weighing four and half kilograms (kg), each with a long solid iron bar and iron dumbbell bar. These added a new and refocused dimension to my fitness program, and I did clapping press-ups.

Pushed up and clapped in midair – 200 press-ups and 400 sit-ups – every day. My training regime, as I dropped on my hands with my head by my stereo and started the press-ups as soon as Intaferon's *Get out of London* or Mel and Kim's, *Showing Out,* began.

No-one could stop me! I wouldn't rest until the song ended. Sometimes, I continued. Until I couldn't physically do any more.

As many as I could, every day, regardless of the company present. "Excuse me" as I dropped on my hands, started doing press-ups, even in our living room, with my brother present, and his girlfriend.

I remembered the great pride and elation of becoming press-up champion at school. Upstairs above the sports hall, a couple of other non-fanatical, normal friends acted as overseeing judges. A full, proper press-up counts if our chests touch the back of a hand, arms extended straight as we push.

I hadn't ever done over 80 press-ups in a minute. My challenger friend went first. The stopwatch began. He counted, "50, 60, 70, 80," in the minute. *Impressive, he's equalled my best.*

"Well done," I said.

I mustn't slow at any pain barrier or tiredness. On my hands, focused. Poised for the start of the stopwatch and the word, "Go!... 40... 60" I increase speed, "70, 80," as I strain "85, 90, 91, 92," as the minute elapsed.

Yes! Press-up champion, by sheer determination, a desire to win. To be the best, as I became indeed more obsessed with fitness and endurance. Zany acclaim, as the one who had to exceed expectations.

Never give up, addicted to the thrill, the rush of power to amaze. Alas, now so weak! Unable to lift my head or body from the mat by even a millimetre.

I loved that physio's attitude. It was as if she knew more than I imagined. She strapped my legs into half drainpipes/gutter splints and attached a harness and rope to my waist to pull me up into standing between the parallel bars, then eased me along the bars.

Awesome, as I walk again with a lot of support, but like a slow, malfunctioning, mechanical robot.

Great to be on my feet, upright, and bearing weight, but so difficult. Immense effort just to move a centimetre, I quickly became out of breath, red faced, so hot, achy and sore; exhausted, would determination be enough? Scary too, having no balance as I clung onto the bars.

I remembered really exerting myself in the other world. Weight training with my friend Paul as Survivor, *Eye Of the Tiger* played and pushing 198kg with my legs from a seated position. More intensive training in a friend's garage after leaving school. I supplied my weights, and Mick had a multi bench.

I enjoyed the friendly rivalry, revelled competition, and relished challenges. Especially from boastful friends, "I'll show you how it's done, P." Brad said with a smirk as he lifted my weights; the arm-curl competition began.

His Herculean effort reached 75 arm-curls. "Beat that, P!"

Twenty arm-curls with only two of my weights equalling nine kilograms, plus the two-kilogram bar wasn't easy. At 50, I became tired.

At 90, the weights were so heavy. "300," I said, with pure determination and adrenaline, my arms so heavy, achy. Now at 400, each repetition is a strain. Requires ever more effort, energy from nothing... 500, 600, 700. *I cannot believe my total.*

Exhausted as I strained and grimaced and reach my 763 arm-curls, total. It becomes physically impossible to lift that heavy bar another millimetre. "Beat that," as I slump onto the floor, barely able to walk, let alone move my arms.

Stopping at 700, not an option... I was an endurance fanatic. I revelled exerting myself to the extreme, never giving in, to be the last. And to do the most. Was this now irrelevant?

The situation now, very different, and myself, but I had to reach the end of those bars as Ratbag, not P. I put in a colossal effort to move along one centimetre. So tired, so weak and no balance, but eventually I got to the end.

That physio's determination and dedication inspired me. Made me so determined, I gave my all in those sessions, then more. My goal: impress that physio, gain praise by showing her what I am made of, how determined I could be, but I'd miss being called "Ratbag!"

Shortly afterwards, another one of my physios, Sarah, wheeled a shiny, red wheelchair toward me as I sit by my room. Her animated face exudes excitement; wide eyes full of joy as she shows how to propel my first wheelchair.

The same colour as the three geared Raleigh® Grifter bike I had for Christmas at eight-years-old. My hand-built, racing bike in later years and my dream red car in that far distant world of the past, too.

Part of me is sad getting my first ever wheelchair; and I may never walk again. But, I can't be miserable. My fantastic new set of wheels, a trendy sports car compared to my yellow armchair I had lived in day and night!

How could I not be the former self I remembered? The epitome of fitness who became so unable? Still, I pushed the bobbles on the rims to propel myself in my chair around the ward, into the bays and sometimes along the corridor toward the dayroom, the stairs and lifts.

And, more progress whilst being fed breakfast, I said my first words again, "More bacon." What a momentous day and jubilant cheers as I began saying a few words.

Dad put peas in my ice-cream to get me to eat more veg and fed me a bag of chips a night from the canteen before the visitors' bell rang to go home, so I'd gain weight.

I wished I could have gone home with Mom and Dad as the hospital routine became monotonous. Breakfast, bedbaths, dinner, ward rounds, and a highlight, as I enjoyed the nurse's company, daily observations (obs). Pulse and temperature written on papers on a clipboard attached to the bottom of the metal-framed bed.

Mainly trainee nurses did this. I remembered them all and the polythene thermometer sleeve on my tongue. My hand, slightly aloft, two dainty fingers on my wrist, on my pulse as they studied their ticking watches held in their other hand.

They were all very nice and dressed in their white outfits. One had comely, big, brown eyes and good-looking. A white hat, like a paper upward arch, perfectly sat on her brown hair and around her head, ponytail, and strands of hair in cylindrical ringlets.

I liked her. There were far less pleasurable highlights. I fell on the floor from a commode chair, banged my head on the chrome bedside. Another night, in the depths of winter, the sliding vertical window of my second-floor room opened with great speed.

Chilly air rushed in, the wind howled. My room was dark, just my dim orange bedlight, window blinds into the ward, shut. Bitterly cold, shivering, with only a thin sheet and counterpane for warmth, as I pressed the call button on my buzzer.

It didn't light up, sound, or flash outside the room. And had always worked, first time. I pressed and pressed in vain, making it ever stranger and scarier in the never-ending cold. *Has Iceman caused this from his distant world?*

I closed my eyes, and went back in time, to a past winter, my childhood, hoping for snow, deeper, the better as I put on my Wellington boots. Rushed outdoors, into the fresh snow, and made snowballs.

Rock-hard snowballs for snowball fights, even though my Wellington boots leaked. My elder friends, Ian, and Paul, built a sizeable snow house in Ian's garden one-year.

It was superb, perfect square walls, six-feet-square and five-feet-high, with a rectangle opening as a door. I helped cut thick, icy snow blocks from dense fallen snow that had fallen on the garden path and froze.

We covered the structure with a large tarpaulin, making it dark inside, but the frosty walls glistened and sparkled in the sunlight that filtered through. An impressive construction project that inspired building, my stronghold from snow and ice in my front garden.

Two people could fit snug inside the snow shelter I made. An ingenious haven against snowball bombardment with a chute to deposit handmade snowballs for whoever made them. A brilliant invention, even for a nine-year-old, as it withstood the hardest, fastest snowballs.

Braving the cold for hours, scooping, compressing snow, freezing wet feet, numbed hands, all for fun, the honour, snowball fighting in our groups. Our road packed with kids seeking refuge from the bombardment, behind trees and lampposts, decreasing the likelihood of being pelted.

I hoped to be in the same group as Ian. He had the best aim and compacted the snow into the hardest snowballs. Although there's no snow in my room now, it's so cold.

At about 7.30am, the morning shift sister opens my door. Shocked at the cold and to see me shivering with the window open. The window is closed.

"You poor thing." As she wraps me in warm, wonderful blankets. I had never been so grateful for warmth and that rescue.

Suffice to say, there was only one thing I wanted, well urgently needed, a cross and chain and I suggested Mom buy me that gift for my forthcoming 19th birthday. My aunt bought me *NOW That's What I Call Music! 11* double cassette albums, too.

I missed my former abilities and would have liked to have been able to walk, talk and other things, but received a variety of special gifts, including an unusual present. A star chart, like in my school-days, made by a kind nurse.

And, I filled it with coloured stars as I completed impossible tasks, like I can hold my fork, I can put food onto my fork, I can bring it to my mouth, I can brush my teeth, comb my hair. It felt good to have the goals, even though difficult, beyond me, as dreams.

So different to grand ambitions long ago, in my previous life, as M|A|R|R|S' *Pump Up the Volume* played from my stereo. And my uncle elevated my bed with the connected footpump.

This song played in heaven amongst angels and stars. Bizarre and uncanny, too, as I ascended toward the ceiling and sky.

It's so different now, practically bed-bound. Still, I was glad for a family get together. Although strange having a party to celebrate my 19th birthday I nearly didn't make.

A stark, unbelievable contrast to a year earlier, my 18th celebrated in a Darlaston pub, The Staffordshire Knot, with friends who stripped me off in the car on the way back to Bilston. It was freezing as I streaked through town in December.

No more outings like that for me, despite longing to be outdoors. To be in the open air, feel the sun, wind, and even the rain. But, I'd become accustomed to living in that warm hospital, and lost track of the seasons despite Iceman's antics and clues from the brief moments I saw the sky from the windows and visitors' clothing.

By the spring, there was an unexpected treat, as I yearn for company. Forlorn and bored as I looked out the window. Two hands covered my eyes. "Guess who?" someone said.

A sweet voice, I pretended not to know. "We're taking you out today, Paul." Two lovely, bubbly student nurses, taking me for a walk around the hospital grounds was beyond wonderful.

Along the corridor, into the lift, savouring each moment with the caring nurses, Claire, and Hannah as we ventured outside. They were great, Hannah with long black hair and refreshingly cheeky, always trying to cheer me and others up with zeal and kindness. Claire, a tall blonde, was more reserved, but still bubbly.

Yes, I was outdoors. On a warm day, fantastic feeling, the

sun's warmth, and two lovely ladies pushing my chair, talking, making me laugh. Hannah stooped to listen as she couldn't hear me as I spoke, and she pushed. "Are you being cheeky, Paul?"

I was all theirs, being pushed in a wheelchair; that didn't matter. Suddenly, the front wheel rolls into a dip in the tarmac, and I tip out of my wheelchair, bang and graze my knee, but I didn't care.

I expected more sympathy and fuss though, as one said, "It's only a scratch." Still, great to be outdoors on a glorious day.

My aunt took me for walks, too, pushed me in my chair and encouraged me to go out. Apprehension and nervousness dissuaded me from venturing any further afield. Being pushed out of the hospital grounds to town, and into a pub, was unthinkable.

How can I interact with ordinary people? People who shall see me in my wheelchair, hear my changed, slowed speech. I overcame nervous reluctance, succumbed. It was good to be somewhere different. Somewhere other than a hospital: The Fisherman Inn in Wednesfield, drinking beer with a straw.

Toward the latter stage of my hospital stay, a stand in nurse gave me a bedbath. I had admired her from the times I'd seen her from afar. Gleeful: *She's in my room*. Black heels, long, light-brown hair, attractive.

What a treat after tepid bathwater, but although I could say a few words, I could hardly speak in her presence. What could I have said? What use is her phone number, if I could ask, and she gave it to me? She wouldn't, but I enjoyed the pleasant company and wished that bedbath could last longer.

More than this, the water on my body, sound of swift swishes, and dripping water as the nurse put her hands into the bowl evoked thoughts of trophies and triumphs in the former world. I wished she could have seen me from the sun-drenched, grassy riverbank as I swam with no fear of the fast water.

Oh, to impress with my physical prowess, agility, abilities; to woo and charm with my eloquence and my mind. My zaniness and even my immense Frisbee throwing skills, ah, my fantastic luminous Frisbee: I spent many hours throwing, and won't throw again.

I had self-learnt many tricks: making the Frisbee return to me, hover in midair, spun it on my finger and amassed a repertoire of catching methods.

Such exceptional skills and talents I had. I'm useless now, stuck in bed, and so reliant on help. There's added frustration, as it's the total opposite to a year earlier; my able-bodied existence, yet it seemed much longer ago, in another dimension.

That night I became melancholy as I remembered making sweet love outdoors, under the stars as the year began, dancing, romancing, sparkling sequins, evocative dance moves, lustful eyes, and scintillating sensations from a lost era.

Mere fantasy dreams, savoured memories of my past life, in another distant world. This brought pleasure, and pain, entwined with frustration. Those experiences could never happen again.

I'd awoken, totally transformed, and accepted there was no escape from that fake, clinical, robotic, alien world. Return to other realms wasn't possible either. The past world was just that, a surreal dream, entwined in time.

Although accustomed to hospital life, not disability, I hadn't tamed the inner torment at being unable to walk. Or do other physical things I used to do as second nature, so effortlessly.

But I was grateful to not scream. Had empathy for others who still did; while I knew the staff and nurses had done all they could for me, I had earned stars and filled my star chart, too! The thing I needed next, specialist, residential rehabilitation, but what further abilities could I gain?

Had I screwed up my life? Perhaps so, from some perspectives, but could I prove them wrong? And, did I have the inner strength to strive on changed? In time, I would hold the view that my life had begun again, as if reborn.

Section IV

WHY?

22.

SLOW ASCENT

My life and abilities had changed forever. Long-gone ambitions and aspirations dwindled away, but I had new goals as I wondered what rehabilitation could achieve? And how much of me had become lost forever?

These were deep questions to ponder while I missed my past life. All I could do, yet, I soon realised, I had to continue.

Keep trying in gratitude for my survival to the best of my abilities and qualities. Soon, in environments different to hospital, more intensive regimes would present new challenges. With new goals to focus on as I progressed. And I had waited a long time for a suitable specialist rehabilitation unit place.

After 13 months, it was strange to leave the hospital environment, and exciting to contemplate a continuing adventure. I had been reborn in that hospital. Anywhere else would be scary and new. Even that place I remembered as home.

The slow recovery continued as a highly anticipated journey by ambulance to Kings Lodge, Derby, began. To a faraway place and I became excited by fresh air and the countryside.

The scenery reminded me of Wales, and a place I had visited since the age of five-years-old, with my family.

I became thrilled to have our own caravan bought from my mom's aunt. A kitchen sink with no running water, wood burner, and gas mantle lights, as there was no electricity.

For many years we went there most weekends, and big summer holidays from school. I relished every opportunity to venture toward the green, inviting hills of Wales.

On route, Mom often spontaneously burst into song with countryside themed hymns, but we never applauded. My mom, brother, and I had greater amusement playing games, like I-spy, choosing a colour and counted every car we saw of that colour during the journey.

It's nothing like in the ambulance, no-one singing, or games either, just scenery, and many thoughts.

I still loved the countryside. It always seemed a privilege to visit that rural scenic place discovered half a century ago by a great aunt.

A place my family and I spent many long summers. The small, quiet site, near an old landmark, woodland, and tranquil river, idyllic stretches of water.

A dusty drive of light-grey stone lay in front of the caravans. Beyond this, a wooden garage stood next to a garden embankment, a wall of green grass and towering eucalyptus trees. The garden had a bare grey patch that looked somewhat odd with no greenery, pecked clean by chickens that roamed in that area.

We fetched water in large white plastic containers from near some stone steps a short distance away from the old mill, and the whole family, my mom, brother, dad, and my aunties collected pine cones that had fallen to the ground from redwood pine trees.

These cones were an excellent fuel for the caravan fire and provided a warm, lasting fire that roared and crackled. While a characteristic aroma accompanied the homely, amber-red glow of light from the burning cones and embers; glimmerings of light that complemented with old gas mantle lights.

Dad made sure we had a fully charged car battery for the 14-inch black-and-white TV, too. He carefully fixed the jagged rusting crocodile clips onto the dull, grey, lead battery electrodes, producing dramatic white sparks, like mini-lightning.

What followed was less dramatic in comparison, but still exciting. As we watched the black, grey screen and listened as Dad extended the two fixed, shiny metallic telescopic aerials from a cream-coloured plastic base.

Meticulous adjustment of these evoked hope and escalating suspense with 'oohs' and 'ahs' as pixelated apparitions formed from the dancing white dots on the dark screen.

A hiss, then crackly voices before the dots dispersed and more hissing, then voices, as Dad tried to get a picture and sound from the white dots and frantically moved the aerial rods in every conceivable direction.

The rigmarole show enhanced the excitement and delight to the extent we cheered when the picture formed, but groaned when it dissipated. Sometimes, Dad lifted the aerial and gained a picture. "Stop there, keep still!" We said.

Perseverance would eventually prevail. We carefully sat down, held our breaths, trying not to disturb the aerial. Dad was determined to get a better picture for the TV.

We became anxious, worried as he ascended and disappeared into the high, leafy foliage, and dense branches of an immense tree next to the caravan.

Many a night, I snuggled up on the caravan bed after drinking warm cocoa. My brother, in the bed opposite on the adjacent side of the caravan, as we both watched late-night horror films on the black-and-white portable TV.

Often, as I nodded off, Dad asked, in a terse, sharp but kind tone, "Paul. Are you asleep?"

I'd awaken forthwith and suppress my annoyance as I glimpsed the TV. "Yeah, I'm awake, still watching tele, Dad!" half-asleep. Then, as I finally fell asleep, *twittwoo-twittwoo* from a hooting owl sometimes woke me. "Mom. Dad." In a whiny, soft tone.

"It's OK, Paul. Only an owl," Dad said.

By then, my brother, fast asleep, and the battery drained, TV off and so offering no comfort, or distraction. Just a faint orange glow from embers in the fireplace behind me. Strange how my brother slept through all that noise!

I lay there, listening to the sounds of the night, whilst wondering if anyone was prowling by our caravan, even under my window. Perhaps the scary films played a part, morning, too long away.

The first awake, and most restless, I lay for ages. Didn't get up, wary not to wake everyone too early; Dad would shout. When I could bear it no longer, waiting for a mini-eternity, I tried to wake my brother up by saying his name quietly and progressively increasing the volume.

Dad annoyed, "Paul, go back to sleep, it's early!" firmly but under his breath. It was no use trying to sleep once awake, except for one-night as lightning flashed.

My uncle interrupted my slumber. Unbeknown to me, a thunderstorm raged. I remember being carried on my uncle's shoulder, half-asleep, to a safer place for refuge from the storm.

The next day, it surprised me to wake on a camp bed. *Where am I*, as I lay awake, anxious not to wake everyone up, but with curiosity I couldn't contain for long? So, quietly ventured downstairs and opened the kitchen door.

The sun shone in, and my two aunts and uncle chattered away. "Good morning, Paul. 'Here, have some tea!" The friendly greeting in a jolly place. Welcomed and amazed, I'm not moaned at for waking early.

The kitchen felt homely. Always warm from the Rayburn®, which cooked the food and housed the fire. Many a day I entered and smelled food, the aroma of bacon cooking, and the sound of eggs from the chickens and ducks hissing and spitting in the hot pan.

I loved those times, and the moon and stars, the bats, and birds. Interests gradually changed and pastimes evolved as years and the summers passed.

Childhood became assigned to history. Sadly, with no warnings of how fleeting and precious those moments would become. Time had stopped and begun again.

Now I am lonely, apprehensive but excited with a strange optimism tinged with sadness as I arrived and saw my new residence.

Still, a nice and modern place, and a warm greeting, quaint country accents excited me further as a nurse pushed my wheelchair. They wheeled me along a corridor and turned into a light, pleasant four bed dormitory.

Where I'm shown my bed, by an alcove near to the toilets and showers, opposite two other beds. The place seemed nice, friendly and had an upbeat atmosphere, different to the hospital, partly because of hearing novelty accents so far away from Bilston, my Black Country home.

Who else will I meet, and am I with fellow disabled in here? Will I get on with them? As I orientate myself. Here goes, as Tim introduced himself; made me more at ease — welcome. Pushed a tea trolley into the room. He walked with a limp and wore black, leather, brogue special shoes that look old and faded with callipers attached and a blue football shirt.

As Tim told me what happened to him, I sensed emotions, anger, distress, and sadness in his broken voice. *He doesn't have to tell me if it's so upsetting,* but soon realised he had to tell me as his voice changed again: faster, louder, vehement from jovial.

Then ever shorter syllables, almost shouting then crying as Tim relived the emotions, "I was beat up, a good kicking, football hooligans. They didn't stop until my skull caved in."

He turned his head, showing the metal plate implanted after brain surgery. This was shocking and upsetting to hear, but I became surprised at how well Tim regained his composure.

He seemed to cope well; relieved to get through the emotional ordeal of sharing his story, but exhibited more distress and anger despite trying to stay calm as he added. "I was happily married, you know. Do you know what my wife said when she left me?"

He shook with anger as he rattled the teacups.

"She couldn't be a nursemaid." Tim lifted a stainless teapot from the tea trolley and poured tea into a cup on the trolley. "Well, I'm here now and doing OK."

He looked to his right. At another man in a wheelchair. "Alex was beat up, too, another kicking, for no reason, unprovoked. Learning to talk again, aren't you Al?" Alex couldn't speak but murmured in agreement. "Left you for dead, too, didn't they, Al?"

I looked across at Alex, such sadness in his eyes. Deep sadness I had never seen before in a human being from hearing Tim's story and reliving his, he couldn't tell. This saddened and angered me; mindless violence, but glad not to be a football fan.

"We look after each other in here. Don't we, Al? You'll be

OK. What happened to you then?" asked Tim.

"Oh, just a head injury."

"Car accident?"

"Yeah, sort of."

Such intrusive questions, disturbing, made me uneasy. I just wasn't ready to give an implicit answer. *Will I ever be?* And felt bad about the unfair trade; Tim had bared his soul to me and I didn't do likewise.

"Good place this is... they'll sort you out," Tim said.

What a fabulous place, as I lay my head on my pillow. *A good bunch of lads I'm with.* As the lights went out and I reflected: *Tim can walk, pour drinks from hot teapots. I can't do those things, yet his wife left him!*

That's cruel, unfair. What chance do I have of future romance? I am more physically disabled than Tim and didn't have his level of eloquence. I thought back, what if they hadn't stopped?

On a night, my friends and I pursued other desires. We walked around, seeking activities to relieve boredom, ideally female company. Girls to chat with and charm, as we ventured into unfamiliar territory, a neighbourhood beyond our patch. Allured by the prospect and intrigue.

"Come on. Let's go to meet the ladies. Come on, P, Cratches," Andy said as he smiled and chuckled, amused by our invented word for ladies. Still reluctant, but tempted by the daring escapade.

"I don't fancy going there. Aren't there gangs up there?" with a smile, as I contemplate opportunities.

"Nah, we'll be OK. Come on," said Tom.

We set off. *Well, there's a few of us. And I might meet a lady.* Andy knew the way, and we soon arrived at a small shopping area lit with the orange glow of streetlights.

The girls were there. Three of them, and we began chatting and being cool. Well, tried to be as we fought anxiety, resisting looking over our shoulders every two seconds! Whilst chatting away though, other youths approached — a gang. Only Andy dared to carry on chatting as silence and tension enveloped us.

Guys older than us and one had a dog on a lead, a bull terrier.

I'd heard chilling rumours of such a character, I won't name, but will call, Chief Thug. They wouldn't pick on us small-fry, and we can reason with them. I became less optimistic as each gang member confronted us, like enemy troops squaring up, and realise I'm trapped.

A short, blond, messy-haired thug with a high forehead and a white shark's tooth earring intently staring at me. Hundreds of thoughts in a microsecond as I momentarily made eye contact. Hostile, but calm, with eyes that evoked sinister fear and alarm. Bang! A white flash accompanies the sharp but dull sensation of pain on my forehead.

Dazed for a split second, stunned by the blow, nutted, as he banged his head violently into mine. Before I know it, I am on the wet pavement. Being buffeted around, being beaten up as the tirade of blows rained down relentlessly.

One was hitting me over the head with a heavy, steel triangular road-sign. The steel, hard and cold. In horrific contrast, the sound of a frenzied dog, and the warmth of its breath. Wet saliva on the slimy, teeth of a vicious bull terrier, desperately trying to bite into my face in-between the momentary lapses of kicks to my head.

Petrified, stricken with terror. It's crazy; I hope for more kicks to my head, the best of three evils. Relentless, never-ending, until I hear, "Fucking pack it in, lay off. You're gonna kill someone one of these days." An angry shout of a girl's voice I recognised.

As the attack lulls, I run for my life — faster than I had ever run. Limitless, unadulterated power, fuelled by pure adrenaline and terror as my bladder empties, pissing myself.

I did not believe or dream I could ever physically run so fast; seemed almost mechanical, automatic. I was like a rocket-powered hot-air balloon, losing all ballast, and taking off at immense speed.

Like a super-athlete! Such speed could outrun anyone, but just hope I can escape my psychotic pursuers and the bull terrier in pursuit. Taking chase as the sound of a metal chain lead dragging against the road and growling, snarling escalates the sheer panic. Terror-stricken, as I imagined the dog catching up, being much faster than human pursuers, and prey.

I arrived at my friend's house, quiet, in shock and angry they'd abandoned me. My stony expression met the aghast, concerned faces of my friends – and the girls.

"I heard and saw the dog; we scarpered." One said as the girls fuss over me. Alas, too shaken by the ordeal to reciprocate, or in the state, for a friendly chat.

"I saw them kicking you and heard the dog."

Another said, "Why didn't you run, P?"

I was most upset my best Lemon Lyle & Scott® yellow bird jumper, ripped, and angered by the ordeal. *How could the gang and leader inflict such violence? Subject such terror to a human being? A show of power by mindless, idiotic kings of that territory, repelling puny invaders for sick amusement!*

Will they ever come after me again? My most feared thought I remembered as I fell asleep, but still disturbed by the previous day's stories; thoughts of the other world on my mind as I woke early, next day.

A nurse opened the door and curtains, and said, "Good morning." Few other words as they transferred me onto a long, black, rubber bed for my first Arjo bath. They lay me on that hard, uncomfortable trolley.

Anxious, as the nurse wheeled me through the corridors, only a wash-flannel and towel covering me as they placed me over what resembled a large vat. The trolley platform clicked into place, and lowered, immersing me into the tepid water.

It's hard to wash in that water. As the door closed, I'm uncomfortable on the hard surface, but excited. The suspense: *Have they forgotten me? It's been a while?*

It was only 7.30am, and relieved to hear the door open. But surprised, as a short, dark-haired female in a familiar white tunic appeared. A physio at my feet again, one physio was enough. "I'm Gillian," she said.

By then, I only had a wash-flannel to cover my immersed nakedness. In different circumstances, I may have been excited, but remembered physios. There'd be no pleasure, only pain! Gillian wasted no time, grabbed my right foot and pressed so hard

I feared the extended tendons may snap.

Is this much force necessary, as I tried not to grimace? It was only the first phase? Immense pain followed as Gillian grappled with my foot, to get a better hold, to exert even more pressure. The pain made me tense up and my eyes watered.

"I've never had physio in a bath before," as I shivered.

"Well, the water makes your joints suppler,... I'll see you later for more physio."

What, there's more?

How can she be so strong? Such torture at this fresh place but, the suspense and anticipation of challenges ahead, kind of pleasurable, although I missed home. A nurse helped me from the bath; dressed me as I shivered, and readied myself for round two, at least mentally.

In a narrow, corridor shaped physio room, I met Gillian again and was soon on my front, on blue physio mats with socks off, right leg bent back, Gillian after my foot again, leaning, pressing on it with all her weight and might. That day I was up walking on the parallel bars, albeit warily, with help.

A tiring day, and, to my surprise, that night they moved me to a luxurious side room with a swanky remote-control colour TV. Very nice, although I missed talking to the lads. The move mystified me – but tremendous – a private room; is this a hotel, or rehab? I got to like that place. Great crowd and atmosphere, excellent food, too.

The sense of satisfaction, too, as I endured intense and gruelling physio, an unexpected bonus. But to my dismay, physio became more intense. Gillian pummelled my foot even more, twice a day! The pain became more tolerable as my tendons stretched, though — progress.

Speech therapy and occupational therapy were different. Making ever-complex and prolonged sounds and bobbing my tongue out was more fun. And less painful.

A strange highlight, Dad drove up with Mom in my car, as a surprise, for me to see. He had fitted the engine from the other car I bought, and I remembered the white flashes as Dad lay under jacked up cars, welding. Flying sparks and noise as he used his grinder.

A more painful memory, Dad and I walked up Prouds Lane, and he proudly lay my papers on the countertop in the car insurance place, "My lad wants to insure his car." He said. Now I can't drive, ride a bike, walk or swim!

Delighted by their visit, but saddened with mixed emotions as they left without me and I missed them. Yet, I was getting to grips with my transformed life. And, enjoyed being at that place.

Still, after two weeks, and 20-years-old, I moved again, to my second rehabilitation unit, Hillcrest, in Moseley, a busy, non-rural suburb of Birmingham.

Less scenic and larger than Kings Lodge, with a wider variety of clientele, mostly older and more staff, the place was OK, drab but pleasant. I missed Derby though, and the rural country atmosphere.

It's strange in another bay, four beds in the corners of the room with my bed at the far end, opposite the toilets and washrooms, near a wide aluminium sliding door to a patio. I met fellow residents. Derek's bed was in the opposite corner of the bay. Victor had the bed opposite mine. His TV was on full blast all night. He chuckled away, then snored.

I couldn't sleep, so I tried to turn the volume lower on his TV once, after they hoisted Victor into bed. "Hey don't bloody touch that," Victor said.

Lonely times, but I got used to the place and watched *Moonlighting* starring Bruce Willis and Cybill Shepherd as a weekly treat. Mom and Dad visited as often as they could and stayed as late as possible; were so kind.

I was glad to go home on weekends. Odd to sleep downstairs in the living room and not in my upstairs bedroom.

As I returned to rehab one Sunday evening and Dad put my belongings by my bed, Derek's family's jovial chatter changed to whispers as Dad, Mom and I entered the washroom. Silence as we returned. My wallet wasn't there.

Derek's children were the only ones nimble enough to grab it.

I couldn't accuse anyone without proof!

I enjoyed chatting with new friends, though. Sue, in particular, a sweet, bashful girl, and wheelchair user, with short ginger hair, who wore round-rimmed spectacles. The physiotherapy students, who collected me every morning, too.

A similar age to myself, dressed in crisp, smart, white ironed breast pocketed tunics and smart navy-blue trousers, they pushed me from the bay. Along the corridors, and outside, to a huge outbuilding and chatted.

The therapy rooms, and gigantic, adapted, kitchen fascinated and daunted me, as the therapy was difficult and challenging. But, I relished the tasks and activities, occupational therapy, in the kitchen. Speech therapy in a small room with a great bubbly therapist.

There were many characters, brilliant nurses, too. Fred, in his motorised chair that looked like a barber's chair, and moved slightly faster than a snail.

No matter how many were watching TV. We knew, as we heard the click of the chair. No force on Earth could halt or sway that sure trajectory. A man on a mission, Fred, that cheeky amputee, would change the channel.

No-one dared stop Fred and his chair, or deprive him of watching the channel of his choice!

He'd then return to his table in the dining room, a can of Newcastle Brown Ale® in front of him, as he chuckled, and sometimes his face turned red from laughter. I couldn't help but wonder what may happen if I was half as cheeky?

Fantastic that Fred went on a cruise to Acapulco with a nurse. Yes, no TV channel changer, bliss.

I often sat by the entrance and one Friday night I saw a man pushing his son, Adam, in a wheelchair. We chatted about physio.

"Adam can stand now, show him Adam." He said. His son, in tracksuit bottoms and a T-shirt, smiled as he stood upright, and balanced. "Good, Adam,... Adam's in a chair now, can't speak. He sniffed lighter fluid once, just once."

This surprised me, as I wondered if I had preferred to be more physically able in a trade for some mental faculties, brainpower, or even fluent speech, and less able. Interesting notions, although grateful for all I can do, and to have survived.

The days dragged sometimes, but there were exciting, memorable nights. Such as, seeing one of my favourite bands, Kool & the Gang in Birmingham, 1989. Masses of people, bright lights and terrific loud vibrating tunes, amazing and great, being invited backstage to meet the band who gave me signed drumsticks.

But, I reminisced about another concert. Two years earlier, at that same venue, workmate Dave had a spare ticket to see the Eurythmics. We drank so much. Surged forwards, through heaving masses of people to the front and scaled the barriers.

So loud, mind-numbing, exciting, daring, being so near the stage, then glee at the end, as Annie Lennox removed her bra! The effort to reach the front, well worth it. I'm unable to surge to the front now, but I did better: Met the band.

Another day, I enjoyed the mind-flexing, memory and cognitive tests, conducted by a clinical psychologist. I astonished them, as I instantly recognised part of an elephant. I'd only seen one jigsaw piece. "No-one's ever recognised that so fast!" they said.

The memory test was simple. Yet, I revelled those few hours of tests; became disappointed as they ended. I hoped to do more, and amaze the psychologist. They sent a detailed results report stating I have a superior memory, like one percent of the population.

I knew I had an excellent memory, though. That night, I remembered a time, as a child. So still, nervous, scared to flinch, or move as one of two angels. Angels, side by side at the far-edge of the stage, and I'm the hot Angel Gabriel beneath the stage lights as I overlook a nativity scene.

To my right is a packed school hall, a sea of faces, awaiting perfection. So, I felt important but silly standing there in bare feet and a long white, shiny tunic to my feet and glittery silver tinsel halo on my head.

I had an important role and so many words to learn. The long-awaited performance I spoke my dwindled but still a lot of lines without a hitch, despite nerves and a pounding heart.

When the second angel recited the words, though, oh the momentary silence. *Remember, remember, I can help; the teachers should have believed me; had more faith in me.*

Enormous effort instilled pride that changed to dismay when, moments before the play, teachers gave a small part of my lines to the angel next to me, and said they had given me too much to learn. It wasn't possible for one person so young to learn such a vast amount of lines.

Oblivious to how I revelled in the challenge of that mammoth task; how determined I was to learn every word by heart to prove a point and astound everyone. They were wrong to not have faith in me. They could count on me! I had accomplished that magnificent feat — no need to doubt!

Of course, I saved the day by whispering the forgotten words to the fellow messenger beside me. The show went on as I used ventriloquism skills I never knew I had. I had no desire to be on stage again, despite the rapturous applause.

Such memories instilled pride. Years on, at Hillcrest, I knew there wouldn't be a day as stimulating as when I met that psychologist. I had other highlights, though, being collected daily by a variety of student physios.

Exciting, even though part of me wished we weren't going to physio. So much physio, so much pain, efforts, as many tried hard to make me better. And I tried so hard, put maximum effort in for so long.

It's so difficult to reach my arms from side to side. I couldn't even sit up on my own. It was difficult to sit even with support on massive gym balls, but fun, although daunting as I'd fall off if the physios let go. I aspired to make slow, graceful movements instead of uncontrolled, jerky movements. It was tedious but important.

One day, with my T-shirt off, I sat as the senior physios studied my back, muscles, shape, and tone. Strangely, I felt like an animal in a zoo, but important, unique, an object of study. Then progressing from the sedate, gentle physio that was sometimes interesting to listen to and hear unspoken thoughts.

It was only a matter of time before I had six student physios at my feet, pressing my bare feet, another pressing on my foot with hers while two senior physios held me and forced me up straight. One of them was very strong and six-foot five, holding my shoulders, easing me back ever further, ever straighter, excruciating spasms of pain in my lower back.

Six girls at my feet, but not at all enjoyable as my body fought against the pain, muscles, and my posture had changed. Physios trying so hard to get me back to the person I once was; yearned to be but could never be; I wished they could have known.

I tried hard to relax, but couldn't control or tame those spasms or pain. So intense, and I sensed the extremes shocked the students, as I sweat. Sheer defiance to fight the spasms, show everyone what I am made of got me through that never-ending session.

I think I gained respect that day. Besides a "Well done," from a senior physio. Much appreciated praise after all that pain, and effort to stand me up straight and get my feet flat on the floor. The same the next day, every day; relentless, but something else instilled excitement, and daunted me even more.

Transferred onto a white plastic seat, winched into the air, then lowered until my feet, legs, and body up to my shoulders immersed into the water. I yearned to dive, to swim, but could hardly move, my muscles so rigid.

Two students and a senior in the hydrotherapy pool with me, I felt pathetic being towed by a female physio. I flapped around, moved the best I could, no longer coordinated, muscles wasted, and somewhat embarrassed by my body, my total reliance.

No longer able to swim, float or tread water. Now with my head back, ears underwater, so muffled sounds. *If the physios loose me, I'll roll, sink and drown.* The water's much warmer than that I used to swim so effortlessly; when I relished any opportunity to swim.

And, had swam in the sea, at Welsh coasts, but revelled the challenges of swimming in the river, in fast-flowing water, a raging torrent; speeding water glistening more often, and wispy white foam formed on the surface.

Fearless, as I dived in downstream and swam upstream,

against the untamed current, the chaotic water, towards the rapids. As far as I could go, as I pushed myself to the point, muscle fatigue signalled me to stop moving my arms and legs because of the immense pressure of the water.

Seduced by such thrilling challenges, exhilaration, and competitive reluctance for not even nature to beat me.

I clambered up the side of the riverbank, flaked-out on the grass that would feel sticky and cool on my flesh as I smelled the air and gazed upward at the pale-blue sky. Senses overloaded, listening to the gentle gushing of the river.

Sometimes, I walked to two blocks of shiny but tarnished, eroded dark-grey stone in the river's heart and protruding from the water: the salmon steps. Shallow rushing water led out to these.

On warm summer days, I sat on them. Dangled both feet in the rushing, churning water after I tentatively walked through the gushing water and slippery moss-like weed underfoot.

Most painful, I remembered prowess and passion, and tantalising riverbank sights upon lush green grass and the dreamy, steamy kiss on the path by the old stone hut. My pounding heart after lustful stares from bewitching eyes, making me swoon, entwined as one.

It's now all so different: I cannot walk, swim, or even sit up and so weak; vulnerable and powerless in an unfamiliar world with no picturesque scenery. Strange, I had dreamed of being in the water with a lady, an unfulfilled fantasy from another era.

I imagined walking and running through the woods, though. Alongside the river's fast-flowing and dark water on the undulating, well-trodden path of grey, brown silt that snaked its way through the woodland vegetation and immense trees on a joined peninsular.

The woods separated the river from the backwater: an interminable stretch of uncannily still water that ran behind the caravans below high embankments of greenery, furnished with saplings, stinging nettles, wild flowers, and weeds: A mini gorge between the caravans and the woods.

Thick protruding ancient roots, long brown spindly twigs and

169

overgrown bramble bushes with sharp thorns obstructed passer-by as if they had a mind of their own.

A mind intent on trapping visitors to the wooded domain before they become enchanted by a painted mosaic of green in the distance. Enveloped and sheltered by immense evergreen pine trees and wild plants forming a lush green canopy, above that filtered light from the sky.

And in front, like a web suffused with bright light, chunks of green from the broad shaped leaves, tapered arcs into points, all sizes, and nuances of colour. Further afield toward the river, changing to a misty, dreamy hue of merged green on barely visible stalks of brown: nature's perfect art.

Sometimes, I stared at the dark water. Calm, yet unpredictable, treacherous; black and shiny water, as sunlight glistened on its surface. Dazzling, sparkling specks around little whirlpools that appeared in the water, like magic.

Inducing a hypnotic effect. Like enticing eyes, peering up at the sky. Portals to deep unknowns, distant and mysterious worlds amid the stars, and outer space.

It was a place that provided much pleasure, only after unease at passing a mysterious stone hut at the edge of the woods, beside the river, and railway bridge. Forsaken without a door, moss covered most of its surface, including the high pitched, grey slate roof.

Inside, darkness loomed, dank, inhospitable. Anyone could have hidden there ready to pounce on innocent 'trekkers' of the path. Had a mad axeman long departed? Relented to nature's effortless triumph and power; his now blunt, rusty axe?

The elements moulded the hut to blend with the woods. Birds chirped, sang joyfully, others scolded with sharp shrills. A welcoming, serenading chorus, resonating through the woods. This complimented the barely audible, gentle, soothing roar of the flowing river that enticed.

Sounds different, occasionally dramatic, as Royal Air Force® low-flying jets roared as they flew over. But some sounds the same, just more distinct. Louder, compared to the lorries, and the metallic clank of empty milk churns I had heard from the caravan. Loud cockerels, and voices, so strange to my ear, as was the distant intermittent shriek of a horn. Ever louder '*clickety-clack*', '*clickety-clack*' noises as nearby trains trundled over metallic railway tracks, bedded on long mounds of loose light-grey, jagged stone.

Railway tracks that run toward the black-painted metal railway bridge across the river. Before this, two stone arches supported the road bridge, and also spanned the river and railway.

In the other direction, past the mill, just below the railway tracks and before the woods, a much smaller arched grey stone tunnel formed a channel for water from the river some distance lower, water that once powered, turned the enormous cogs on the old grain mill but now trickled through the tunnel feeding the backwater.

The water by the mill, dormant and still, a rich rusty brown colour, discoloured by the innocent pollution of large rusty cogs, of a once busy water mill belonging to a bygone age.

Precious memories and such challenging, painful sessions, but I still loved the water and adorable physios. Admired the strict ones who seldom smiled. I enjoyed speech therapy, too. It presented a fun, refreshing change to the rigours of physio.

My speech therapist, Sally, had long, brown, curly hair, rosy-red cheeks, and a great sense of humour. She made me laugh as she encouraged me to make repetitive sounds, mouth movements, and every tongue movement imaginable. My speech therapy exercise book contained vowel sounds, alternating vowels, and a plethora of sounds.

Sometimes I felt silly. Bobbing my tongue in and out; side to side the fastest I could. Sally was great, and she promised to take me for a spin in her car, a red Ford® Escort XR3i cabriolet, my former dream car at 18.

What a present to look forward to as the weeks ticked by, months passed. Then one-night as I settled in bed, I heard shouting, moaning and echoed screams from another room. Fred had passed away, and out of respect, we were reluctant to change the TV channel.

Another resident, John, walked with a Zimmer frame. He was blind, always wore smart jumpers and polite, said thank you as a nurse guided him and helped him sit on a chair.

Sometimes he exercised, run on the spot whilst waiting to sit. He was amazing, and I wondered if I would ever walk on a Zimmer frame.

Outside the dining room, a fellow wheelchair user, Mr H, stern, authoritarian and wise, but he always sat in his room, beckoning, nodding his head as I trundled past his room. Strange, I imagined he was the king of that place, in some circles.

They all passed on, and I missed all of them in different ways. I would miss friends and the friendships too with fellow disabled people, and the common ground we shared.

I knew I was different, though, to others there with various disabilities. Nobody else had acquired a head injury the way I had. Or experienced coma; some were permanent residents, with little chance of returning home.

Yet another reason I felt lucky; glad to have survived as Sally helped me into her car. Roof retracted, engine started. Wow, the breeze, the sun, the posing, embarrassed — well, almost.

An amiable lady taking me for a spin; was she a speech therapist or a secret agent on a mission to thrill and please? Exhilarating ride, but Sally apologised; she only got up to 70 mph. What an excellent farewell leaving present, to my delight, the first of two.

They planned a pub outing; a farewell get together. The sun shone; my best T-shirt and shorts with pretty physios in summer attire, no uniforms and taking turns to push me to the pub: Fantastic.

Out-of-this-world as I sat in that pub in Moseley. Surrounded by those lovely ladies, tanned legs, refreshing drinks and even better company. The luckiest man alive, and most envied. For a day, at least.

Funny, I grew to love physiotherapists after initially hating them. I became fond of the kinder nurses, too, and other staff. I would miss them and new friends.

Pleasant and painful memories entwined with unreal, cruel memories of my past life, but tumultuous emotions, as the world of before beckoned.

23.

DAYCENTRE AND LEARNING

*A*cquisition of a head injury, coma and being so ill totally changed my life. And facing physical disability, unable to do the things I did so easily before; in a wheelchair, with impaired muscle movement and affected speech, was very daunting.

The prospect of leaving hospital and anticipation of adjustment evoked apprehension and fear as I truly believed the world would be such a lonely, harsh place.

Such fears and negative emotions became founded as I was partly right. Strange and frightening, too, but the slippery slope had to end somewhere and profound change led to a new beginning, a second chance.

Still, two-and-a-half years in hospital and rehabilitation units was a substantial period that seemed longer as I'd experienced timeless coma events.

I couldn't imagine another life. Or that I'd miss those times or places, although unforgettable. Besides apprehension, and the fear of being discharged brought. I imagined periods of boredom, frustration, and restlessness. And although I'd progressed, the fizzling out of challenges bought the realisation of monotony and daily routine.

Most of my old friends had moved on and I wasn't as mobile. Changed upon venturing into the world again, I realised I had to adapt, reinvent myself. But how, what will I do? How will the world see me? How will I cope?

I couldn't do any physical jobs ever again. Will I ever find romance? Have sex again, ever dance, be happy? Do half I did before; achieve anything?

These questions plagued me as tortuous quandaries, since I woke from a coma, irrevocably transformed, and becoming a wheelchair user. It was even more tortuous and harder to accept the stark facts; the possible circumstances that led to **my suicide attempt**.

The stigma of self-infliction was doubly difficult. How could I ever deal with these difficulties? Maybe the best way was with bold defiance and steely determination. How great was my desire to succeed? Was I still the same resolute, resilient individual?

As I faced the presented, profound, physical, and psychological changes, I was unsure I'd ever deal with the associated immense challenges. Having to rely on others almost constantly, for almost everything, daunted me, too.

As did frustration at confinement evoked by physical inability and restriction. I couldn't just go to town, or even open the front door myself; I needed help and someone with me.

It was as if returning from a long, profound, life-changing journey to a sad world with nothing for me. Or anywhere to fit or do. So alien, foreign and harsh, every aspect so irrevocably different.

I had irrevocably changed too; my perceptions, how I interacted. I saw the world and people differently. This brought a greater, fuller appreciation and realisation I had taken my abilities for granted.

Amazed as I watched people and realised just being able to stand independently and balance, let alone walk, was incredible.

To dance, lift a drink to my lips, swim, drive, run, cycle, write with a pen or even hold a pen; speak eloquently and fluently, without effort and mimicking any sound effect or accent, were things I did so well.

A plethora of incredible and truly remarkable feats I did by second nature, that I'm now unable to do become miraculous in the face of my ineptitude. So, the future is bleak?

More receptive, though, and as I didn't excel as expected at school. This presented a time to re-evaluate a future I couldn't initially imagine. I remembered I loved early learning, became a bright pupil, at least my teachers said. There were tormenting memories, too.

The reading ability of a 14-year-old at seven, at least, according to my mom, as the school headmaster told her. Yet, I dreaded reading class, became even more timid and nervous as the teacher hated me!

Why won't she choose me? I'd read well with fluency and impress her. She may be a little nicer, if she gave me a chance.

My wish came true, and I beamed with delight as I eagerly left the class, and closed the classroom door with the empty box the teacher asked me to take to the headmaster's office.

So into the cool corridor and bowed my head. In preparation to run and return as fast as possible, excited; elation with the immense sense of relief, out of that classroom.

Thrilled, away from the anxiety and fear. *Yes, I will prove I can do that simple errand. She will be over the moon. Things will be better when I return, successful, and cannot fail.*

Doubly pleased for respite from that one class I hated. *She chose and entrusted me with an important task.* The task represented my only chance for that teacher to like me. All my hopes, everything depended on my success, but I just wanted her to accept, and like me.

Alas, disaster came so swiftly; my pace abruptly ceases because of bumping into someone, and I drop the box on their feet. To my horror, no other than the headmaster's feet in shiny black shoes. "I'm sorry, I'm sorry," I said as I sob.

"Don't worry, Paul, it's only a box." As he tries to console and comfort me.

No, I had failed that one entrusted task; my one and only chance, there wouldn't be another. So, my only chance to prove myself to that teacher, lost.

It wasn't a big deal really, but to me it was as that class I hated and dreaded became even worse.

I would never forget that day and failing, becoming inconsolable. The headmaster called my mom for a meeting at school and said I shouldn't worry so much; it was trivial. Still, I worried, and was quiet, reserved and shy before then.

Despite such emotions, I enjoyed a book we read in class, *The Little Wooden Rocking Horse,* but became frustrated and confused during class. Most of the other kids read slower than me and struggled with long words. I wished to help and prompt, it wasn't appropriate to do so. Sometimes I read ahead.

I remember standing up, pushing my chair under the table, putting my hands together and saying two prayers in that class, before home time with the sense of relief from the anxiety, overwhelming, as I closed my eyes and I knew the teacher couldn't pick on me. The prayers comforted me.

I said the same prayers at my bedside before jumping in bed. Before the man in my mind, appeared, I was quiet, shy and battling with emotions and insecurities. The freak tried so hard; a worrier with other pressures that sapped my self-esteem. Why was I taunted, tantalised, by an older and mischievous character who lived nearby? He was always getting on people's nerves.

I put up with the torment for so long — until he dared touch my Raleigh® Grifter bike; I loved my bike. "Let's have a go, Walters," he said.

"No," I kept saying, but he became ever more threatening and hostile.

"Touch this again and you'll be sorry!" As I trembled with anger; leered at him. Really hoping he'd push or hit me, anything, but not for him to touch my bike!

He still tantalised and riled me, ever more defiant, unrelenting from my response, and touched my bike again. Rocked it without a care, even tried to force it from me.

Enraged, I wanted to kill him, cause harm, erase. We started fighting outside my house, rolling around in the road, frantically trying to get the better of each other.

My fury got the better of him. Somehow, I held his head firmly in both hands and kept banging it on the kerb with all-my-might; in a frenzy, having no control, pure hatred.

After a while, I stopped. As if a thick fog cleared instantaneously; as all my senses returned upon seeing the pain, the frightened facial expression and I heard the spectators' gasps.

An eerie calm enveloped me and the street as I focussed on his distraught, pallid, unsmiling face. My grip loosened, and all-anger dissipated. I didn't intend to hurt him. I only wanted to stop the torment.

That former figure, to earlier stature, toppled and pointing his finger at me with tears forming in his eyes as he trembled, held the back of his head with one hand, and said in a broken voice, "One day I'll get you back!" I knew he wouldn't.

Spectators had gathered around by now. "Oh no, there's blood!" one kid said. As they spoke these words, tears trickled from his eyes. He turned momentarily, his head gushed with deep-red blood everywhere, on his clothes and on the pavement.

Afraid, and filled with dread as I watched him slowly walk away, like a destitute aged person, limping along our road with head bowed and still with one hand in place, trying to stem the blood flow. I won that fight, taught him a lesson all right, but didn't experience any victorious joy.

More kids on the estate arrived. Even a girl I liked throughout school. Such strange, freakish accolades.

In contrast, the boy's mom came. "Look at what you've done to my son." She said, protesting. Shaking all over before hearing those words, my legs like jelly, terrified and disturbed by the unleashed, uncontrollable inner rage.

The change from being that placid pacifist who never caused trouble and tried to resolve arguments was frightening. Yet, ending tyranny justified the resolve in exchange for all-consuming worry for what I had done.

So, the torment continued in other guises as I became shyer, withdrawn, with even more worries. I even stopped going to Boys' Brigade at Bilston Baptist Church, despite fabulous activities and fun, and I found the best and most unusual hiding places, like under the stage.

But as soon as they mentioned marching around streets with a band, I had to leave. Filled with dread, and became nervous about being at school.

Despair and anxiety, I had an upset stomach nearly every day.

No way out, or solution; I had to keep attending school. So it was strange to be where I was born in 1968.

A West Bromwich hospital, in an isolation room, a welcome change. Enormous glass windows to the front and side, a jug of curious, pink liquid, labelled 'DSK' on an oblong white sticker next to my bed.

Doctors found nothing wrong with me, so they attributed the upset stomach problem to nerves. The dreaded nerves!

And I was OK after that, apart from nervousness; being shy. Shyness had always plagued me, as I became ever introverted and worried about almost everything. All this fitted in with my quiet, withdrawn persona.

A year later though, I became more settled and inspired in another English class, competition intense to spell ever longer and complex words, and by age nine, I remember winning a fabulous prize for being the best speller out the boys, a pencil sharpener of a globe of the world.

Weekly tests, 20 spellings, and 100 maths questions based on times tables. In a group of boys that used to get about 98, sometimes 100, correct! Those ultra-competitive maths tests, a challenge we revelled in, eager as we revised times tables in our heads and recited before the number-crunching began.

Years later, in that different world, I realised I had two basic options. Do nothing or learn? Study was the only viable choice, and I knew this as I attended a daycentre with various activity rooms for art, woodwork, printing, and computers.

It seemed outlandish to meet other disabled people, an anxious prospect. I learned of a vast variety of disabilities. Stranger still, to learn again: Basic computing, word-processing, and I spent time in the art room, although unable to paint or draw.

I studied English, too, wrote stories, an essay, and letters and via the daycentre, studied progressively more advanced computer courses at college, then at a local polytechnic.

Wonderful to be learning again, and the acquisition of knowledge instilled confidence. The daycentre became a base to learn and experience, but after learning, I always returned to that base camp. Great staff encouraged me and even inspired. Pete in the art room in particular, wise and knowing, as if he'd studied every subject, and funny too.

He oversaw masterpieces at his desk by the window in the large room. Taught his room's occupants to paint. Some poised with paint-laden brushes and intense concentration. Some, like me, chatted, but Pete guiding, nurturing regardless.

"Welcome to the office," sometimes "orifice," he said to amuse, as I entered.

I'd approach the desk and chat. Update Pete about learning progress, studies and sometimes mention women. That long-haired philosophical guru of everything always advised, there with other great staff.

Whenever I entered that masterpiece creating place, and even though I loved science, I thought of my third year of secondary school. Choosing subject options, not a simple task as I was top, or near the top in academic subjects, even art, and achieved very high marks as I drew great pencil and pastel sketches.

I disappointed my art teacher by not choosing art as an extra option, and despite the passion stemming from painting the mangle rollers and the fencing bright-blue at my nan's at age two, as my aunt gave me the paintbrush. Everyone will be pleased with my efforts. My creativity, painting so much, so fast, I must paint the entire fence.

Still, it was difficult to decide what subjects to study. Or what I wanted to be, a fence painter, maybe? But I chose history and two sciences, then dropped history to study all the sciences, physics, biology, chemistry.

These academic decisions would gradually become less important, as emotions shadowed learning and logic. Things may have been different if I had chosen art, my teacher encouraged me to pursue. Did they see talent?

Now, unable to draw, write or even hold a pencil. I had no talent, unlike the talented artists in that art room.

I thought of my school-days and a similar, but different transition as I further pondered the past, before coma.

24.

THE LATTER YEARS

*A*s I reminisced about that first summer after leaving primary school, I became apprehensive and buzzed with excitement. At 11-years-old, as I approached a transition stage in adulthood. Namely, going from primary school to a large comprehensive school, and I stayed at my aunt and uncle's house, in Wales, a perfect place to relax.

And away from Bilston. Daunted at first, I hadn't ever been away from my family apart from organised school trips to places such as Cirencester and Chester.

My aunt kindly gave up her room for me to sleep soundly. Still, I became perturbed by the open loft and night sounds of bats scratching.

I didn't expect my stay to be so enjoyable and memorable. Or anticipate the importance of jobs my uncle allocated for me to do. Each time I heard my adopted and appropriate nickname of "Oddjob," I smiled.

At first, I was nervous and tentative about entering the chicken coop each morning. The cheeky chickens walked round my legs, and brushed against me with surprising force, unashamed and fearless, at least at feeding time.

So, I gingerly walked into the chicken shed. Sprinkled corn on the shed floor before collecting the eggs from their nests and, sometimes to my surprise, from other places.

The fresher laid eggs were warm to touch and clean. Others, when out of the shed, muddy. A mixture of colours and patterns, too, some were white as the whitest clouds in a summer sky, others pinkish brown, others with darker brown mottled patterns.

Collectively, the chickens made quite a din, and striking,

I could tell when they were cross, angry, or just being sociable with fellow chickens and to me, the human imposter with their food. One of the white feathered, free to roam chickens, Buzby, sometimes visited us in the kitchen.

Every morning, I traversed the garden to collect the milk and newspaper, even though the garden lay on a sharp incline. An important errand and an effort to get to the top, despite the makeshift steps, chopped away into the hard soil bank. The long, dark-green grass, glistened with morning dew as I strode upward.

The top of the garden led to near the main road, and a heavy wooden gate, and a clay terracotta pipe. Covered with a cut piece of concrete slab, the enclosed pipe was a handy and inconspicuous receptacle for deliveries of milk and newspapers.

Sometimes, I discovered the concrete cover misplaced, undoubtedly because of a rushing milkman or paperboy. When this happened, I often found the milk with holes in the silver foil top. Neat little holes, triangular shaped; birds, the culprits, after the cream on the reverse of the top.

That strenuous but important daily ascent was well worth the prize. An idyllic view from high, at many miles of scenic beauty spanning beyond the woods and river to a sea of green fields separated by boundaries, forming a patchwork carpet of grassy green far into the distance.

A sweltering day, and another important job as I basked near the greenhouse. My aunty and I popped freshly grown and picked peapods. And I marvelled at the art, scraping the peas out into a colander.

A huge galvanised bucket full of peapods for shelling, and a never-ending task, but nice to eat a few straight from the pod. Delicious and the freshest you could get! So many pods, shells, and peas, and I ate so many, my jaw ached.

In my spare time I made a chess set from off-cuts of wood, cutting the pieces, filing and meticulously shaping and crafting with tools and a vice. This endeavour and perseverance in making my masterpiece instilled pride. I became tired, but completed all 32 pieces.

On my last day, as dusk approached, my uncle and I walked past the caravans and into a secluded area for a lesson that made me feel important. Manlier for the magnitude of trust the task involved. My uncle carried his uncocked, unloaded shotgun and as we walked.

I glimpsed at the black barrels and polished woodgrain of the butt. Nervous as I knew it was important and might be vital one day. "It will kick, so you must know how to hold it," as he inserted the shotgun cartridge into the barrel, closed the rifle with a click, and helped position the rifle safely against my shoulder.

Nervous as I steadied the cocked rifle and positioned the butt firmly between my shoulder and upper arm; aimed the barrel into the sky as instructed and my finger around the trigger. Poised in a nervous anticipation as I tentatively squeezed the trigger.

Such a loud bang! Louder than I expected and glad my uncle told me about the recoil: As the gun fired, it forced back into my shoulder. So cool, but scary. *Wow, I've fired a gun, something unique I'd only get to do in the country with my uncle's expert tuition.*

I had an excellent week. Helping-out as I heard the birds, saw beautiful trees and scenery every day. Unforgettable moments and cherished memories.

In a few days, I would start secondary school, and those days in Wales helped me to prepare and made the major transition of leaving primary school to go to a large secondary school less daunting.

Still, I was anxious but ready, proud on my long-awaited, and highly anticipated first day. I felt special and unique, too, knowing the speed of light to be 186,282 miles per second and fully equipped with my Fisher Space Pen®. Thixotropic ink, pressurised, hermetically sealed cartridge.

An infinitely superior pen, and I knew, too, as the front door knocked, I would be the only kid in school with the means and ability to write underwater and on the moon!

"I'll look after Paul, Mrs Walters, don't worry." Paul said, and equally proud of making sure I got to school safely.

It was exciting and strange sheepishly walking to school, up the lane into Bilston with an older friend. His blazer lapel upturned, hiding a prefect badge, just the straight brass pin visible, but Paul would flatten the lapel and show the smart shiny green-and-gold-coloured badge if needed.

Paul said, "Hello," to so many as we ventured onward past Bilston Baptist Church, God's Acre, St Leonard's Church, the Orchard, then Swan Bank and Green's sweetshop, and Stump pub, onto a wide paved area toward Fraser Street. "If anyone picks on you or cheeks you, tell me. I'll sort them out, don't worry!"

"OK, thanks," I reply. We were soon at school, a mass of old, dark-red brick buildings.

So many people, wide corridors, the smell of old books, old-fashioned wooden white frame windows, chatter, and noise as we found our way to a huge school hall. Anxious excitement as I waited and wondered.

What class will I be in and did I ace my exams? Will my classmates be friendly, sociable, clever? Silence followed the cacophony of chatter as everyone in the hall listened intently.

I waited ages in assembly to hear my name read out. The longer I waited, the more anxious I became, as I knew the classes started with the top Alpha classes, then A, then Beta, B.

Well, I wasn't in Alpha, A, or any class, so I stayed behind to tell the teacher reading out the names. Paul stayed with me for moral support. 1 Alpha A, yes, in a top class!

On that first morning, our class merged with another. A room with small, white windows, chairs, and tables, and I sat at the back by the white, rough-brick cream gloss painted wall. In dismayed concern, at pandemonium, kids shouting, walking around and ignoring the teacher's increasingly desperate instructions to sit and behave.

That nice teacher, out of control, frantic as a horrible scruff-bag kid, defies her, squares up and hits her in the face. Hits a teacher, I want to comfort as she sobs. *What is this place?* So different to my adventures playing in the sandpit on my first day of primary school.

How can this place be a school? Ready for outer space but primitive, unruly anarchy. Later that day, our class moved, and it pleased me the class became less rowdy, controlled, and more civil.

Unlike the playground, like a hazardous jungle! The wisest option: sit on the wall or stand in groups. Males who dared not keep a low profile would be at risk.

Often, I saw lads grappled to the ground, legs opened wide. The group lifted them into midair, then run and rammed the open part of the victim's legs hard and fast against sapling trees, aptly called 'Bollocking Poles.'

Such unbelievable, barbaric, and unexpected mad challenges disappointed me, as I just wanted to learn. But I soon settled in and survived the first year. I even enjoyed most of my classes and new subjects such as technical drawing, religious education, geography, metalwork, woodwork.

And an essential and obligatory bag of multicoloured, flying-saucer shaped Fruitella sweets in my blazer pocket from Green's shop, sometimes sugar-coated cola cubes.

I hoped the second-year would become more enjoyable and challenging. It was partly as a lifelong, innate fascination with space inspired me to write a special and important letter overseas.

It thrilled me to see that large brown envelope displaying the NASA post mark. Pleased to get a reply and many glossy, full colour space pictures, but dismayed they didn't send any UFO pics.

Such was my passionate, curious desires for intergalactic liaisons; my 40x magnification telescope, my prized space pen as used by astronauts, knowing space facts and talking about space so much, attracted the nickname of "Prof." Alas, far from it, and few cared about the velocity of light.

I had gained an O Level I wanted, a B in maths a year early and naively considered maths, physics, and other sciences to be the only subjects that mattered. I only tried in the subjects I liked and considered important. And even shunned the opportunity to study an extra O Level in statistics; I messed around in that class for the entire year.

Besides, my funky, amazing space pen had run out of ink after six miles of writing. Alas, I couldn't afford a new cartridge. Yet diminished ink was uncannily proportional to dreams and growing desires!

I had reached the latter years of school, and had had several girlfriends, despite shyness. Shyness fuelling new dreams; yearnings drifting to fantasies, mainly of the most sought-after girls in our year: The most attractive, but often the least refined. Girls, the lads, talked about most.

A partial dream came true one day, in English class. Our teacher organised the desks, so we sat around the four walls of the classroom with girls opposite boys instead of tables facing the front. It was bizarre how popular I had become.

A lot of the girls in class indirectly asked me out during the year; they were good-looking. It got even better though, by pure chance, sitting directly opposite one girl I liked most.

But there were many girls I liked in my various classes. Was I on another planet, or stupid not to capitalise on my popularity? Especially whilst studying William Shakespeare's *Romeo and Juliet*. I didn't get into it though.

I never went out with any of them, although lovely. Even arranged a date to meet, but half an hour before, overwhelmed by shyness, I phoned her to say I couldn't make it. Although I could have. She was the loveliest girl, too, and I yearned to meet her, but didn't. That dwelled on my mind for years.

I missed the excitement and former simplicity of kiss chase, now on a grander scale with more complex rules, emotions, and passion.

But, realised I was learning the flirting game, as I noticed on frequent occasions, upon looking up from my book, the vision of beauty across the room and sometimes momentary stare, then a cheeky smile, as if embarrassed. So, I looked at my work. Pretended to write before lifting my head to glance again.

Sometimes, we glanced at each other, evoking mutual beaming grins. Quiet laughter as our eyes simultaneously met.

The tension and thrill of that unpredictable flirting game made sitting opposite the girl I adored better than sitting next to her.

After class, I sauntered behind her with my friends. Inhibited by my bashful nature, entwined with fears of rejection that I may have got. Anyway, I doubted that calibre of a girl would be even remotely attracted to a conscientious, brainy type like me. Nevertheless, I seized any opportunity to impress.

Resorting to my charm and wit, a gift of making people laugh, as a joker who tried to gain attention, although somewhat jaded. Deflated by knowledge of romantic attachment. Then elated as she asked me out.

On an overcast Sunday, in winter, we met by the bus stop, as arranged. The bus arrived; I led the way upstairs. A test and delighted; worked like a charm. She sat next to me, holding hands on the backseat of the bus, and she reached her hand to mine. *Yes!* I hoped she would.

Later that day, it felt wonderful on the sofa together. Hugging and kissing each other; in my embrace, and such sweet, soft lips upon mine, God must have had something to do with it, listened to my prayers. In fact, intimately close in each other's arms. Entwined with the girl of my dreams at last.

Evening walks around the estate weren't long enough. Amorous antics, intimacy, fun, and laughter. *Am I the luckiest man alive* as we caressed and kissed beneath an umbrella and sheltered from the rain?

Smitten; striving to be the exemplary partner, and I didn't want to rush things! Or be considered shy, inexperienced for not recognising initiative requiring moments. *I can't say I'm anxious I may have made another girl pregnant! Have two babies on the way to two women.*

No inkling the goodnight kiss, by her backdoor, was also a goodbye kiss. She had chosen another, but I wouldn't have let her go so easily. Might have even grovelled.

Acted differently, said more if my friends hadn't been upstairs, listening. *If only I was older, with a car, and rich. She may have chosen me if I'd succumbed to the sultry stare as we passed the secluded garages!*

Maybe, but she wasn't who I liked most. And, as dreams faded and changed, I realised the infinitely sweeter, purer, more everlasting romance. If only I'd chosen the girl I stood up, sadly, her lips never to meet mine.

Who cared? I'd discovered drink with twisted motives of endurance: drinking the most. Being the most radical and unpredictable.

Every Friday night, a friend and I would walk to Bilston Town, hopefully to get a favourite and potent tipple, Olde English cider. The first visit to that off-license, I was so nervous about getting that lovely green plastic bottle.

How will I walk in, lift it without straining as I heaved the brew from the shelf? Oblivious that the drink will soon be more precious than liquid gold. As sweet as any kiss as I placed the bottle on the counter. I spoke few words, just waited, hoped for a price and request of money. Success, but did this signify failure?

We would walk to a secluded place on a windy, grassy hill below an electricity pylon, and overlooking the Grapes Pool and the same field, my prefect badge fell. I should have looked for it; scoured the long grass. But that never entered my mind.

Other things stimulated my mind. An addiction to the smooth, sweet, cool liquid, my head back, as I drank the lovely, potent tasting alcohol. That too rapidly brought enlightenment. Escaping the monotony, the heady humdrum of a crazy world, as a wise, all-knowing philosopher.

Crystal clarity with euphoric moments of false bliss disguising pain. The answers to the deepest mysteries of the universe, graspable. So savour and rejoice, the magic elixir. Each sip, more addictive than the last.

But never enough to quench or satisfy. Temporary peace, never solace. Just sadness entwined with masked happiness.

All as we lay on that cold grassy hill gazing up at the stars in wistful wonder, dancing, spinning, rotating, swirling simultaneously toward an inner or outer void. Not thinking about tomorrow, or wanting to escape from that unique moment. A moment no other had ever experienced, or ever shall.

School on Monday though, but I looked forward to Friday. Suddenly, everything seemed strange, but right. And, despite unease, as I didn't exert myself to learn the French language.

A lovely female French teacher, too, and a relaxed atmosphere in that class. We often spoke, if only to ask the person next to us how to pronounce specific words.

Such antics and behaviour signified the start of dark-times as my senses became dulled, aspirations dampened as ambitions dwindled away in the encroaching shadow of dark-times.

If only I had realised how powerful, and surreptitious the influence of alcohol was, its potency. So I couldn't refuse an opportunity to drink, dance, and romance. Any adventure to revel, escape the bland world of boredom, to stimulate my mind, have fun.

I remember going to a party at a community centre, the splendid music, the dancing, and the pretty girls and passionate kissing. But I became too drunk to walk; could only crawl on the pavement.

A Good Samaritan helped me on the bus. I got home somehow, despite my intoxicated state. At school, Monday morning, still in a daze, a girl from the party approaches, and chuckles. "You enjoyed the party," as she looked over to the doors. At a blonde girl who looks at me with a sheepish expression and blushes.

"Aren't you going over to speak to her? She was all over you... and did a good job of those love-bites," as she reaches me, inspects the bites, and sniggers. Proud but self-conscious, embarrassed and worried as I couldn't remember, "Really?"

So, there I was, in my final and most important year of school. High expectation of accolade and achievement, glowing school reports mentioned high ability, potential, and words of encouragement and to try before it's too late. I didn't care.

The discovery of alcohol and girls a year earlier heralded the start of a beguiling revolution, and hindered progress I should have made.

Academic aspirations became unimportant. I'd had enough of

school life and counted the remaining days. Enlightened as I knew there was no point, or viable, good reason, to try. Or purpose, as there were no jobs. Besides being born in the wrong country to become an astronaut!

So, doomed as others ridiculed those who tried hard, and those who excelled became unpopular. It just wasn't cool to be clever! A carefree attitude and acting foolish, the in-thing, as opposed to behaving sensibly and showing intelligence.

The pretence, difficult at first, but became easier; gradually moulded, became second nature. Wise advice and words I would invariably remember from school, wasted on me, and any attempt to change my viewpoint. No appeal would dissuade or change my little solid philosophical ideas.

The insecure, wanting rebel was right, perhaps for fears of being alone and so the downward momentum increased.

Adolescence loomed. And, the future beyond school for which I was inadequately prepared. Regardless, the springboard platform was ready, and I didn't fear the unstoppable tide.

So wise, with good maths and physics and chemistry O levels, I made the most effort for, plus a batch of CSEs. What more did I possibly need?

Such unnerving memories, these were, but I also remembered by my fifth year, school was no longer a priority. It had become a mere boring chore. Few lessons were fun anymore.

It seemed I had two lives: life at school and at night. Two worlds, poles apart as both aspects of life became increasingly disparate, diverging; two separate, conflicting dichotomies represented by an internal battle.

My divergence, driven by rebellious tendencies and antics, and began in my fourth year as part of a gradual transition. A transitory phase, I believed, might make me popular with females. And, gain a greater rapport with fellow rebels, all despite unease and the downside.

The displeased, frowning teachers who once looked upon me with pride, and poorer prospects that were once exceptional, and the likely origins of my downbeat, divergent path. A path embracing negativity and total opposite of all aspirations, all that is healthy and good, wise, and right, but ignoring my mind; my rosy future.

My quest for popularity was misguided though, as I needed to make progress and excel, but was less bothered and didn't. The group that actually mattered, who I should have impressed, teachers; I should have focused on academia.

I didn't care about respect or ambitions of cleverness; trading for a bit of madness as I wandered around the streets with friends. Watched videos, *Back to the Future* and *Weird Science* were the best.

And, I listened to music in friend's houses. New Romantic Human League, UB40, electro-funk and dance music of the time that moulded and blended with the harmony of that mid 80s era.

I enjoyed break dancing and learned a few moves, spinning on my hand and back. I wore my black, grey, and white, trendy Patrick cagoule, and tennis shoes as essential street gear. All a novelty at first, preceded by boredom, monotony, with little to occupy us.

To keep up with fashion, I found a paper round at a Bilston newsagent. Why not earn and save up to buy some nice clothes? A smart, woollen, golfing jumper as my first goal and then various bike parts to build a bike for a dream tour for which I probably won't ever be ready.

The newsagent was a large, bright shop. On arrival, the boss, wrinkled, tall, scrawny, and expressionless, but spoke in a quiet, reserved voice. "You have round six and ten. It's £4.20 a week. Be here by 7.30 in the morning, Monday to Friday, 4pm six days a week, and 7.45 on Sunday mornings."

My first day, eager and excited as I entered the backroom at the newsagents, a hive of activity as five other lads loaded their paper bags with newspapers. And rushed out of the shop. On their way without acknowledging me, as my second load of newspapers slapped on the table, causing a mini earth tremor, and a strong, brief, breeze.

The smell of newspaper ink wafted up my nostrils. "Here's your 58 papers... Here's the list of addresses." The boss said as the papers made my bag bulge. *The others have about 15 papers? I have so many, 58!*

I could just about lift the bag, and struggled to get it onto my shoulder. How would I mount my bike? Let alone ride it, carrying all that weight: half a tree?

Determined to not falter outside the newsagents in view of the boss, with a mighty heave and push on my bike pedals, I was away. Wobbling and swaying from side to side as I rode. A block of flats, then houses along Mountford Lane, by the Fozza. A paperboy from the same shop zoomed by with an empty paper bag, then another.

What? They've dumped the papers? I've only delivered seven papers! But hey, my bag's lighter. So onwards, as I covered an ever-increasing vast area of the town. Another paperboy zoomed by, coolly riding with both hands off his handlebars.

Hands back on, to steer as he passed, turned his head and stared back at me, adjusted the strap of his empty paper bag. *My bag has a never-ending amount of papers.* Two hours it took me; so overworked as I arrived home, put my bike in Dad's garage.

Again, in the morning, out at 7.00am. The crisp, cool morning air, and darkness, shiny black roads, passing dark alleys, and the bright white lights of the newsagents, a welcome sight as was the warm air that hit me as I entered the shop.

The next evening, I dared ask one of the unsociable paper lads how many papers they delivered. "28," one said, another, "32." *So unfair, 58 papers a night,* but I persevered. On arrival, I checked the amount of pages in the paper.

Mondays, Tuesdays, there'd be 28 or 32 pages. As the week progressed, the papers contained more pages, so heavier.

The first Friday papers had 58 pages, one paper was heavy, unbelievable. An Olympic weightlifter would struggle with such weights. That stern boss taking the piss.

One morning, a strange, orange glow lit up the dark-blue morning sky by the Fozza. As I ride nearer, I see huge, fierce flames and billowing grey smoke against orange streetlights. Red fire engines and water jets shooting high into the air, then descending into a factory that's ablaze. The same factory an older friend told me made nuclear warheads.

All that slog, delivering half a tree a day and full trees on my bike on Thursdays and Fridays and weekends for £4.20 a week was hard, but I stuck it out and saved money. Twenty-eight papers, what wimps, I delivered more than twice that every day!

It was grand to be earning a bit of money. More independent and with my mind more occupied, school felt different. A friend set me up with my next job, for even more money, £6, a week for loading a video van.

The ride back and forth to Wednesfield was more distant. Tiring, but exciting prospects. My friend and I, at a marvellous house where the videos and video van were.

We listened to Ashford and Simpson's *Solid* at high volume, crystal-clear sound from a topnotch Hi-Fi, loved it and the occasional day off school.

That day, I helped load the van and lifted many large, heavy suitcases, full of videos, to put onto the shelves. Then locked up, armed the alarms. So added pressure with the responsibility, but nice being trusted.

Suddenly, the days I enjoyed, looked forward to and felt excited by learning seemed long ago. More disturbingly, I remembered voting for who we thought should become school prefects. The careful deliberation that went into who I voted for: my choices.

And, the delight of others who voted for me. The honour of being chosen and feelings of pride and importance. My animated face glowed as I polished my shiny emerald green and golden brass prefect badge on the shiny, black, ironed lapel of my blazer. How could I have ever-wilfully removed that badge, that symbol of immense pride?

The deputy headmaster, unimpressed, whacked me with his acclaimed stick. With that strike, I joined the elite, notorious group of rebels who could tell the story of the whack in vivid, slow, syllabic detail. Smugly rejoice with no shame as a fellow rebel, but ever alone.

Losing my prefect badge was pretty shameful. Throwing it away, foolhardy and sadly symbolic of throwing away respect of those who chose me, trusted, declared their faith in me but more poignantly, self-respect.

Well, and truly off the rails, in a rash attempt to show off, as I hurled my prefect badge with all-my-might into the air on a massive field of lush, fecund green grass. Although crazy to insult and shun, the very stars with my discarded symbol of pride.

It presented a valuable symbol I never looked for, or treasured enough. That was weak, too sensible, and sadly, as time passed, it became harder to find as the grass grew longer.

Alas, my ever diverging path, but I had to be radical, crazy, uncaring, and strong. That set and chosen path had to be trod. And I had taken the first step on a downhill trend. Part of this entailed other interests and night pursuits with my evening circle of friends, amongst which my nickname became "P. "

College would be different to school. Focusing on the subjects I enjoyed most at school — certainly the best plan. Something to look forward to with renewed hope as the days passed.

Before starting college, I had a summer holiday in Wales to enjoy, a rest from school. The bike tour in a few weeks' time would represent mammoth challenges, too, and tests of tenacity — if I ever got my bike ready.

25.

CROSSROADS

I'd loved bikes since Dad played *The Pushbike Song* by The Mixtures on his record player and I raced around the coffee table on my trike as a toddler. I even sang along and copied the sound effects, amusing Mom and Dad.

My passion for cycling continued into my school-days. When I left school, a lot happened within a few weeks of leaving. I had been excited and enthralled hearing about bike tours and thought of my friend Ian's animated face.

Laughter as he told me amusing stories, but of exhausting touring and gruelling climbs up the hills of Cornwall two years earlier.

Amazing times, adventures, immense enjoyment, and challenges, I could merely dream of such aspirations. It was back in my fifth year of school when I heard rumours about another bike tour.

My mind cast back to that time in French class when one of my teachers confirmed the rumours and mentioned he was planning a cycle tour of North Wales. This filled me with excitement and sadness for my deep affinity and affection for Wales, and knowing I couldn't go, heartbreaking.

From that moment, I hankered and daydreamed. The vision in my mind of when I rode to Halfpenny Green on my very heavy Raleigh® Grifter BMX type bike as Ian bellowed at me to get up Goldthorn Hill on a sweltering day of blazing sunshine. I was so tired and thirsty. My reward: a cool drink at the top and the memory as an accolade.

An unfriendly, cycling rival gloated as he taunted, "You going on the tour, Walters? It will be hard. Think you can beat me up the hills?" Such provocative questions.

He had a top bike, naturally. Virtually no chance of me going. Still, I paused before replying, "Maybe." To rile him as he expected a "No."

I would have loved to meet that brazen challenge, but added, "Just teasing, no bike." I didn't have a suitable bike for touring. My bike was nowhere near good enough, too small and far too heavy.

Still, out of politeness, I expressed an interest in the trip. Told the teacher organising the tour, I'd love to go, and loved Wales. Alas, my only chance of going, if I got a lighter bike, all the equipment, panniers, and paraphernalia.

This seemed an impossible task. Especially as a new bike alone cost about £200 without all the equipment. My family couldn't afford such a bike.

So, the tour I yearned to go on, a mere fantasy, a dream. Desires to go intensified; relishing the challenge from the boastful classmate and beating him would be sweet too, but if I didn't beat him, at least he would respect me more.

Soon after, though, in the mini jungle and high grass of our back garden near Pluto, I see a strange object sticking out above the high grass. Pluto was what we called my dad's old grey Austin® A35 as it had a colourful but now tarnished cartoon character sticker of Pluto, the dog on the passenger door.

Curiosity compels me to pick up the object that resembles rusty metal. It's actually a rusty old bike frame. I examine the frame, and to my delight, noticed an old faded and partially missing Reynolds 531 tubing sticker.

Many cycling enthusiasts talked about 531 tubing, how good it was, and lightweight! What a rusty treasure! No idea how it got there. An ambitious plan came to mind. A long shot, but I may be in time. Maybe I can clean the frame. Have the rust ground off, sanded. Have it sprayed, then try to save up to buy the many bike parts.

I told my friends about my lucky find, but they were bewildered by my enthusiasm; by anyone, with even the slightest optimism for such a long shot. They were right. My story was so incredible and

I still only had a frame and handlebars, nothing else, but the odds, pessimistic doubt fuelled my determination.

Still, I persevered with my plan, although the chances of my grand ideas coming to fruition were remote. I paid £17 to have that rusty frame shot blasted, sprayed, and stove enamelled in a bright, dashing, pillar-box red colour and gradually bought parts each week.

It took a long time to raise all the money for the various bike parts with funds from my £4.20 a week paper round.

But lugging half a tree a day on my old heavy bike acted as a bonus training supplement, and slowly but surely, that old rejuvenated frame looked something like a bike. Alloy quick release wheels, 52 42 chain-set, 28 14 rear sprocket, alloy pedals, and Shimano® rear derailleur for changing gears.

I bought plastic mudguards, toe-clips, snow-white foam handlebar tape, brakes, and a comfortable saddle, rack, and so on, from a fabulous bike shop in Bilston, Victor's. And, luckily gained a second-hand set of panniers from veteran tourer and friend Ian for £5. I meticulously built my bike in stages, and by myself.

New parts, chosen on price and durability on an old frame and handlebars. Great, although heavy compared to the more modern bikes destined for the hills of Wales, with thin racing tyres, I considered impractical. But "Yes!" my fantastic and very own hand-built dream-machine was ready.

This instilled pride, especially against such stacked odds and to have paid for it all myself. The acid test was lifting one's bike with your little finger. I could just lift it, although heavy compared to the others that had cost £200 upwards.

Great to have a suitable bike, but I required more to be a cycle tourer, proper cycling gear, clothes, paraphernalia, I couldn't afford but Dava borrowed me his smart red and yellow Raleigh® cycling jersey with top zipper and large rear pockets to hold essential supplies, sustenance, bananas, and packs of essential Dextrosol®.

He gave me his red and white, striped, woollen hat, too, Liverpool football colours, not a proper cap but warmer and an old cagoule. I only had the cycling jersey and hat, so I would have to wear sports training shoes and tennis shorts.

Just one more ominous hurdle, training, but there's no time. It's only a few days until the bike tour, so I'm thrilled and appreciated someone told me that riding up Hurst Hill to Sedgley only once on a bike would give anyone a heart attack. I rode up and descended five times! That was the extent of my training.

Then, one day before the tour, whilst riding back from Dava's, being brought to an abrupt halt presented a mini disaster! My gears had broken and moved sideways into the spokes of my back-wheel!

So disappointed! All my efforts, in vain. Devastated, so sad to see the gears had bent the fore-end that the gears slide on to, I couldn't believe it. Such an impressive bike frame, unusable.

We called my teacher, who came to see me and console me about what had happened to my bike. He was sympathetic, saddened, too. Powerless, but I just had to accept I couldn't go on the tour.

My bike was beyond repair; no-one could fix my bike. A crushing, demoralising development, as we all became downhearted. Dad, though, showed sudden and unexpected enthusiasm, as his eyes widened. "I have an idea, a brainwave.". Legendary for saving the day with his ideas, he called brainwaves, but I was baffled.

Dad lit a blowtorch, and I became more upset as I watched and smelled the newly painted paint burn away as Dad heated the frame until the metal glowed red-hot. He then bent the metal fore-end back, extremely carefully, as he said, "This may break."

Anxious moments of anticipation, hope, and suspense as the teacher and I watched the metal slowly bend just enough for the frame to hold a back-wheel and gears.

Dad said, "That may just hold. If I bend the metal more, it may snap and might anyway, once it cools." Wary, but delighted, at least I won't miss the start of the tour and great if my bike survives the entire week.

I only needed a new gear derailleur and my friend and fellow cyclist, soon to be novice tourer, had a spare set of fabulous

Suntour VX gears for only £5. Luckily, there was just enough metal frame to hold this vital bit of kit firmly in place.

Fantastic, but only time will tell if my bike frame and I will withstand the rigours of North Wales for seven days. Will I cope, be able to keep up, let alone climb mountains considering I had had very little training or preparation?

Elation overwhelmed me with the granted opportunity to at least try. Proud, again to have built a fabulous bike from a foundation of rusty treasure, perseverance, and toil, paid for myself.

My bike was far from the best, but a symbol of my pride. Dad's hallmark, too, from his brilliant idea that salvaged all. The one thing I had forgotten, rim-tape, I just hoped not to get punctures after every mile. Most of the other bikes had Tuffy-Tape between the inner-tube and tyre to help prevent punctures. Mine didn't have that luxury.

The turn of events, an emotional rollercoaster, with times of suspense — I wanted to scream. The last-minute soul-destroying drama intensified the emotions; made me more eager, intrepid. The next day, a grand journey of adventure would begin.

So, on a warm August morning at the height of summer in 1985, outside school on Holland Road, we assembled. A group of 13 lined up, sat poised on their prize bikes, most togged up in all the gear and displaying smooth Lycra® cycling jerseys that comprised more colours than the rainbow.

Some in Lycra® shorts, novices, and veterans with bulging calves, defined muscles and determination.

Odd being in my tracksuit bottoms, I didn't have any smooth Lycra®. But had my red and white woollen hat instead of a chic, peaked cycle cap. So not as streamlined as the others.

Still, I stared in a contemplative trance of humbling reflection at the first of hopefully many grey open tarmac roads outstretched in front of me.

Before pressing on my pedals, I was proud to make it that far. I just hoped boundless determination wouldn't ever abate, and that I had enough tenacity and power. Would we all make it back?

Thirteen men set off for Anglesey on our pedal powered machines destined for North Wales. As for the bragging rival, who taunted and cajoled, asking if I was ready and he would beat me up every hill, he didn't even start the tour.

With a push on the pedals, the journey began, a leisurely modest pace but gradually built up to an unbelievable extent and pace. I tired after less than two miles and my bike, heavier than all the rest.

Undoubtedly, the leaders were showing off; a speed burst they won't be able to maintain! We hadn't even reached Wolverhampton and were barely into a 48-mile journey to Bridges.

Day one had well and truly begun. A shock to the system. A thrill as I venture onward, further than I had ridden in a day. So tired. What can I do? Awesome, yes – keep pushing – hope for hidden inner reserves to spur me on as we climbed, heading for a well-known landmark.

It's a chosen place for CB radio enthusiasts to reach further afield; such was the height of that mountainous terrain. And, a never-ending ascent had begun by the school. *How will I deal with even the slightest incline, let alone mountains?*

We were soon marvelling at picturesque countryside; the sun shone on those country lanes, but we didn't fully realise until Craig had his first puncture. A puncture so early on, unbelievable but the upside, respite, reflection, and sunbathing whilst we made repairs. The journey resumed, and we were near the notorious Long Mynd.

Lower gears, slowing under the strain, so hard, the first climb had begun! Grass, all around, and as we ascended, the picturesque panorama presented itself. The Long Mynd, would it beat me or any of us?

A long ascent, a breath-taking prize. We dismounted at the top and gazed at the scenic delights. So hot but a welcoming gentle cooling breeze fanned us.

The following day we would travel to Plas Rhiwaedog youth hostel near Bala Lake and pass through Welshpool. I hoped to see my uncle or aunts, but the chances of being there at the same time were remote.

Day two represented a milestone. A significant day, as we crossed the border into Wales, ventured ever deeper into the countryside. I knew we would pass through Welshpool but didn't know how close we were, as I'd never experienced the hilly, winding mountain roads.

One hill was so steep, it shocked me, as we climbed, and naturally, the experienced veteran cyclists, with lighter bikes, were the first to reach the top. The steep ascent and descent represented a real challenge for even them, but was tame compared to the challenges we would soon tackle.

As I reached the top and descended, I heard a loud bang, crash, the yelp. And screeched to a halt only to see Anthony, a grazed and furious veteran tourer, pick up his bent £200 bike from the road, and throw it at the suicidal dog before he chased it while shouting obscenities.

Angry that the dog caused injuries, wrecked the tour from his point of view. He'd have to return home on the train. Highlighted hazards, and we'd have been doing about 35 mph. A dog running out of a farm gate was scary and hard to avoid.

We became warier as we neared Welshpool, but I was the most confident, enthused, as I volunteered to ride to the railway station with the teacher and Anthony. An excuse to ride extra miles, to reminisce, and I knew the way.

That road, so familiar as I had travelled along it in Dad's various cars so many times. As I rode, I brim with excitement as right away I recognised a passing car and the number plate.

The Vauxhall® Viva stopped ahead of us. "That's my uncle," I said with pride, as I beamed with delight and extra pride. *My uncle knows I have cycled to Welshpool on my bike in only two days.*

Lucky to see my uncle and Anthony appreciated the lift to the railway station. At Welshpool, we soon found the baker's shop and replenished our energy with pastries and cakes.

Onward, deeper into Mid Wales, destined for Llanrhaeadr's Pistyll Falls, the idyllic beauty spot I visited four years earlier. Excited to visit again and to peddle the entire way. The village and approach just as I remembered, but on this occasion. We climbed to the top of Pistyll Falls. Looked upon the raging, sparkling torrents.

Superb, and the swim in the water-pool I'd swum in years ago. It had been a magnificent day that exceeded the wildest expectation, more so at the grand sight, serene, crystal-blue water of Bala Lake and the warm sun on our backs.

That night we stayed near that picturesque lake at Plas Rhiwaedog youth hostel and enjoyed chilled drinks sitting outside a pub.

The next day would be a whole new adventure. And test us in many ways as we travelled ever deeper into Wales. Pushed on, ever higher, across increasingly mountainous terrain — the infamous Dinas Mawddwy.

A long mountainous trek, along a steep, winding, undulating mountain ride with fields on either side; I reminisced.

I had travelled there many times in Dad's cars and caravanettes. His old caravanette buckled under the strain. Slowed to a snail's pace, steam bellowed out of the bonnet, eventually crawling, then stopped.

There were no lay-bys, sheer drop at both sides of the road. The handbrake under strain, not holding, creaking as we slowly edged backwards. *Dad can't reverse! Oh no, terrifying* as a line of cars queued behind us. I would always remember the fear and excitement when Dad bought a second, newer, more powerful caravanette.

Like many cars, even that struggled. Then the excitement and amazement of being woken by the gentle '*whoosh*' and '*roar*' of the sea from my vinyl bunk bed above the front seats. And, to see the beach and waves as I peer through my curtains on the seafront at Barmouth. On my bike, that route was just as tough.

We made it and passed many sheep in the green hilly fields, looking on and calm. They'd seen it all before, as they grazed in the rugged terrain.

We pushed on, and the day had barely begun. But would be the hardest yet. With tough tests, and against the elements as we ascended.

The climb and ride to the foot of Snowdon and Pen-Y-Pass was particularly arduous. A seemingly never-ending ascent that began after a full day's riding. The rapidly dwindling light of dusk presented a second race against true-time as the Earth turned and the sun dipped below the horizon.

Ice-cold stinging rain and frozen cheeks from the driving raw wind so strong my bike swayed and wobbled. Each turn of the peddles harder, ever heavier as I pushed on, exhausted, but the increasing, unbearable fatigue fuelled defiant determination. Stopping and dismounting – not an option! Ever higher.

I remembered the outdoor pursuits holiday at Towers, Capel Curig a year earlier, a beautiful mountain covered in chunks of white quartz of various shapes and sizes.

Determination to bring a quartz crystal home as a memento, as large as I could carry, became an obsession, as everyone said. "That's too heavy to walk 10 miles with!"

Then the chilly rain on my face reminded me of the Tyrolean traverse, and the watery mist from gorge walking. Canoeing on an icy lake, so black, still and cold. High mountains and trees surrounded the lake, an awe-inspiring idyllic location.

The instructors warned us not to capsize. I risked a telling off to experience capsizing and swim in a wetsuit. *Will it keep me warm?*

The frigid shock made me gasp as I became immersed in the water, momentarily upside down. The invigorating, but tiring swim, energy-sapping in my water-logged wetsuit, but I was warm as I continued.

Now, soaking wet through to my skin, I was more tired and colder. Drained, fatigued, achy with cold, hard, fast rain stinging and freezing my face and legs. I did not stop to rest. That gruelling, energy-sapping climb, utmost respect for that majestic landmark, but the highest mountain in Wales would have won if I had stopped.

I made it first up, and despite having the heaviest bike. Well, the first of the novices, close behind the teacher, the true king, and master cyclist who briefly congratulated me as he, too, was so pleased to have reached that summit and looked exhausted too, in his green patterned cycling jersey beneath the grey sky.

When I dismounted at the top, exhausted and saddle-sore with red-raw inner thighs as I didn't have the proper cycling shorts, other parts of my legs are like icy jelly, numbed flesh; knackered! *How will I lift my bike?* No idea where the energy came from to put my bike into the youth hostel bike shed?

So tired after being buffeted by the harsh elements. My clothes soaked and my panniers leaked from prolonged periods of rain during those past days, and that unrelenting day.

Too weary to celebrate that epic achievement or enjoy any euphoria. I placed my underwear on the top bunk bed I claimed and, on the window to dry, broken in the corner.

I climbed onto that top bunk, wet and cold, shivery by the draughty window, but slept soundly in my wet clothes, despite the howling winds whistling and rattling the window. I woke refreshed and ready. *Yes, I've made it up to the edge of Mount Snowdon.*

The highest point of the world I'd ever reached by peddle power. I didn't worry about trivialities: Are any of my clothes, underwear still wet? And after the arduous climb of the previous day, quietly confident no mountain or ascent shall beat me.

I just hoped for better weather, couldn't believe it had rained constantly for two entire days in August! Still, I woke with upbeat, high spirits. Enjoyed the much-needed breakfast, and invigorating fresh mountain air, as I took deep breaths.

Smelled the morning and gazed upon the sheer magnificence. Beauty of the mountain before us and the lush green, unsurpassed loveliness of the valley, fields, and treetops meeting a perfect pale-blue sky.

Gruelling work, an arduous climb, and the first part of the prize money cannot buy unfolded in front of our eyes, all around us.

Up so high, we could almost touch the clouds. A beautiful, awe-inspiring and humbling location, it felt a shame to descend, but that was the hard-earned second part of the priceless prize.

An exciting bonus, no rain. It had stopped; the winds had eased. Moments to savour, but we made our reluctant farewells to Mount Snowdon as our descent began. Speed built quickly, exhilarating and wonderful, the mountain air gushing against us and with us.

Sent us on our way ever deeper into North Wales, lush, breath-taking scenery into an incredible, unspoilt wilderness on a grey tarmac path. We ventured onward toward the coast. Great, the gushing wind dried us out.

Hard though, the ride against the wind and driving rain, winding roads, long climbs, then scenic rewards and satisfaction, until we arrived at a village. Stopped for supplies and respite, but a newspaper headline gutted me; changed my upbeat mood.

Dismayed, Madonna had married Sean Penn: "Who is he? Never heard of him! I wanted to marry her!" At least when I wrote to her. Anyway, we had nature's simply beyond perfect prize from the edge of Snowdon.

The ride went on; the rain came again, the wind against us as we sped ever-onward. Beside jagged rock walls as we rode, and taking turns, enjoying the slipstream, at the rear of the pack, edging ever forwards to lead, at the front of the pack.

Close to the rear wheel of the bike in front, requiring intense concentration, focussed on the mini wall of water displaced from the tyre and revolving upward momentum.

It's great as I'm dragged along by the narrow pocket of air, the slipstream from the riders in front enabling me to conserve precious energy, a welcome, and brief lull from the gruelling rides, but my turn at the front as leader would come that day. *Will I be fast enough, strong enough, ready?* I hoped so.

It was an incessant struggle across a great distance. Conwy and Swallow Falls in a day, both magnificent. The power of the water, the constant whooshing and gushing, immense gravity driven jets buffeting from part-eroded rocky channels, forming a cool white mist on our faces and many magical mini rainbows.

We climbed in that forest area and revelled in that environment. On the descent, Craig went too fast, lost control, and became another casualty with a gashed and bruised knee after a collision with a tree.

Jon noticed his bike frame had cracked, too, after negotiating the rigorous, rough terrain, trying to get a splendid view of the final waterfall we visited: Aber Falls. We were tantalisingly near the coast, near to Llanrwst.

Our intrepid merry band dwindled further as two more abandoned the tour, with their injuries and cracked frames, so we all chipped in again for two more train fares back to Wolverhampton. *How many of us would return on our bikes?*

As we approached the village, Alan and I had a mischievous idea. Shorts down, buttock cheeks exposed and on display throughout that sleepy place. In front of me, two white buttock cheeks moving as we peddled.

Wanting to laugh, but I did my best to keep a straight face, nonchalance as I say, "Hello," to onlookers with aghast faces; stunned open mouths everywhere as two crazy and cheeky Englishmen rode through the Welsh village.

We progressed, ever-onward. To Llanrwst, and the Ffestiniog Railway, with its magnificent, immense black metal engineered, steam-snorting beasts from a bygone age. Our bikes, a mismatch of power, man, and peddle-powered machine, as we continued our journey along the coast to Bangor.

To reach the North Wales coast by pedal power instilled a tremendous sense of achievement and pride suffused with an overwhelming emotion of seeing the blue sea. As we crossed the bridge to Anglesey, we knew we'd made it to our furthest destination and would begin the journey home.

On the way back on our penultimate day, we passed the Welsh border and rode under sunny English skies. Then through a small town too scenic to speed through as Alan and I saw two lovely girls ahead, on bikes.

We heard a "Yelp" as we passed slower than our group. I suspected they had pretended to fall from their bikes to gain our attention, to make us stay and talk; as if we were visitors to their land, visitors they'd like to entice and enchant.

Their plan worked. They had probably heard about antics near the coast, mountain conquering and buttocks. How could we leave a damsel in distress even if she fell off her bike on purpose to get our attention?

We showed no concern as the group sped off, left us behind, gone for dust. Stopping to chat with girls on a serious bike tour with tight schedules may not go down well with the teacher, and others more senior in the group, but couldn't resist their charms.

We flirted a little, sped toward them, then slowed and leaned, as we stood on our pedals, acting like peacocks or knights in shining armour, gallantly controlling our steeds whilst exhibiting no fear and suppressing escalating worries about being left behind, lost near the Welsh border.

Despite imagining a scene of much scolding, the group reaching home without us, and exclaiming to the world: "Oh, they stopped to chat some girls up!" We entertained the girls, succumbed to their charms for as long as we could, or rather dared. Well, we're in flat, England; we can speed and easily catch up with the rest.

Only after ensuring the maidens were safe, we sped off at maximum power. Pushed on ever harder and fought the hesitancy at the prospect that the rest had turned off without us, leaving us to continue on our travels into unknown foreign territory.

Soon we surpassed our usual comfortable cruising speed of about 15 mph. Desperation and determination as we raced to catch the posse, in overdrive to a new level. The clink of the gear levers, our battle-cry, building into top gear, my feet spinning round faster and faster as we take chase.

Heads lowered, breathless and in pursuit. Chasing for too many miles, still nowhere in sight? Must think of a plan. What to say when we met? If ever? "Crikey, they must be motoring! Or they've turned off... Shit." Alan said.

How can the group vanish into nowhere? They haven't gone this far? We're lost, and no road signs, but as I slowed, eased my pace, there's a firm pat on my back.

A startling, welcome pat from the teacher who had been chasing, as head of the group, trying to catch us for 15 miles and only caught us as we eased the pace.

So, pleased, relieved, we didn't know the group had made a slight detour; hid on a side road to await us, and play a trick on us because we went babe hunting.

The less mountainous terrain of England allowed greater speeds, though. Wonderful and so easy after coming out of Wales, conquering Welsh mountains. Reunited, too, great as we sped onward, on our way to a place we stayed at the outset of the tour: Bridges youth hostel near the Long Mynd.

We arrived with an enormous sense of triumphant achievement tinged with melancholy sentiments: it was the last night of the tour. And, the last of our youth hostel stays. We weren't far, Shrewsbury, a mere 40 miles from home.

That night, as we lay in our bunk beds, I read out an erotic story from a girly magazine one lad had bought for a laugh. The comedian I was added intonation, various accents, and sound effects. Putting everyone in hysterics.

But, at the conclusion of the story, I said with a serious tone, "Beware of the one who calls himself Terry Wogan, for he is a Zillon from the Planet Tharg!" As I mimicked a favourite Rowan Atkinson sketch, "Zak the alien" and reproduced an almost identical voice; I earned the nickname of "Paul The Zillon Walters."

Six unforgettable days and tomorrow the last day, the last ride. I slept well, content I'd amused and entertained all.

A week of hard slog, but there was no rivalry or malice. Just friendship, as we were a team with one goal. To ride as far as we could. Enjoying the tour, the countryside, idyllic sights and all with peddle power and determination to keep going.

I never stopped pedalling, and unlike two of the most expensive bike frames, my old rusty but trusty frame with a bent fore-end precariously mended with a blowtorch and Dad's ingenuity stood the tests of time, and all rigours of the tour.

As I got home again, soaked from yet another of those peculiar, rainy, August days, I staggered upstairs, lay on my bed and rested my aching sore legs. My entire body ached while my mind spun with memories of precious moments and stories that instilled feelings of pride mixed with sadness as the tour had to end.

Mighty hills and mountains through valley and vale, in the rain, sun, and wind, as we visited many idyllic and humbling places.

Waterfalls and to the sea along the coastline to Anglesey and back, rode 347.8 miles, even as the only one not to have a puncture, despite forgetting the rim-tape, and my mended frame. Thanks to my wonderful, genius dad.

Surviving that week required colossal amounts of determination, motivation I wasn't sure I had, although success itself came by making it to the start line. Every day presented a bonus. Completing the entire week — a dream. Particularly as one of 10 out of 13 to make it back safely.

Such immemorial accolades of priceless mementoes became stored in my brain, forever as the ultimate and best school, leaving-gift anyone could want.

It was relentless with intensive tests of endurance, but immensely enjoyable. A grand achievement and boldness as I strived on to new wider pastures, into the sun. The refreshing dawn, but poorly prepared for the presented, stark reality. I thought back to those times.

It was fantastic to be free from the daily drudgery of attending school, but so strange. Still, a fresh start for a man of the world who'd soon begin college to study advanced level mathematics, physics, and computing.

The prospects and opportunities excited me, and being the cool, clever, popular swat I couldn't be at school may increase my chances of romance. What a fantastic, fresh start, and outlook, a grand future ahead.

And, as I recollected that past summer of physical conquest, my current, and foreseeable achievements become insignificant compared to my former stature and prowess.

How could I have changed so much? Lost so many abilities and become so inept and unprolific? Will even the smallest mountain beat me? More memories returned.

26.
ADOLESCENCE

*T*he transition of leaving school to begin study, again, provided a period of leisure, recreation, and reflection. Time to prepare mentally for the vast forthcoming challenges, changes in my life, as I grew older.

As for earning, I went from paper round to a Saturday job. At a butcher's shop, with a strict boss, and hard and relentless work, I cleaned, scrubbed, swept and mopped floors, and washed up sharp knives as the most ominous task for a measly £8 a day.

Not enough, as sickly smells suffused my nostrils as I washed out blood-stained containers. This was the most unpleasant task, after Friday night drinking and severe hangovers.

The only perk: delicious sandwiches for breakfast, but I soon lost my appetite, as on one sweltering summer's day, a bag of ox liver split open. Dark, red, smelly, sticky, blood, soaked my jeans.

The pungent, vile smell combined with my hangover from the previous night's drinking made me sick straight away. I grew to hate that Saturday job at the butcher's. There had to be a better job!

A superb job in the market followed afterwards. Good pay, too, excellent compared to my earlier jobs and relatively simple work for such likeable people. They were sociable with great senses of humour.

Brilliant, although shyness hindered me at first, in an outdoor market stall, interacting with so many people. But plenty of girls on the market, too — a wonderful bonus, and such fun, outdoors chatting, as we waited for customers.

Especially on warm summer days, when the market was busier. I watched, learned, and with encouragement, I overcame my biggest hurdle of serving customers as I conversed, gained confidence. Even measured and cut the coverings in a straight line with sharp scissors.

We fetched a large, heavy, metal-framed trolley from the garage, pushed it up the hill and crossed a dual carriageway. Then I loaded the trolley with strong, large cardboard drums, and long, heavy vinyl rolls, contour worktop, and wall-coverings and pushed the laden trolley to and from the stall and across the busy road, leading to the garage.

Loading and unloading the van was easy, although heavy work, and even harder to hold back heavy loads on the descent. But I relished the challenge of those physical endurance tests, and good to be outdoors.

Friends come for me as the market closed and hindered, but amused me with their mischievous antics. Tom lifted the heavy barrels off the truck I had loaded. "We'll help you!" Jokesters: so I had to reload the truck.

Less amusing on sweltering summer Saturdays, but I enjoyed that job and the money. I bought a leather coat from another stall for £60 and wore it everywhere — a bargain. Cold beers on Saturday nights became even more refreshing. My social life was busier, too.

And, worldlier than when at school, on an ever upward high, relishing progression from that juncture. Less shy after experiencing romance and the joys of working outdoors on Bilston Market.

Still, determination to spread my wings during that summer before college drew me to visit Welshpool. It made sense, too, a natural progression as I was there during the holiday transition period at 11-years-old. As I left primary school, into secondary school at a crucial stage in my life.

Great to be at that special place, five years later with my cousin Dava, a week's holiday in our caravan. I'd enjoy the trees, scenery, and countryside.

Basic accommodation, no TV, or electricity, or running water, but a plentiful supply from the tap, near the steps, and birdsong for entertainment. I hoped Dava would be appreciative of the idyllic setting. As I showed him the river area and rapids I had swum so many times, I hoped to see Mandy and Lisa I met a year earlier, too, but wasn't optimistic.

Proud and excited as Dava was a fellow, powerful swimmer. It was a lovely, warm summer's day as we dived into the water, swam and revelled in the friendly competition.

The cool water, welcome and invigorating as I swam underwater, but, as I pushed my head above the water's surface, I glimpse at a woman with blonde hair sitting on the grassy riverbank.

This was totally unexpected, as I recognised Mandy and signalled to Dava with a quick, coy shout to him, as if I wanted to race. But then glance at the riverbank, to avert his gaze as we swam.

We stayed in the water, though. Revelling, as we put on a show of prowess and power.

Swimming fast, surface diving, disappearing beneath the water, and staying underwater, holding my breath as I swam quite a way before surfacing. Lunging upwards toward the sun, like a dolphin, and for fun and for our special audience, of one.

No inhibitions or shyness — in a watery paradise I knew so well. Even though I had considered that girl out of my league a year earlier.

I relived that first encounter as I swam and glanced upstream to the railway. Anxious as a past vision entered my mind, two girls sitting on the railway bridge, basking in the sun.

With my best burgundy Grandad shirt on and baggie open-pocketed jeans with buckles by the ankle line as I wandered. Hands in pockets toward the woods and river as I walked, then gaining pace and direction.

Mandy did most of the talking. She looked bored, and I wished to change that. Both girls looked much older than me and attractive. Lisa more so, with stunning looks, brown hair, and wearing a nice denim skirt with suede, velvety hemline above the knee; so pretty and oh sweet, oh so kissable lips.

Intimidated by beauty, I dared not say much. Or try to speak even though, occasionally, she looked up and smiled.

Tantalised, aroused, my mind in overdrive. I so want to stay with them; be in their presence. With them until the sun went down; all night. Under the moon, the stars — bathe in starshine, as we listen to the water. See the moon set and each sunrise.

Alas, regrettable missed opportunities, dashed destinies. Nervous and stuck for words, embarrassed, as I shivered with excitement. But, so timid and I felt terrible, torn. *Stop, no, relax!* "I have to go now," as I looked at the floor. Hating myself more with each spoken word.

Especially as it seemed as if they were standing by for me to respond. Make them laugh, make a move.

But I didn't, and as I walked away, my heart thumped to a sad beat and with each step, emptier, sadder. Wondering and wanting: *do they want me to turn round and come back?*

I crave to turn round, to see them again. *How slow can I walk as I dawdle?* Hoping they'll call me back or follow me; different hopes, but similar desires?

Even sadder, it was as if they were waiting, just for me. What a fabulous, uncanny gift, and in my special place, I had sat many times, gazed at the river, scenic delights, and now beauty, attraction like never experienced.

Destined to meet, then walk away from my wildest dreams and desires. Why couldn't I just return to them? Say anything, be there. Near them, relax and be myself or very different just for once? I hated myself, my shyness! Such an unfair affliction that caused much frustration and intensified yearnings.

I so wanted them, either or both, alas, a mere dream. I just hoped to see them again. And to be less shy, if lucky enough for a next time, and there she was.

My next encounter, imminent as we clambered out from the water; hurriedly got changed. Mandy, still watching while she sat on the grass. I greeted her and introduced Dava before we sat near her on the grass.

She walked to one side and spoke with Dava whilst I remained seated on the moist, cool grass, leaning back on my arms with my legs sprawled out and gazing at the fast-flowing river.

Dava returned. "She fancies me; I'm not bothered and think she likes you, too."

"Don't you like her?"

"She's OK. If you like her, talk to her!"

"Shit, what shall I say?" as I grinned.

"I dunno. Anyway, I might go back soon."

Attracted to her, but, I wondered where Lisa was, my natural first choice. My shyness a year earlier presented an ever-greater challenge: slimming the chances. *Hope she likes me enough. Maybe she'll at least talk to me, be interested and not overly put off by my past immaturity.*

Mandy sat beside me, in the dappled shade of an enormous redwood tree facing the river. Demure and glum as she gazed at the water. She looked mature, but I wasn't as shy as before, or as inexperienced.

Dava said again, "Try your luck, P… See you later," as he started the trek back to the caravan.

This prospect seemed out of the question. For a while anyway; the tantalising sight of tanned legs meeting the hemline of a short white tennis skirt and accompanying thoughts overpowered my reluctance to try, and fear of rejection.

The visions of her standing up and walking off as I approached, leaving me embarrassed and forlorn, filled my mind.

I approached and sat near her on the grassy riverbank. "Hello!" I said. Nervous, but pleased, her gaze into apparent nothingness shifted towards me. "All right, hello." An acknowledgement that excited and caused me to contemplate daring more than a tentative glimpse.

My senses overloaded; momentarily mesmerised as I succumbed, made a swift, but bolder, lingering stare at her big, wide blue eyes, embellished and adorned with bright-blue eyeliner. *She's gorgeous.*

An unfamiliar song played from a stereo beside her.

"What are you listening to?"

She turned to me, ' still with a glum expression. *"Like To Get To Know You Well,* Howard Jones, he's brilliant!*" Yes, she answered me, looked at me, didn't turn the volume up, and start singing.*

"Do you fancy coming for a walk?"

She glanced at me again, still looking moody, probably from interruptions to the music. But her expression gradually changed to a warmer one. "A walk. Where to?"

"Oh, how about along the riverbank?"

"Yeah, OK, I'll put my stereo in the caravan. Won't be long."

Bounding with joy mixed with disbelief. *What will we do, though? What would we talk about?* The more I thought, the more I worried. Yes, she'll accompany me on a walk, just us. By the riverside, I expected nothing more.

Such a question, difficult to contemplate moments ago, let alone propose. Proud and bold, but tantalised by emotions tinged with anxious anticipation. What may or may not happen, as I asked her to accompany me to an unknown destination.

She returned sprightlier; more cheerful, with a wonderful smile that made me swoon, filled me with joyous pride with a lovely female as we walked by the riverside. But uneasy, as I hadn't ever walked along the riverbank with any girl, or anyone.

It's fantastic to walk together, under the warm sun, beside the ever-gentle babble and whoosh of the river. We stroll further away from the fast-flowing rapids, downstream, along the lush green grassy riverbank at a leisurely pace. *How far dare we walk,* as my heart pounds faster with each step?

Mandy said little, making me more nervous. Even more attracted as she walked beside me, so close, her tanned long legs brushing against my legs and waving blonde hair.

Everything, so new and rapidly changing. Fresh, exciting, amorous emotions, as I looked upon her tanned complexion. Explored more with my gaze.

Beyond which I dared a moment ago, but always returning to those pretty, and now sparkling, comely eyes, adorned with blue lashes as I hoped and expected our eyes to meet. Such lustful yearnings entwined with a sultry glance.

Somewhat intimidated by glamour. But excited as I received all sorts of signals, filling me with delightful feelings. Our pace quickened as we progressed further and further downstream; beyond the realm of the caravan site, away from prying eyes.

Her hand grasped mine, as I beamed and became more at ease. The sun shone fiercely; the grass grew longer, untrodden, unvisited.

Where are they going? Onlookers must have thought. I knew, even though I hadn't ever walked that far downstream.

"It's nice here! Let's stop here to rest!" I said with added confidence as we sat on impulse.

Heart pounding as I contemplated a bold question and thought, *Nothing to lose.* "Shall we kiss?" Aargh, so stupid in hindsight, I shouldn't have asked! Our lips kissed.

Passionate kissing and caressing ensued. Mandy seemed relaxed, not at all nervous. Older and more experienced, as she teased me with her tongue, kissed me; I hadn't kissed like that before, so sensual.

Our breathing quickens with each second. She lay beneath me with her long, sexy, fleshy legs slightly arched.

The tempo of the passion moved up a few gears as we playfully kissed. Despite the public location, but farther downstream, in the long grass, by the river, as the sun blazed.

Superb to be next to nature, although anxious, in a partial state of shock at the ever-transpiring situation. Thrilled, over the moon, smiling as we walked back to where we met, holding hands, and more affectionately kissed.

After a farewell kiss, I hurried back to the caravan, shaking with excitement. Like a kid, who'd found a treasure trove of chocolate. An expression that said it all as I arrived. "Hey Dava, I spoke to her; she likes me too!"

"How did you get on?"

"We walked by the river... lay on the grass."

"Well done, go for it!" As he packed his bag. Wales wasn't his scene.

Annoyed, he got bored so easily, didn't allow time to settle. Disappointed and saddened about his departure. This meant I'd stay on my own for the rest of the week. More concerns entered my racing mind. Mom and Dad may worry and might even turn up to bring me home.

Such prospects daunted me until I realised the opportunity for further passionate antics, sending my imagination into frenzied excitement as erotic visions entered my mind.

I will have to be so calm, show no excitement and resist temptation to beg, implore, "Look, please, don't fetch me! I am fine. It's great, here by myself in the caravan, fresh country air, and the trees." The time for that vital phone chat had arrived!

"Hello,… Mom?"

"Hello, Paul, are you OK?"

"Yes, thank you, fine. And you and Dad?"

"We're OK. Do you want us to fetch you? It's a big thing for you, on your own in the caravan?"

"Nah. Don't worry. See you in a few days."

"OK, if you're sure you're OK."

"Yeah. Tara-a-bit, then."

Yes, let the fun and frolics begin! As soon as Dava left, I called for Mandy at her caravan. We spent hours on end at my caravan, overwhelmed and powerless to resist such passionate opportunities.

Mandy and I went for more walks, on sunshine drenched days, by the river and toward the railway bridge. To quiet places, idyllic havens I'd discovered as a child.

Secret pathways, and one was via an opening in the undergrowth and brambles, past the bridge and river. To a thick old, grey stone wall, and a 6ft jump onto a rough, downtrodden, muddy path below I had been many times.

A place for intimate passion, and other wonderful places to explore and such deep, sensuous, dreamy kisses under the sun as I shared my heavenly domain. Dizzying pleasures, sensational, I just hoped a train wouldn't speed by or slower ramblers.

Splendid company and a few more excitement-packed days at

the caravan. Great, too, to prepare my food, fetch water, light the stove at night and the old gas mantles.

I wasn't afraid of night sounds, the hooting owls or trains. Yet, still loved being woken by the dawn chorus, beautiful song from birds of the woods, heavenly, cheery sounds rejoicing the light of a new sunrise.

What a tremendous week. So special, and new, I had left school, travelled, and experienced an adventure, without my parents. The distinct highlight, romance, and thrilling times as I conquered shyness.

Extraordinary, and ever-exciting, as Mandy and I made plans to meet up nearer home. After the holiday, I rode over on my bike to her house one glorious, sunny Saturday morning, after work.

On arrival, as I stood at the front door. *Is she here?*

Such a contrast now, and comfortable, but nervous and strange, as I composed myself. Hoping for pleasure and fantasy to continue and transcend to another level. *Will Mandy open the door or someone else?*

Tingling with excitement as I tapped on the door, and a glowing, painted vision of beauty appeared and greeted me with a beaming smile. I ventured inside, into a cool hall. Welcoming after the ride in the heat, delighted and relieved by the warm greeting and reality.

I sank into the black leather sofa. Leaned back, perched on the edge of the cushion as Mandy sat close. We knew why we had met.

Now was the long-anticipated time. Tension, a thrilling new game; poised for passion. A short skirt, tantalising leggy sights, a glimpse of a bra strap and tanned flesh, excites me even more.

Our first kiss magically broke the ice and reminded us of earlier encounters. And I envisaged further, ever more enjoyable moments as we drank cider, chilled from the fridge. Refreshing after the hot ride, and relaxing us, as we kissed, tasted the cider on our lips, numbed by the chilled drink.

Ever intense and more aroused, as we fondled each other, writhed in ecstatic excitement. Eating each other, devouring the most delicious food ever — mouth-to-mouth, entwined as one.

Deep kisses, as she ran her fingers through my hair. We touched each other and undressed and playfully teased each other as we enjoyed that fabulous encounter.

She was irresistible and mine. Unlike when I first saw Mandy and Lisa basking in the sun. Fantasies and regrets as I scolded myself for not being more forward with Lisa. I hardly spoke to her because of shyness and lack of confidence.

Didn't think I had a chance of becoming even friends years earlier, let alone romantically involved with mature, attractive women!

That summer of 1985 was the best ever, the bike tour, no more school, romance, and I had my market job. The music, too, with the apt song of the summer, Stephen Duffy, *Kiss Me* as I approached adulthood.

For sure, I had no chance of attracting any lady now, a partner, soulmate. Or of romance, yet still hoped. Dreamed, and I would begin new pursuits in the wide world. While an additional indifferent aspect to my life would feature more.

27.

TRANSFORMATION

*D*uring coma, many from the clergy visited and perhaps religion, the power of prayer and many blessings at those critical times played a part in surviving coma and life afterwards. Religion embraced me, although it had embraced me all along, just not as a significant part of my life.

Although far from devout, not Catholic, it was a privilege to visit Lourdes. Excited, too, to experience the South of France. And Lourdes' historic origins fascinated with mystery and stories of miracles.

The film *The Song of Bernadette* had moved me. It focused on Bernadette, a girl who saw apparitions of the Virgin Mary in 1858.

Well, I had become disabled, and so inadvertently become a candidate to visit that holy place, and I improved after a blessing in hospital. But was it too late for me?

Still, I relished the opportunity to experience Lourdes. With an open mind, grateful for fund-raising efforts and coffee morning donations from kind people who didn't know me, but cared.

Would I spring up and walk? Abandon my wheelchair or even move or talk like I did before in my able-bodied existence? Experience or witness a miracle? Despite these wild dreams, insurmountable wishes and irrespective of whether I was beyond saving, part of me went in pursuit of inner peace, maybe new friends.

We left Digbeth, Birmingham by coach at dusk, destined for Lourdes and in our bright yellow sweatshirts with a smiley face emblem and the words "Smile God Loves You!" My dad and I on our way to Lourdes, our first pilgrimage, and first visit abroad, to France amongst veteran travellers.

We arrived at Dover as night descended. Greeted by a massive ferry and enveloped with a splendid buzz of excitement on a busy deck of that incredible vessel.

Cars, coaches, lorries and so many on their way to the lifts, more homely upper decks. Our group stood out as a tremendous mass of yellow jerseys and Mac, the master orchestrator; in a navy-blue nursing sister's uniform that reminded me of a hospital.

She was stout and stern, magisterial, overseeing all like a wise old mother hen keeping her fledgling yellow chicks in check, but we were all on a ferry; cooped up on a ship deck.

For decades she had done this, travelled on so many journeys; organised pilgrimages. Saw that disabled children experience Lourdes, despite obstacles, logistics, and negative attitudes. It was new to Dad and me.

Novel as we sat, observed as part of a more seasoned group, tended to by experienced helpers. Some instructed by Mac, an austere lady perhaps as she had great responsibility, looked after everyone.

Yet, behind the serious exterior, no harshness, as in reality, Mac was the most caring person anyone could wish to meet, warm, and friendly.

Excited, at my first, ferry trip and restless to see the sea, experience the outdoor decks, it seemed crazy to ask Mac's permission, but knew we must. Dad asked; and received an acknowledging nod. She was the captain, and we both felt relieved.

So, Dad and I entered the lift, but the lift doors opened onto a deserted nightclub with sparkling mirror balls suspended from the ceiling and many switched off disco lights. The place I loved to be. Where I danced and drank, but in my former life.

I remembered a past holiday. Our crew danced in a line to Steve Walsh, *I Found Love*. In rhythm, side to side, clapping, spinning, fantastic to tremendous, the entire dancefloor following us.

Part of me wanted to stay and reminisce, but we pressed the buttons again and emerged onto the sea deck and moved forward to the white rail and sea beyond. A strong, fresh breeze and crisp, moist air with the salty, cool sea spray as the boat rose and fell.

Riding the waves as we sped along, breaking the dark, peaceful sea. An invigorating experience to remember and savour as Dad and I returned below deck to reintegrate with the group after ruffling our feathers.

We soon arrived at Calais and were back on the coach. Disembarked and on route to the South of France. Excited on my first trip out of the UK. Overseas, although only across the English Channel. I leaned my face up against the cold, misty window, trying to enjoy the French sights from wide multiple lane highways.

To our right an elderly lady, wrinkled with long hair, tied back in a patterned headscarf as she held her Rosary beads and chanted, "Hail Marys..." while she moved the beads along in her hands.

The TV screen at the front of the coach flicked to life, played a video of Pope John Paul the second, praying in many languages for many hours. Such wide roads, unfamiliar road signs, placenames, péages as we continued south.

A true pilgrimage to Lourdes, but so tired and sore, my legs ached as I remained on the coach all night; frazzled as the lights of France flicker as we pass. Daylight, welcome and long-awaited, and refreshed as I woke.

A full day of travelling; we arrived at the hotel Corona, on a narrow side street. Alarmed to see steps to the entrance. But lots of experienced, strong helpers quickly lifted about 10 wheelchair-using occupants up those steps.

They showed us to a quaint, small, but adequate room. Unpacked, then downstairs, via in the lift for croissants and coffee. Quaint and strange to hear spoken French language and dialogue.

A first busy day ahead of us and we would visit the domain. Our group assembled, a procession of wheelchair users and helpers dressed in yellow and two-by-two up the hill, then through the red doors of an outdoor lift leading to lower street level a scant distance from the shops and domain.

Inside the domain, calmness, and overwhelmed by peace, and a tremendous awe with power to put the most troubled minds at ease.

People kneel as they pray, with hands clasped tightly, bound by emotion, devotion, unshakable belief and immensely focused faith. Some, transfixed on the statue of the Virgin Mary, set in a cave. Heads bowed but all in prayer, focused, with the most personal of thoughts; words in hope.

Mesmerised by the sight and sounds, trickling water from channels and inlets of the open-plan dark stone cave walls. Those on stretchers, screaming, others silent with twisted bodies.

But still hoping, crying, praying for fellow humans and the world. Petty worries and most are insignificant. A place that shocks you into putting your troubles into perspective.

Outside, though, near the gates to the domain, innocent evil lurks, devious and ready to strike the unwary and vulnerable, the unaccustomed prey for pickpockets. Around the entrance to the Grotto, like flies around dung; waiting for opportune moments.

Blue signs on white backgrounds warn of such dangers. Other signs tell you to cover up when entering the domain. Then vast arrays of shops, intense, glitzy lights, highlighting religious merchandise.

Those shops, commercial parts of Lourdes and lights, reminded me of and resembled Blackpool. The glitz and bright lights of the souvenir shops. Silver artefacts, frames, and crucifixes that gleamed, and images of the Virgin Mary and Jesus and other religious artefacts.

It was strange to see busy bars below bright-blue and red neon signs in a religious place, behind packed tables laden with tall, wide, shapely glasses containing bubbling frothy beer. Packed pavements meeting streets that bustled with life and even revelry and drunkenness but seldom song, out of respect for the bell tolls.

Revelry, a lesser extent for the helpers, at least when on duty and who worked so very hard lifting, carrying, pushing wheelchairs; pilgrims including me though, weren't there for such places.

I still dreamed, though, and remembered the mention of various churches, the underground basilica, and St Bernadette. Most intriguing, the holy water baths, but I was excited and anxious as I entered the baths, a stone building with many curtained cubicles, cool moist air.

I cannot walk down the steps and how will the helpers safely immerse me into the holy water? It happened quickly and efficiently. In the baths, helpers helped me undress and draped a blue, thick canvas cloth over my middle.

They positioned another thick blue cloth underneath, then inserted two wooden poles through loops in the cloth, forming a cradle.

Two burly helpers dressed in black rubber aprons lifted and walked with me in the swaying cradle; as they took the strain and positioned me over the grey stone bath before lowering me into the water.

The utter shock at being immersed so quickly. Ever intense because of being submerged for longer than expected as the icy water took my breath; I gasp as I shivered.

Ecstatic euphoria followed, as they lifted me upward from the water, and put a statue of the Virgin Mary in front of my lips to kiss. I shivered, but no sooner than I entered the water I was dry; no need for a towel, as I experienced a delightful feeling of warmth entwined with elation.

A sensation of vitality, warmth, and euphoric contentment, cleansed and refreshed as I ventured outside. The sun blazed, and I remembered the cold waterfall so far away.

That night, a million candles shone, a mass of bright yellow candlelight and silent chant, warming hearts and the universe. Brilliant light, glowing as distant as the eye can see, like earthly stars replicating the myriad of stars in the heavens.

Lights as beacons overpowering the black void, on the steps, on the bridge, everywhere. It was sheer blackness apart from the candlelight; beautiful light in darkness. Candlelight like dancing fireflies as the procession moved, and some waved their candles in the air.

Light cast bright shadows on faces amid prayer. Light, sound, and emotion that proved magic is real, and hope.

Some dare whisper, most become enthralled by touching

moments of heart and soul. Love, hope for humanity, symbolic of each glowing light as spoken prayers play in many languages via loudspeakers and church bells peal and toll.

A potent plethora of emotions, suffused to bring fullness and near tears. To shock us into the realisation of others, of suffering, of pain, and fear within hearts, as serene peace transcends as if a spell was cast.

I imagined those with hands clasped in private prayer, probably not for themselves, but for others. The state of the world, combating evil, easing suffering, those in pain, and solace for tortured minds, those in turmoil.

I prayed for the same. *And let miracles be for those in the greatest pain.* Who most deserved, the worthiest and considered it miraculous I was there with my dad. Foremost in my mind were thoughts of my close family, too.

Whenever I entered private unconditional prayer, without personal wants or desire, I wondered who the audience was and where did my thoughts and words go; who listened? Was it the heavens, the cosmos, or an inner universe?

And how about the millions of prayers entwined with starry candlelight, piercing and radiating into darkness, thoughts conveying energy, faith, despair and hope?

As less devout, I seemed out of place, unworthy. As though I didn't fit, or deserve to be there, among those with rock-solid, unshakable faith, but I still prayed.

Well, clasped my hands, and closed my eyes, spoke in my mind. As I did as a child, as each primary school day finished. Then at my bedside, before sleep, but those prayers I learned, recited and spoken.

On another day, by coach, we experienced the French countryside. We travelled to a ski resort at the foot of the Pyrenees.

Such a warm day and surreal to see the majestic snow-capped mountains as we enjoyed our outdoor picnics, a delightful place, as the days passed. We also visited Nevers and stayed at a convent overnight on route back to England.

At that convent, St Bernadette lay at rest, in a glass casket;

perfect and frozen in time. In the evening, many drank wine in the enormous kitchen, sang and feasted on cheese Dad and I didn't like. We slept on either side of a small room. The calm; quietest night, but the opposite of eerie, as the experience, indescribable and I felt safe with my dad.

I returned to Lourdes the following year, but with a designated helper to care for me and help. Lonelier without Dad, it was more of a challenge.

But I met girls. By the grotto, a friendly French girl came over and spoke to me, and, later in the week, a gorgeous nurse approached. She had long blonde hair, elegantly wrapped in a bun and covered with a pretty, intricate white lace hat.

Delight and disbelief as she speaks to me, approaches from afar. It amazes the surrounding males. Lourdes isn't a place for desires.

Rather, reflect, accept in gratitude, think and pray. Pray for others, but I still had fantasies. She was attractive, so part of a prayer answered; no room for desire in prayers. Can I compete with the more able and eloquent?

On the return journey to England, on the bench seat near the compartment door, I smiled as I posed for a photo next to a lady helper. A momentary cuddle of friendship as she lay her head on my shoulder.

I wished they could have taken more photos. But felt useless; I couldn't get up and walk. The night approached; they lowered the window blinds.

Later, when tucked into my bunk bed, a senior helper laughs from the corridor outside my room as he tells Mac what another helper said. "Paul wanted to stay out last night at the Grotto. We said he could, but at 6.00am."

Unaware I was wide awake. Dismayed at their presumptions, the now unable me, I used to be up at 6.00am for work. It wasn't too early. I stayed silent. They didn't know me.

Silent as my anguish and frustrations worsened as I thought of a girl I had written to all year, a mere carriage away. Powerless, stuck in my bed so close, but yet another world away.

Too bad I couldn't talk niceties in the corridor, or join the party. The fun party, so near, but so distant. Laughter and celebration as the party cubicle door opened and closed.

I lay awake, thinking about everything, dwelling, reflecting, and trying not to brood as the door opened. Mac came in, perched on the edge of my bunk. "Are you OK, Paul?"

"Yes, I'm all right, thank you."

"Enjoyed the week?"

"Yes."

"Lourdes isn't like Blackpool."

"I know," and out of great respect, admiration for that wise lady, I said nothing else, despite many evoked thoughts.

Still, in some ways Lourdes was like Blackpool, bright lights, bars, alcohol, frivolity, many women, and seductive sights. Sadly, but perhaps rightly, it seemed not for those sick in wheelchairs.

Though that person, in some respects, had changed physically. He was still able-bodied, albeit only in the mind. Saddened at what he was, although he should have been grateful? Yet he closed his eyes, but didn't escape as his thoughts drifted to a past-time.

Phenomenal, fun events of Blackpool at 16. Filled with anticipation and excitement as he entered the club with his best mate, Bedduz, a club called Shades. Great dance tunes, Madonna's *Into the Groove* played and the place chock-a-block as I stood in awe thinking these ladies are out of my league.

Seductive sights were all around, adorable ladies.

"Look, all these babes!" As I feasted my eyes.

"P, your babe mad!" Bedduz said with a grin.

A male approached, older than us, about 18. "Where you from, lads?" Bedduz didn't answer, instead turned his head to me, but I dismissed his alarmed expression as he said, "This chap, at the bar; there might be trouble."

"Why?"

"Are you thick or what? Blackpool supporters hate Wolves supporters. If they find out where we're from, we're dead!"

"Nah, doe talk daft! I'm not going from here. Look at all these gorgeous women!"

Bedduz looked downhearted, sombre at my nonchalance and desire to party. "Oh, fuck it, let's have a laugh and get pissed, man!"

So, we bought our beers and sat on the sofas in the club. Then sheer delight and surprise as a stunning lady with long, brown hair and in a long figure-hugging skirt appeared.

Ever thrilled as she gave me the eye with a sexy smile and sat beside me. I returned the stares with lingering looks; so lovely and aroused, just by looking into her bewitching brown eyes.

We started kissing. Sat together on the sofa, luscious, soft lips, pressing upon mine, ever deeper kisses, as our tongues touch and play. The most scintillating kisses ever driving me insane with desire, as her caressing hand wanders from my neck, lower to my stomach, inside my shirt, then lower, stroking my thighs and in-between my legs.

At first, I glanced away, to shun suspicious, voyeuristic, jealous eyes, then returned to, kiss. Dreamy, deep, sensuous kisses, seductive as she teased and pleased.

Tantalising fingers, stroked my inner thighs and sneakily moved upward, between my legs beneath my Bilston Market designer cardigan.

Delighted, I shivered with excitement as she unzipped my trousers. Fondled me with her hand, touching, tantalising and kissed and sucked my neck as Baltimora, *Tarzan Boy*, and Billy Idol, *White Wedding* played.

Incredible and in ecstatic disbelief, such passionate antics, daring exploits, neck covered in love-bites. Ian was angry with me the next day and embarrassed, knowing he and his family invited me on that weekend away. He was right, too, as he waited with me for moral loyalty.

The sexy, vampire-type lady stood me up that day. I waited and waited, thinking and hoping she'd turn up soon, greet me with a kiss and more; the silver rope chain I gave her overnight until we met again. She kept the jewellery, but sent one romantic letter.

The train sped through France, ever northward toward the English Channel and Calais, rattling and swaying on its tracks.

As I shut my eyes to sleep, I thought of that party and lovely girl so near but so far; I cannot walk to and of the former party animal. Of Lourdes, candles, and neon lights, serene bells, bars, and prayers whilst wondering why Mac said the words she did.

I visited Lourdes four times; each time felt unique, but always special. I didn't get up and walk. Nor did I see anyone cured. But how would I know?

Faith and the dedication of the helpers, friendships, and the common goal to transport and care for the sick amazed me, and as I experienced the faith, powerful emotions, and atmosphere with all my senses.

Devotion of faith: tightly clasped hands in prayer and tears from souls of those more disabled than me through no fault of their own profoundly touched my heart in a life-changing and spiritual sense. Self-affliction of a suicide attempt seemed even more inane and emphasised a reason for survival.

I made many wonderful friends from the Birmingham group, and Christmas parties at St Anne's, Birmingham, were great. I wrote to Mac, too, and she gave me the label of Casanova, probably for attracting ladies in France, without knowing about other holiday adventures in my previous life.

28.
NEW HORIZONS

*R*ehabilitation, holy water, and experiences of Lourdes made me eager to travel and experience more culture. The changes in my life brought me into contact with others as I became more adventurous. I met more people with disabilities.

Romance returned to my life; fresh challenges, goals, and academic ambitions. But even with my reawakened, bolder spirit, and gained wisdom, I remained unfulfilled. I still attended the daycentre. My base camp, as a place I associated with learning. Childhood yearnings to learn science returned, too.

The rekindled passion for physics I had had ever since I became enthralled by an inspirational, great, and favourite teacher at age seven. That one day, in science class, set up a demonstration I found amazing.

The teacher attached a vacuum pump to an empty oilcan. We hear the whir of the electric motor of the pump, crushing the oilcan. *So what? The air's sucked out of the oilcan, so it crushed.*

Not exactly, the oilcan crushed because of air pressure, blew my mind. As did, afterwards, when I watched a long balloon fly across the ceiling at high-speed. A balloon with cut off straws attached to it with string threaded through, acting as a track as the air shot out, propelling the balloon.

From those moments, I was hooked on science. English, and everything else, became unimportant in comparison. I loved spelling and swimming, though. School became much more appealing, with more inspirational teachers and challenges.

Out of school, too, as a kid, I spent hour upon hour round Ian's house. An old, wooden shed, stood at the end of his garden. The rickety shed door in a narrow, muddy passage, only accessible after clambering over a variety of overgrown flower bushes.

At first glance, the shed contents looked drab and chock-a-block with junk. The brown-grey grime obscured windows were so grimy they let in little light.

Beneath the window was a dark wooden bench of oak. The showpiece in that shed, a smart blue space-age chair that resembled something out of a science-fiction film, or even Star Trek®. That chair for no less than a starship captain.

Ian had the privilege of sitting in the comfortable, high blue captain's seat. I stood and observed that proud captain, but sometimes took part in exciting and crucial decision processes: what chemicals to mix next?

Like mad scientists, we worked away, mixing a bewildering amount of substances, chemical concoctions. Pungent and volatile as our creations reacted so vigorously; we laughed until we cried and run for fear of an explosive eruption from many stained test tubes.

Ian had a replica phaser ray gun, and a fantastic electronic project kit, too. You could even build radios, light-sensitive alarm clocks. Most exciting was a bugging device. The only trouble was hiding the wire. Such superb missions, all highly important, but I hardly ever got to sit in that captain's chair.

At home, I did experiments of my own. Marvelled, building a crane with a functional winch with string and pulley hook from my bedroom window, suspending my powerful magnet to the floor outdoors.

I was also proud of my box of electronic parts. Resistors, transistors, an old mercury tilt switch, and my prize exhibit, Dad's crystal-set radio, and a sugar bag full of old TV valves; fascinated by the intricate metal structures inside the glass tubes.

The most interesting, a broken cassette player, I took apart and studied the electronics and mechanisms. Curious, I plugged it into the power supply.

Two silver prongs, empty because of a missing fuse, intrigued me so much, I touched them as an experiment. My arm, my body, received a sudden jolt from the 240V. It was unpleasant, but the thrill and excitement to experience that shock and live on, addictive.

I experimented more; gave myself more shocks. Amazed by a strange fulfilment that's unique, special, as I'd gone beyond even the most complex electronic experiments. Beguiled by the craziness, a passion to endure like no other. Years on, I was still as radical, daring and inquisitive.

So, I had to learn about science. Despite disability and nervousness, self-doubt. But the head of science at a college I visited wasn't receptive or optimistic about my interest in physics.

Discouraged by their negative attitude, as they emphasised the practical nature of science. And suggested computer courses might be a better career choice.

Undeterred, I enquired about an Access course into Science at another college and experienced a more positive attitude.

Even when I discovered the course led to study for a degree, I continued, despite being daunted, did my best, went through the motions, to study sciences. Physics and computing, I only had to pass the Access course. I did just that.

University presented immense challenges, doubts lurked in my mind. Some thought the Access course was beyond me. Memories of triumphs spurred me on with self-belief. Especially one very exciting day and the most enjoyable ever as our class joined with the other top classes, and brightest kids to form a special class called STYLE.

Great, being selected, yes, and in a different classroom buzzing with brainwaves as they allocated us into groups of four. A box of newspapers in front of each group engrossed us all, and soon perplexed by a set challenge against the clock.

Build a free-standing structure using the newspapers, no other materials allowed. *Yes,* and blank faces in every group.

Ahh, after a few seconds, I set tasks to my group members, baffled expressions as I asked them to roll up newspapers. With six newspaper tubes, three formed a tripod, and I tied the top with thinner sheets of paper, twisted to strengthen them.

More newspaper cylinders slid in the tripod, into each other as high as possible as we pulled the inner rolled papers higher. Incredibly, our tower reached almost three metres. Dwarfing the best efforts of the other groups. A great triumph, particularly as none of the other groups had even the faintest idea, and baffled as they watched us, and our tower grew. Why couldn't every day be fabulous, other classes as stimulating, half as challenging?

Degree study subjected me to fresh challenges, provoked fabulous thoughts, and stimulated my mind in ways I never imagined. Yet, a greater challenge was getting to lectures in various buildings on different floors via old-fashioned lifts; I had to wait for a caretaker to operate.

Flights of stairs, as a wheelchair user, presented an added stress, too. Such obstacles made daily study tougher, but enriched the adventure.

I wouldn't have got around or coped without daily help and support from my dad. Every day was a struggle. Never-ending mental and physical rigours, always something to do, so an endless mountain climb, just in the first year!

After a while, I set my heart on a personal ambition, letters after my name and every day, I dreamed, hoped and visualised graduating in my cap and gown.

Times my mind buzzed with knowledge outweighed times of stress and hard slog! Leptons, hadrons, charmed quarks, gluons, muons, oh wow! Millions of neutrinos were passing through the earth and our bodies each second. Incredible stuff, things everyone should know.

Laser Interferometer Gravitational-wave observatories, (LIGOs) to detect these theoretical waves, atomic clocks, quantum mechanics, superstrings, and the quest for the Theory of Everything!

Fantastic, but Albert Einstein's special and general relativity theories blew my mind. As did the mathematical formulae. *What, "moving clocks run slow," "moving lengths contract?" The Twin Paradox, where one twin rockets from Earth and ages less than their twin?*

Those days were outstanding. And, a revelation, as the ideas and concepts were profound, beautiful, intricate and complex.

Science strengthened my belief in the existence of a creator, God. So, the opposite and conflicting views: science versus religion, logic versus faith seemed somewhat wrong, as mysteries eroded with enlightenment from combined knowledge as the two dichotomies entwined.

Then, as I watched the physics lecturer write 0.00000 on the blackboard and continue with zeroes across the board, then a 1, I became intrigued. As captivated as when I observed the oilcan implode as a child.

I become even more amazed to learn that number, was a percentage related to a theory proven to be the most accurate known theory.

This was the pure essence, proof of why I had loved physics and space. Those indescribable, special moments encompassed knowledge and beauty I wouldn't have experienced if I had heeded the advice not to follow a physics path.

I revelled in those lectures but struggled with the maths, strange symbols, theorems, and concepts, perhaps as I didn't initially grasp the significance but memorised many formulae.

Childhood zeal for astronomy, to go into space as an astronaut made sense. Although I didn't aspire to that, I could think, dream and gaze at the stars. My mind could reach them, and other worlds, previously unknown, and understand a little of how the universe works.

It was 1993, the end of the first year at university. Frazzled but with fresh, wonderful knowledge, I spent a weekend at Lowestoft, a UK destination. A long journey in an old minibus. Arranged via the daycentre, the holiday with others with disabilities and elderly ladies. A carer and drinking partner attended, too.

I didn't expect to become enchanted on the first night! In a club, by a female, dressed in a lovely skirt and wide-brimmed straw hat. She danced provocatively, as music played and frequently stared with sultry eyes; smiled as our eyes met.

Lovingly draped her arms around me, to my glee, as I approached. We held each other whilst moving in rhythm to slow music in a slow dance, sweet perfume, soft warm skin against my face, cheek to cheek but so wanting our lips to meet.

"It's my birthday today... I'm 23." She said. *I'd so like to party with you; give you a present.*

As we headed for my chalet and my carer pushed me, she seemed uneasy. "I'm forbidden to visit clients' chalets," she said. This, enhanced the excitement and expectation as desire beckoned.

We arrived at the chalet, and she sat on my lap. Her loose-fitting top partially exposed her breasts – a luscious sight as we kissed and caressed. Lovely, soft warm breasts, velvety skin to my touch.

"Shall we lie on the bed? We'll be more comfortable!" I said.

"Yes, all right."

I am helped onto the bed. Tremendous as Tina lay on top, and we kissed and swooned. Too bad I needed help from my friend and carer who said. "I forgot my chalet key. Don't worry, I'll sleep on the carpet. I won't disturb you two." He liked Tina, too, jealous of my success.

"You sure you haven't got your key?"

He pulled his trouser pockets inside out and grabbed a pillow. "I'm locked out, and can't sleep outside... Can you be quieter? I cannot sleep; you slobbering over each other all night?" He said as he settled on the floor.

Much to my deep annoyance and in a strange shock, I didn't respond with words. Tina rushed to the door. "Wait, don't go. He didn't mean it. Stay!" It was no use. The chalet door closed, deeply upset, robbed of passion, and I ached for her.

The next morning, I nursed my bruised ego and knew that I must try to rectify relations; resume the rudely interrupted passionate encounter from the previous night. Nervous as I entered the shop where Tina worked. *Will she remember me, and understand me, if I can speak clearly enough?*

The contents of the shop aisles are interesting. Well, that was my cover as I wheeled along, for my aimless perusal for nothing in particular.

From time to time, a discrete glimpse over to her at the counter and my heart pounded almost from my chest as I fleetingly see her wonderful, warm smile as she served the customers and try to assemble the words in my mind for the imminent moment I speak.

Patient as I awaited my chance, anxious with expectation as I browsed the aisles. And the moment I become overwhelmed. *Shall I leave?* Yes, the ever-dwindling queue no-one else entered the shop. I wheeled toward the counter, and our eyes met.

"Hello!" as she closed the shopping till her eyes lit up and widen.

"Hello how's work going?"

"Oh OK, I'll be knocking off soon."

"Ooh, and have you got any plans?"

"I was going to feed the ducks. Do you want to come?"

"OK!"

I bought duck food from her in a brown paper bag. She fetched her coat and bag and we left the shop. She strolled beside me as I wheeled carefully along the inclined path toward the water's edge of a pond.

"Last night was nice; pity you had to go."

"Yes, it was nice."

"We could go to the chalet again."

"I can't, but can help you get back; want a push?"

"OK, yes please," as I lifted my hands off my wheels and she started pushing my wheelchair."

Overwhelming emotions quashed fears of being caught, though, as we ventured ever nearer to my chalet. Relieved and excited as she opened the door.

Still, she was apprehensive; anxious as she sat on the bed, rekindling memories of the previous night. She looked toward the window, fearful a fellow staff member may see her.

More at ease as we chatted, and I gazed at her pretty, glowing face, her lovely frame inside a well-fitting white stripy blouse. "Last night was awesome! Pity it had to end!" as I neared her, and we kissed; such soft lips.

I so wanted to resume what began the previous night. She looked sad, but her facial expression changed to a smile, then to a mischievous grin and a sultry stare.

She placed her hand onto my bare leg and moved her hand, stroked ever upward, "Are you nervous?" with a cheeky smile and a lustful stare.

"No!"

Her hand moved further up. "Are you nervous now?"

"No, still not nervous; keep going."

Her fingertips stroked the inside of my thigh and ever higher, above my shorts in between my legs, briefly. "Nervous?" As she chuckles, and grins. *Wow! Not nervous.* Aroused, and immense attraction, I so wanted her, that lovely, bubbly sexy lady. But it seemed more like a playful game than sexual.

Nothing else happened. This heightened already intense emotions and desires, and made the end of the weekend heart-wrenching. But we exchanged addresses and promised to write and meet again.

The ensuing long-distance relationship blossomed. Amorous letters and endearing phone chats, but the days apart were hard. I pined for her every second.

Startlingly, she said not to phone her as she'd phone me. We talked for hours; she even sang Madonna's *Crazy For You* and *La Isla Bonita* over the phone, every word.

Gentle, barely audible whispers swooned through the wires and the phone to me. The forthcoming Madonna concert: Blonde Ambition tour of 1993 seemed a perfect place to meet up next. We counted the days until we would meet.

The long-awaited day arrived. *To get up the coach steps, I'll need help from the coach driver, although my brother's on the same coach with his girlfriend. Me and Tina will be away from them in the venue's disabled seating area, too.*

On arrival, there were so many coaches, a car park maze. *Will Tina be at The Arch?* I sat anxiously, waited as my heart pounded with excitement and anticipation.

Two warm, soft hands cover my eyes from behind me. Silence for a moment, "Guess who?" Wonderful, and greeted with an affectionate, sweet kiss.

Tina pushed me into the famous Wembley Stadium I hadn't

been to before, and into an elevated, enormous viewing area. Madonna was excellent. The show started with her descending from a dancing pole, naked, at least it seemed, from afar.

Spectacular, one of the best nights of my life! A night dreams come true, doubly so in amorous, pleasant company.

Tina sat on my lap during the concert, our hands wandering, exploring, tantalising and teasing in the darkness. Our arms around each other, entwined and caressing. Her warm, wonderful fingers inside my jeans, and mine stroking her inner thighs, under her long, flared, split front skirt.

We sang and so much chat; frantic, lustful intimacy, as we touched each other and passionate, lingering kisses in a fabulous frisson. The lights, the heat, the vibrating sounds.

"Shall we go to the loo or somewhere?" she asked.

I craved to, and thoughts of erotic fantasies filled my mind. Oh, being straddled by smooth bare legs, gripped, bare breasts in my face, holding her so tight — sensual ecstasy.

But, I didn't want to miss any of the Madonna concert, so certain Tina would visit me, that we would share many special moments together. So sure, she was the one. She had to be. What a fabulous night!

The wonderful exchanges of love continued: endearing letters, the long intimate phone calls and cards, and sweet poems mentioning speaking softly on the phone, comparing my heart to a warm robin redbreast in wintertime.

Those poems, so real and true, as if a magical and wondrous link existed between us. Barely a second of the day passed when she's wasn't in my thoughts. When she wasn't charming me with her presence in my mind. I wanted no-one else but Tina.

Then, without warning, no letter, or phone call. I worried and pined so much. Elated when the phone rang. *Yes, that's Tina*, as Mom answered the phone.

"Paul, someone on the phone for you!" I rushed to the phone, filled with joy and anticipation of hearing Tina's voice. An unfamiliar, agitated voice spoke. The voice of a man.

"Hello, is this Paul?"

"Yes, who's this?"

"You don't know me, and this may come as a shock. I'm Tina's husband! I know all about you... I've found letters from you!"

"Oh, I didn't know Tina was married!"

"She met you at the Madonna concert, the day after I had my reverse vasectomy. Can you imagine how I felt when she left me to meet you?" Said a now broken, upset voice.

"I didn't know!"

"She's lied to you all along, and to me... I've had one divorce and can have another."

"Tell me one thing. Have you slept with her?"

My mind raced. As I contemplate my reply, *No, but I wish I had have done, and could have. No, he had suffered enough?* Part of me wanted to say "Yes" but I was glad I could truthfully respond, "No!"

A moment later, rumination and annoyance: *"No. But I could have!"* I should have said, and after they'd divorce, Tina would come to me. *If I had, she'd be here with me now, in my arms* and imagined that bubbly female's legs astride my chair, bouncing up and down, my head between her breasts; on my face, oh the passionate kissing, love-making.

Maybe she only wanted a baby? My baby, but would she even have told me, or her husband, the baby wasn't his?

So many tormenting "What if" questions! The bitterness, the hurt, heartache, longing, and yearnings entwined with the utter disbelief and disappointment. I still yearned for her. Despite her deviousness, but how could I have been so wrong? Wrong after being so certain she was the one?

I loved her dearly; I would have done anything for her, even moved on a whim, at the drop of a hat. Overcome any obstacle – together, not alone!

I chose to not miss even a moment of the Madonna concert, declined sex as I was so sure Tina would visit me and of plentiful fun times. Alas, many fantasy thoughts, how it may have been, how happy? The bliss if I'd had said "yes" to the tempting invite, not waited.

I was even more upset to be second best, shunned, alone, and used! While saddened anyone could be so blatantly deceitful, cold, selfish, but I learned a lot and became tougher, wiser and far less trusting. Cruel false hope presented a turning point in my life, as though I had to reinvent myself without changing, adapt, refine.

But, did she think I couldn't have pleased her, or assumed inexperience?

Such disappointment urged me to be more adventurous. Ah, a proper holiday the following year, before uni. *Warm sunshine will help me forget the soured romances.*

Mom, Dad, and I went to Majorca in 1994. I didn't enjoy the packed bars and nightlife, saddened as I reminisced about my former self. Drunkenness and revelry, with fantasies of debauchery, I had moved on from, evolved.

I missed those times and envied them, and those who could dance. As many danced to Whigfield, *Saturday Night,* similar to I had years earlier, in unison to the Fatback Band, *I Found Love.*

The most exciting day, though, one morning after breakfast, as I emerged into the open-plan gardens and saw two people playing chess. Delighted by a fond interest, I avidly observed the two players.

One spoke Spanish, then broken English, asking if I could play. The other, native Italian, called Claus playing Migel. I played the winner, Claus; we shook hands. He had friendly eyes that intently studied the board.

As I moved the chess pieces, he muttered in Italian and said as I moved my Queen, "Questa, muy importante." The dialogue fascinated me and added suspense; I hadn't ever played a non-native English player.

So different to playing chess in Ian's house at 13 whilst listening to Michael Jackson's *Thriller* and Black Sabbath's *Paranoid* album on full blast. Tremendous! I had only ever listened to Mom's Abba, Elvis, Gene Pitney, and Gilbert O' Sullivan songs.

I often beat my older friends, and excited all with the amazing positions that arose in those games, and hoped to do the same against my Italian opponent in Majorca. The game progressed.

I made a super move; Claus clapped, "Bravo, Bravo!" he said, smiling.

The following day I played Migel, this time indoors, in a large empty hotel lounge, to a small audience. A stunningly attractive travel rep called Francesca sat perched on the arm of a sofa, long blonde tied back hair, lovely tanned legs in a grey smart tight skirt high above the knee. She watched the game as Migel and I played. The added pressure, and I moved more tentatively than earlier. *I hope she plays the winner.* This boosted my play even more. My heart raced – expecting resignation – still victorious, as Migel toppled his king. Frustrated, but gracious, as he shook my hand. Forlorn, Francesca didn't play the winner.

I didn't want that chess game to end as Francesca watched, for fear she may leave. My lovely audience, I hoped, studied my moves and became as enthralled with my mind. Those moments were better than watching the waves.

We enjoyed the week, so much, that same summer, Dad and I, travelled to San Antonio in Ibiza. A dreamy, magical place I loved; where I could relax. People less inclined to rush about, and amazing nightclubs, perfect beaches, meeting crystal-blue water.

It was great to meet a friendly Australian family, who invited us to a picnic on Cala Bassa Beach, and picked us up and drove us there in their hire car. Dean, a tall police officer, his brother a Bondi Beach lifeguard and Dean's wife Sam were lovely.

Sam and I sat on the moist sand by the water's edge and overlooking a perfect blue cloudless sky meeting a perfect horizon, the sea. Sam's arm round me, because of my lack of balance, and I enjoyed the most delicious, succulent, baguette sandwich ever, in the sun as Dad, Dean, and his brother swam by the shore.

Then I held onto the back of a white pedalo. Sam sunbathed and watched from the beach as Dean and his brother pedalled out to sea and into an open cavern; Dad swam ahead. So hot, and the water felt great, splashing on my body.

Ever further from the beach, splendid. Privileged, although I felt pathetic as I held on so tight as a seafaring passenger as the pedalo swayed and bobbed up and down in the white-water wake.

If I fall off or lose my grip, the Australian lifeguard will rescue me, don't worry.

Lucky as I looked up at the blue sky. The warm sunshine on my body, legs in the cool crystal-clear water, partially immersed as I listened to the lapping waves, but dearly missed swimming and remembered 13 years earlier.

A time, I felt full of pride. Passing my swimming medals up to gold by age 10, when my prowess shone in the water. I loved and enjoyed swimming.

Understandably, my face beams in my second-year of secondary school as our form tutor tells us about a forthcoming swimming gala, and asks for any ideas who to choose as boys' and girls' captain?

Within a second, someone I considered a strong swimmer nominated me, another seconded, followed by more fellow swimmers. Overwhelmed, as others selected me, and an honour: Team captain for my class, but daunting.

I knew my class well, though, the swimmers, at least, strengths, and qualities. The team almost picked itself, and I was fast and strong, at least equal to and possibly the best all-rounder. What a team! But were we the best?

My hands gripped the cylindrical, metallic side bar, just above the water at the boundary of the 25 metre pool in Bilston Baths. There's silence apart from my thudding heart and the sound of water, gently buffeting and lapping against me, as I focus on the pale-blue tiled wall.

Poised and primed, waiting in nervous anticipation, so tense, all that faith in me, to race... The shrill sound of the whistle instantaneously launches me from the wall with an almighty push. Submerge, kick, surface, swim as quick as I can — remember technique, efficiency and not to splash so much.

The loud, then muffled, cheers as my head emerges and submerges in the water, excites me, fuels adrenaline as I stretch a lead. And ease into a fast pace as I transfix on the white, grey-coloured ceiling and large white round lights as I propel myself faster than ever before, in a swim.

A close finish, but think I narrowly won. Second in the relay, fast in other events, and flawless dives from my team boosted our points tally.

Outstanding, but I doubted we had done enough to win. Such tension and suspense as they tallied the results. Rapturous loud cheers and seeing classmates' delighted faces as they jumped up and down at their balcony seats indicated victory.

With the elation and cheers, as they confirmed our class form as the winners. I excelled then, at 12-years-old, before cheering crowds on balconies overlooking the pool. Nice, but I was too shy to look. So, swiftly glimpse across, and waved in acknowledgement; overwhelmed by so many faces.

What an amazing day! Happiest day of my life! Unreal as I left the baths, but escalated to a euphoric triumph as I walked outside and ecstatic as I felt the warm sunshine on my face. My happiest day, in time, became one of the happiest, most memorable moments of my life.

Yes, our class won! I helped lead them to victory, at least my teacher said in my school report. It felt fantastic to climb onto the school on stage and hold a large silver trophy aloft jointly with the girls' team captain whilst the whole school cheers.

Delighted, but embarrassed. Uncannily, like I felt holding onto that seacraft. A great day, although disabled, and helpless to do so much. I knew, too, such accolades were distant dreams.

Sadly, I could no longer swim or walk, but, holding onto the pedalo in the presence of wonderful, kind people, perfect! A fabulous day on the water by Cala Bassa Beach.

Nights to look forward to in the Spanish heat, and at the friendly Rainbow karaoke bar where I sang. Rowdier bars, great shops, and beautiful sunsets, but Dad and I enjoyed finding quiet cafés every day. I loved Ibiza.

That summer would be unforgettable and recuperation before my second-year at university started.

The studies became progressively easier, at least in the areas I enjoyed most. Later on, at a more advanced stage in the third year, a space-time module with complex mathematics made sense;

I understood the zany maths. And excited by novel thoughts.

I struggled to understand cosmology, the complex maths. But I got an 'A' for a more complex Einstein's special relativity module. Other subjects became ordinary compared to space-time.

It was a privilege and delight to study those subjects, to meet other students. University nightlife, great, too. In my last year of study, I revelled as I explored whether machines could ever become conscious and wrote my dissertation.

Determined to succeed, I followed a passion. And in 1996, I graduated with B. Sc (Hons) Applied Sciences; I achieved, despite adversity and against negativity, after being initially discouraged; some thought I'd fail.

Great acclaim, and I proved a point. Yet, I returned to the daycentre, and became a committee member, although ineloquent. We discussed a variety of issues. Eventually, the focus became a passionate and torrid battle to prevent the daycentre from closing.

My role, crafting letters and combating with words. Activism and friendships that lasted 20 years and beyond.

And a daycentre holiday became the most memorable, as I visited Pwllheli, North Wales, by minibus. On the way to the coast, it felt very special to travel through Mid Wales, as I recognised familiar places and names. Fond memories flooded my mind.

I had so looked forward to, and became excited as I travelled to second-year summer camp, at age 12, on that school trip to Llanrhaeadr, during the height of summer, to a part of Wales I hadn't ever visited.

Excitement escalated as we passed through small Welsh villages on that journey to a secluded spot with a nearby stream and surrounding mountains.

A perfect place I knew I'd love and was even more thrilled and appreciative as I heeded the advice of an older girl. "Oh, I camped there. It was great, but, ugh, the flies. Horrible flies… Make sure you take some flyspray!" as she pulled a face.

So, I packed and remembered the flyspray. *They'll soon hail me a saviour for thinking of bringing an item no-one else would.*

We laid the large green canvas tents out on the grass, guy

ropes attached and wooden poles inserted. Yes, our tent was up, a temporary home for the next seven days. Our tent faced the girl's tent, and behind their tent lay the stream, behind us hills and grey rock mountains embellished with greenery.

What a great tent in an awesome spot, excitement as we unpacked, put our clothes in large pockets at the sides of the tent, our sleeping bags unrolled.

My sleeping bag, second from the door as one of four, next to fellow, backstroke rocket in the pool who helped to achieve victory at the swimming gala, by the door. Pankaj on my right, and Martin at the tent's other end. Unpacked, beds made, time to enjoy and explore!

We sat, huddled around a glowing campfire, ate delicious marshmallows and hot roast potatoes from the kitchen marquee and listened to ghost stories as the sun descended toward the horizon and darkness fell. The warm flames of the campfire gave our faces an orange glow. It was a long, excitement-packed day.

With our tents made, I reached into my tent side compartment. One vital thing I had to do before trying to sleep. So brandished the blue aerosol but didn't initially see the toxic warning label as I sprayed a copious amount of flyspray, filling the tent with noxious propellant.

"Phew, what's that? What the…" one said.

The commotion in our tent attracted the teacher's and everyone's attention. "We can't sleep in there. Walters has sprayed something, it stinks, sir," Gary said to an unimpressed teacher who'd approached.

"Open the sides quick, lads. Walters, what have you sprayed?"

"Just flyspray, sir."

"Why?"

"To kill all the flies." *Obviously, what a silly question.*

"More like kill us!" Gary said.

"What flies? It's nighttime," the teacher asked as he held back a smile and added, "It's getting late. Shut the flaps. Get some sleep."

Disheartened by the major overreaction. *Oh well. In a couple of days, everyone will want to use my flyspray!*

It was fantastic to wake in that tent the next day, to get my towel and soap, and to wash with the clear, cool, refreshing water from the nearby stream. Great, being closer to nature, to experience simple living.

I had so looked forward to seeing and standing beneath the Pistyll Rhaeadr Waterfall, too, the highest in Wales. In awe of the ice-cold water falling 240ft, freezing my brain. Numbing my mind as I stood directly beneath that torrent of water in a sheer test of defiance, endurance, and madness.

What a challenge and renowned competition that sounded too crazy to be true. A challenge older kids spoke of that excited my core.

It's so cold. I'm poised to dive into the water to swim, although I wished to stay to savour the euphoria. Grand but futile triumphs, as my body shivers inside a cascading watery cocoon, with tingling excitement and determination to withstand those icy rigours the longest.

Seven others, and I began that punishing endurance test. "Argh, it's freezing." Someone said.

One-by-one, other contenders, sensibly, gave in, returned to the camp and warm sunshine. Amazed by the immense pressure and to be alone, as the last, I stayed. Determined and in defiance of the unrelenting deluge, the pummelling deafening roar, louder than the crazy world as I stood firm.

Steadfast as I held on tight to the rocky ledge despite nature trying to repel me from the stony platform. As I resisted and interrupting aeons of nature, eroding rock, carving a river, a future chasm.

Through the watery mist, I stared at the pool and teacher. He stared back, waiting for me to give up, or falter, and imagined he thought I was crazy – and I'd give up – I didn't. I wouldn't budge; I awaited acknowledgement of winning the endurance test. That teacher though, strict and short on praise, shouted, "Come on now."

Relieved, as he spoke; elated by the victory, and also pleased to prove what he may have thought regarding my madness. Even then, I paused, pretended I hadn't heard him; nonchalance as an extra show of endurance before I clambered from the stony platform and triumphantly swam across the green-grey pool.

I loved to swim in that pool, my muscles stiff, but the water, warm and inviting compared to the frigid deluge as I swam to the silt bank. More's the pity; no-one left to cheer me, but so proud, my grand prize, a free Mars chocolate bar from the camp shop. That presented one of the happiest and proudest moments of my life.

The next day, we ventured into the Welsh mountains on a long mountain walk. The grass, the lush greenery, and forests, such a gift to be there and experience nature's beauty. Excited to see a lake in-between the mountains.

"Anyone fancy a swim?" One kid said, as banter and camaraderie. I couldn't shun any opportunity to swim.

The lake, nature's perfect mirror of the lush mountains and blue sky with fluffy whiteness from high clouds. Reluctant to disturb that harmony, intact for aeons. Yet, I was first into the cool, stillness, like an intruder into that unspoiled, tranquil water as envious non-swimmers watched.

Green lily pads floated near the lake's centre. The black water's surface glistened and shimmered as my hands parted the water, forming rippling waves. An aberration in that perfect nature's mirror.

The second-year at secondary school, at age 12, was marvellous and memorable, perhaps because of excelling in many ways. I jointly won the swimming gala trophy and a Mars bar. No praise about flyspray, though. Such reminiscing instilled pride and evoked a smile as we neared the North Wales coast.

Pwllheli, would be as special as those memorable days on distant shores. Sleeping in large wooden outdoor dormitories next to a large house facing green, Welsh hills made it an idyllic location. And a beautiful secluded beach at the front and the sea.

Amazing as a carer rowed us out to sea in a plastic inflatable dinghy. Such a summery day as the boat bobbed up and down, met gentle waves, lapping against the boat beneath a pale-blue sky with a few pure white clouds above a curved horizon.

Humbling experiences and there were nights of gazing in awe at the wondrous stars above and across the sea whilst listening to waves breaking on the shore.

The biggest prize, the sea views upon a rocky platform at the edge of the Lleyn Peninsula, Bardsey Island, facing us in the distance. And, in the other direction, magnificent views of Wales; fields as an earthly patchwork quilt beside a sandy path to infinity toward England.

Presented with a beauty I had never experienced or knew existed. But just being there was enough. Breathing, living as I shouted in the strong sea breezes, grateful for that moment. Made possible because of kind carers who knew what I wished to experience, see, hear, and feel.

And, like on other holidays, gorgeous women kissed me and uncannily, both said in dulcet tones, "I couldn't help that. You're so handsome!" Nice but frustrated, as I wanted more, but persevered.

29.

ANOTHER PLAN

*A*dventures in sunnier climates and holiday hotspots were enjoyable, and the chess. Especially at those times with leggy spectators. Sadly, no romance, but I had glorious moments to savour. Enlightenment as I studied subjects I'd only dreamed of excited me more.

Attaining my degree, against the odds, despite a total life change and adjusting to disability, instilled pride and purpose. Represented a massive goal encompassing an obsession to prove all doubters wrong. Those who disbelieved. Looked down on me, and to put things right.

My return from a divergent path, after being so astray on the downward spiral, was great, too. Like being back on track, although in a totally different place in the cosmos.

Blinkered, rebellious defiance had blighted ambition, shunned opportunities and great potential. Without doubt, I'd reached the bottom and began an upward ascent, but how high could I go?

On passing, it seemed like reaching a plateau that brought uncertainty, bewilderment, and frustration about flux-like indecision. Where do I go? What to do next? A state of limbo, strange nothingness. No green, welcoming pastures loomed.

Many revelled in their 2:1 degrees. Some cried with joy, visions of grandeur and endless job offers, the best vacancies; their entire lives mapped out. Focused; sure with precise plans and goals.

I had aspired to that level, but obstacles faced me again! As though in a race to achieve further academic status, or follow a chosen career path.

After doing so well, there was pressure to meet high expectation. I pondered graduate opportunities. Browsed glossy career brochures. Swamped with information. *How can I progress with huge logistical and practical problems?*

Communication, transport, and support: hurdles even with my mind in its expanded, wiser, all-embracing form. Unable to decide, I met with a disability employment advisor. But, I sensed they didn't know how to advise me.

Strange being there as I completed a test to determine areas of interest, career direction, in a room at the far end of the open-plan jobcentre in Bilston.

The place my older, more streetwise friends called the joke shop, and I remembered the dawning and depressing realisation they were right; puzzlement to the fuzzy moments of clarity. That was the 1980s, though.

Still, years on, I gained information. Little else, apart from stagnation as I mulled over options.

My mind flitted back to the joke shop. Funny, alarming tales tinged with despairing sadness, and I remembered the boredom. Uncanny, there's still little to amuse me. Like then, but it's worse, as I cannot do as much. Or frequent the places I used to visit.

To occupy us at night, my friends and I often wandered around town and sometimes into the deserted market. Greeted by row upon row of bare scaffolding; an eerie mass of cold, grey tubes protruding upward from empty wooden tables where we sat.

We did pull-ups on the scaffold structures. Sometimes in winter, the canopy-covered structures glowed from white frost forming from the cold. Desolate, it was a contrast to the hustle and bustle of daytime market days. People milling to-and-fro along decorated aisles beside coloured canopies.

The market was alive! I loved the characters, their banter, and Black Country sales pitch, gift of the gab, and down-to-earth rapport. The distinct aromas and smells, chocolate, pear drops, herbal tablets and rainbow drops from the sweet stall.

Sawdust and meat, fish, and poultry, fresh eggs, and black pudding as you walk toward the treat of sweet perfumes, fragrant flowers, and fresh fruit. Suitcases, graphite, and wooden pencils, new carpet, linen and sizzling onions, English mustard, tomato sauce, bacon, fried eggs and burgers, near the sparkling jewellery I wished I could afford; there was something for everyone.

Occasionally, we chatted with and entertained girls, and sometimes walked to our friend's house all together. Especially when we couldn't afford to hire a film. I still dreamed of Madonna, although there were romantic encounters too, with non-pop star idols. Unforgettable nights, but most nights were boring and uneventful.

At first glance, one evening the market was its usual deserted self. Yet, whilst casually walking as we often did, we saw three distant figures, sat at the corner of the market.

Two of the figures, recognisable as female. The group of us, Dava, Tom, Bedduz, and myself, stopped and sat on the market benches a few aisles away. We're pleased as one figure walks toward us and we realise it's an older male friend who sits with us.

I jog to the next bench, closer to the girls, and become excited as I realise they're attractive ladies. The older friend said, "Ah, I know them. I'll call them over, shall I?"

"Go on then." Despite my anxiety and shyness.

"You like them, P. I can tell." as he smiles and jumps from the table, turns to us and adds, "Leave it with me," and jogs over to the girls, then runs back to me, "One of them likes you."

As we walked from the market, passed the Hop Pole pub onto damp pavements, sparkling orange reflecting light from streetlights above, I felt calm. No expectation; even as we reached a more secluded, dimly lit area, I didn't imagine how that night would unfold.

Trembling with excitement and anticipation as she smiled and walked behind a high wall. *She's waiting for me, her lover, unreal.* My heart thudded as my cohorts gave me some details as they knew the girl.

Surreal, unbelievable as I walked behind the wall. Entering a large open walled area. There she stood, tall, shoulder-length hair, a pretty face in the shadows and gently smiling in anticipation.

Waiting for me, just me, and only me. *Is this real?* The pressure to perform, to please enjoy and savour.

"Hello," I said as I approached and neared the far wall where she stood.

A brief, passionate kiss as she stood against the wall. Alluring perfume suffused with the damp but fresh smell of autumn leaves. Caressing as our kisses deepen, deep, sensuous kisses and soft lips, escalating the excitement.

Her legs against mine. Such soft, warm breasts I fondled as we partially undress each other, her warm touch, her skilful hands driving me crazy with desire. So aroused, as I complied with the suggestion of my more experienced soon to be voluptuous lover.

Behind the wall, away from prying eyes, a thick carpet mosaic of autumn-shed leaves for us. And, there she was. A luscious woman: inviting, enticing, sensuous; warm as I teased to heighten the excitement and anticipation.

So warm against me as we shiver with pleasure. Marvellous, with rapturous delight at the intensity of intimacy; the closeness, and in a mutual ecstatic union. In harmonious rhythm, breathless and giddy with sheer excitement as the night unfolded. An ordinary autumn night became one of the most memorable nights of my life.

A wonderful treat beneath the stars, and envied by less desirable friends. "Jammy bastard," one said. *Wow, I'm more of a man;* vanquished a major fear of being a virgin for my entire-life!

Yes, I wanted to run, jump into the air, "Yes!" Exultant, that woman chose me; my animated face beamed. I didn't care that some of my immature friends laughed as they jumped high to see us behind the wall and explained the visions. Ah ha, the same who filled condoms with water for amusement.

Soon after, my friends said, "Oh, she missed games today… Pregnant, argh up the duff." As they sniggered. *They're trying to scare me.* At least I hoped they were, but something they said certainly did. Ahh, no – unbelievable – apparently my raunchy rendezvous was with Chief Thug's girlfriend!

That sadistic, power wielding maniac and his ugly thugs

would hunt me down. I carried on with my life but with perpetual worry at the prospect of him getting me again one day. This is nothing compared to the dog. I still heard it — unleashed in my mind and hoped it would never chase me again.

This unexpected twist filled me with dread. But how cool was I? Notorious, being chosen for sex and desired above everyone else; like natural justice, considering the attack, and the fear of the unleashed dog.

Anyway, I just had to put that episode behind me, bury that fear. Strive on and not allow anything to undermine that fabulous and monumental milestone moment. Alas, sheer elation preceded much stress: *Have I got a girl pregnant?*

Extreme worry about this intensified turmoil, and inhibited me as I trundled on at school. Refocused on learning with a dedication to fitness. And, I did press-ups. Any activities to help me forget the foreboding distinct possibility of impending doom, the sheer terror.

Strange that school suddenly became appealing; I focused on studying. But feelings transformed to loneliness suffused with yearnings: *When will I have my next wondrous encounter?*

A decade on, I still wondered, as I reached an epic milestone. A milestone and juncture, like then, even with changed abilities. With no woman or defined career path, I enquired about another innate passion: writing. Great to enrol on a creative writing course, but bizarre being at the same college I attended after leaving school.

I remembered voices, visions and saw ghosts from the past and before meeting Cathy, as I approached 17 years of age. A happy period because of an exciting transition as I became less shy, more confident.

It was a crucial period of transition from leaving school to a distinct path, study, or work? I'd experienced so much, yet so little, with short-term plans and indecision to match. Forwards into an unknown, and less certain future. A future that can sometimes seem cruel, but yet be so kind.

To my delight, during my first week at college, I heard a

voice call out my name as I walked along the corridor, a voice I recognised. I stopped, turned, and smiled as I saw the girl I had met on a summer bike ride walking toward me, Jane.

She looked smart in a skirt and heels, long brown mousy coloured styled hair, much nicer than on the bike ride. Her face beamed at me as we chatted and chuckled as we reminisced about the bike ride. I impressed her; I remembered her name and couldn't help but smile.

Asking her out. She accepted. We were to meet outside the college that night! What a great and eventful day. I put on my best gear and arrived at a college in darkness.

My heart raced as we sat on the grass, on that lovely warm summer night, heady feelings of passion as the sky darkened to a deeper blue. The smell of summer in the air, mowed grass, flowers, and the asphalt from tarmac paths and roads, baked all day in the sun, now set.

Wonderful to be in the open air, as an increasing number of stars pierced a painted dark-blue sky and I settled on the grass. "Hey, where've you gone?" Jane asked with a chuckle.

"I'm still here... Look at those stars. I wanted to be an astronaut; you know." As I gaze upward.

Jane lay down as I sat up, wiped the moist grass from my hands. Jane, still flat on the grass, as I turned to face her. "Can't you still be an astronaut?"

"Nah, well maybe," as I lean on one elbow and kiss Jane. Such soft lips, Jane responds by pressing her lips on mine, kissing back... "You don't waste much time, do you?"

Elated and I cannot believe I'm there at college and kissing under the stars. Passions heightened, rapt. *Is this night real or a dream?*

Jane waited for me outside my various classrooms; I enjoyed seeing her eyes light up as our eyes met. The attention and anticipation excited me, made me feel like such a stud. A sweet girl waiting for me, wearing sexy skirts, heels, and outfits — my own secretary-type-girlfriend.

We saw each other almost every day. Had lunch together,

chatted, smiled, and exchanged playful and sexy glances. And walked to various places, sometimes lay on nearby grass together and always had brilliant fun, sensational and sensuous; smitten with desire and romance, often in quiet places.

My desires and fantasies, real on such hot days, and everything was so different, refreshing, exciting at the end of summer. The free time slots took some getting used to, but were sometimes fun-packed.

More so, as the nights become longer and darker, autumn approached. College by day, the streets at night: two different extremes to adjust to and learn. With increased opportunities for tremendous fun, often in the autumn, wind, and rain.

So many places, much laughter, spontaneity, and excitement: college, discos, drink, and on the nights I didn't meet Jane, I met with friends. Most of whom I spent time with in my final year at school differed from my school friends within school, who had set ideas, plans, and aspirations.

None were at college like me and some of these became trainees for various employers, worked or joined a YTS. One of my friends urged me to join a YTS; and with free transport, £27.30 per week, coupled with apparent poor prospects of finding a job, even with qualifications, the path seemed obvious.

Such notions nurtured growing restlessness. Led to discontent as college lost its attractive appeal, the freshness worn. And, while options presented a period of indecision, so soon after leaving school; a quandary, I became disconcerted. *Is college for me?*

Part of me, lost and the options on offer, didn't seem too good. It puzzled and troubled me as I had become oblivious to common sense and somewhat blinkered; feasible options didn't seem like options at all. But I lacked knowledge, and my character at that period wasn't moulded.

A lot to learn, but I didn't realise, as I became distracted; enticed and allured by desires for finer things. And, whether the decision was an inspired stroke of wisdom or foolish, I left college after four weeks. Alas, desires ubiquitously replaced dreams and lowered ambitions.

The radical shift after such a short time played on my mind. The move caused a great deal of upset at home too; my mother disapproved. She had such aspirations in me to being highly educated with the perceived premise that education would lead to a cushy, high paid job!

Such high hopes dashed, becoming distant dreams, but I embraced the new; start earning, train and improve my prospects and still dream, even though more difficult to attain, onto that recommended YTS!

Every day on a minibus, sat on long bench seats opposite stern, staring, cool, gum-chewing youths in zipped up Parker coats. I still saw Jane, who started work in Bilston. We met by the market at the bus stop, out of work, a short walk from my drop-off point on Mount Pleasant.

However, one-night Jane said that she'd be OK by herself, and not to meet her. The suddenness, strange, suspicious, so I turned up anyway and saw her talking to a lad; I approached in silence and glared ahead; the atmosphere was tense.

"Hello, Jane, all right?"

"What you doing here?"

"I come to see you... The minibus drops me off round the corner... I always meet you out of work, don't I?"

"Yes, I suppose... Good day at work?"

"It was OK." As I glance across at her silent companion.

"Do you know each other?... An old friend, aren't you?" As she looks at the chap beside her, who nods.

"No, don't think so. I'll see you tonight though, Jane. Best be off now."

"OK, I'll see you later." We kiss farewell.

As we met that evening, we weren't as amorous or jovial. Jane said again, the lad's an old friend she'd known for years, as she chuckled.

I left it at that. A few days later, I turned up earlier. Hid by the bushes, as I watched her meet the same boy. They got on the bus together, and as it pulled away, I saw them. Sat together on the back of the bus, close.

Right then, time to act: I ran home, three-quarters of a mile like a madman, through the house, opened the garage, got my bike, then rode with great speed to where I knew Jane walked when she got off the bus, time of the essence. I had to beat the bus. Get there before the end of its two-mile journey.

What a race, but I made it. With a few seconds to spare, I sat on my bike in the dark in the pub car park. By the bus stop, awaiting the moment of truth as I stare toward the road, the amber glow of streetlights and white headlights.

As Jane saw me, she changed her walking step from slight prance to tentative; I don't think she wanted to face me!

"Hello, Jane," as I approach with a stern expression.

"What are you doing here?"

"To meet you. Was the boy there?" as I hold back vehemence.

"No, I came back by myself."

I knew differently, of course, and threw my bike down. "I just saw you meet him."

She looked surprised, thinking? *How could he have seen me and got from Bilston so fast?* Jane hastily walked away toward her house – as I shouted verbal abuse – in a rage.

On the Saturday, I rode to her house after work on the market. We talked; it was over. I couldn't believe it; narked, disheartened, yet wiser, and with treasured memories of pleasurable times.

Sadly, the market became less busy, too. There wasn't enough for me to do, but I'd have helped for free as I enjoyed that job; the excellent company. One of the delicious sandwiches was enough. I'd miss my job and Jane. The weather, getting colder; winter was well on its way.

Undoubtedly, my next girlfriend would be better and I'd excel on the YTS. In the meantime,... I made my own sweet elixir. My paper round and Saturday jobs brought precious and hard-earned money.

I bought the equipment to make home-brew, beer. The 40-pint fermenting bin, brew belt to warm and ferment the beer faster, hydrometer, keg with a carbon dioxide cylinder, I became an expert brewer. Superb and home-brew kits from Bilston Market were much cheaper than drinking in pubs.

The only problem: I drank my brew before going to the pubs. I'd be half-drunk before getting there. Once, though, impatient and frustrated at having to wait so long prompted an experiment: I drank half a keg after two hours of fermenting!

The after-effects weren't good, but I got drunk. Had some laughs. Before I rested on my bed and looked at the Sepecat Jaguar jet-fighter.

And, the Eagle spaceship from Space 1999 suspended from cotton of various lengths to imitate flight as I reminisced about the hours I spent making and painting those model kits. Oh, how my hobbies had changed, and dreams of becoming a pilot.

Changing times, pastimes, and a change of scenery as I walked to a new pub, The Gospel Oak, a few miles away, with my friends. It was beyond Bilston, toward Tipton, but well worth trekking to – fabulous place, great disco, and lots of girls.

Two pints of my potent home-brew and beers at the pub made me drunk, but I felt different that night as I walked home, quiet, insular as I strolled back to Bilston.

My mood suddenly changed to anger as I lashed out, punched at a glow of light. At a shining light that shone through small obscured window panes of glass to my left.

I see shards of glass on the ground and by a white polystyrene cup on a desk, a black uniform, and a peaked hat. A moment later, my arm's being held as an abrupt voice said, "I've called the police." I didn't mean to put my fist through the security guard's office window!

My friends said, "Let him go," and get up close and physical, then add. "Run, P."

After a moment of stunned realisation I had done something bad and very wrong a split second later, I didn't run or resist, although I felt bad about shunning their efforts. The police soon arrived. Their walkie-talkies, voices, beeping and the dashboard lights illuminating that car, which was much warmer than outside.

My mom and dad soon arrived at the police station, and Mom, furious. When asked, "As your son is 16, we don't have to take his photograph or fingerprints, but will if the parents' request."

"Yes, take his fingerprints! It'll teach him a lesson." Mom said. So, I held up the numbered card but didn't smile for that picture.

An ever-streetwise drinker, but a chaotic mess. I lashed out in a mad drunken moment at that chosen life, struggling against the shackles of alcohol, perhaps rebelling at the rash and ill-chosen path.

Had my mom been a cow or authorised a valuable, cruel, but kind lesson? Maybe I had had enough of lessons! The shackles became tighter; I tried harder, still drank, but less.

That night, as I closed my eyes, I remembered a past summer, at Welshpool on the other site, with second cousin and Frisbee throwing partner, Colin. We heard rumours and talk of an evening event. A disco, which drummed up excitement.

More so as we approached a large marquee in a field. Thrilled by bales of hay for bench seats, disco lights strobing as Miami Sound Machine's *Dr Beat* played, and beer flowing from the kegs on the tables at the rear of the marquee.

The beer, warm, but refreshing on that summer's night. Great dancing, frivolity, excitement as Colin drank a whisky and asked, "Wanna try?"

So, I did, so strong, it burnt my throat, but the potency felt good. Hated the taste.

The next day, somehow, my uncle found out and called me over to his house for a chat. He was a man of few words.

"Paul, I heard you had some whisky. Did you like it?"

I knew the importance of my answer and felt so glad to reply, "NO, hated it, terrible taste." As I cringed and felt physically sick.

"Good. Get a taste for that and drink enough of it; it'll kill ya."

With that, my uncle continued with his jobs, ending that serious, manly conversation. So glad I disliked it, and great to talk without a lecture. Now though, I was P, and wondered if my uncle would have approved of my home-brew.

That was, then, a different world. Now I was studying again.

Creative writing had begun, and I completed a one-year internet course in only 11 days! Quicker than anyone before, as an extra fun challenge; easy after university studies. Still, it led to an adult learning achievement award.

Further, higher-level courses soon ended. After 12 years of studying, what I had achieved gratified me, but I was still hungry for knowledge, excited by the doors to opportunity knowledge, seemed to open. Yet, during 1998 and early 1999, a part of me became despondent and tired.

I found it so hard getting into gear, but tried to keep busy. Perhaps frustration at being stuck, fixed to that plateau despite great academic achievement against the odds, and perturbed by lesser goals; not having a next substantial project, or goal, to focus attention.

It had been two years since graduating, a perplexing momentary pause that warped-time, like trying to get a grip on a swiftly spinning fairground ride.

Fears and many worries as I strived on, changed; wiser, tougher, less sensitive, more carefree, but still troubled by loneliness. Frustration, whilst stuck indoors, stagnating, with feuding thoughts and taunting memories.

I dwelled on the games I played after school as a child. With two girls who lived at the bottom of our road, I talked to and enjoyed amorous frivolity. They liked me, and both asked, "Paul, who do you love most?"

"Oh, I like you both!" At which one of them got upset. Rode off and watched scornfully from a distance, as I fought awkwardness and embarrassment.

Soon after, at school, a similar dilemma: Who to chase in playing kiss chase in the playground? I often caught the same girls in that thrilling, amorous game that made my heart pound.

How did the playgrounds change so much? Later on, too, I must have been popular, reminiscing. Three girls from school often knocked on my door. What did they see in me? Looks, personality, character, sense of humour, prowess and all I could do?

The muscular, toned, press-up champion, cyclist; that funny, witty soul who entertained in more ways than I knew or imagined. Important, though, to forget the dynamic, eloquent, vibrant person I longed to be. That romantic renowned for falling in love too easily! I still feared loneliness. Hoped inner charm returned or exuded. Or that my personality shone, despite my acquired, severe, anoxic brain injury, and disabilities, physical impairments. *How would I meet anyone? Get to know anyone? Would any female ever see past my wheelchair, see me, like, even love me?*

One girl became fond of me, around the time I started at the daycentre, my first romance after I emerged from coma. Lovely to be adored and admired and experience affection.

As disco lights flashed in rhythm to the music, I sat next to my lady. So thrillingly close, we chatted, laughed and drank; swooned as we exchanged compliments and holding hands with a lovely female again, wonderful.

Then arms around each other, a sensuous embrace, as we kiss; tender meeting of lips as beautiful eyes looked into mine. Scan my face as painted eyelashes flutter; a lustful gaze. Yes, the upward ascent had well and truly begun.

So what I couldn't walk and a permanent wheelchair user, I had the belle of that ball on my arm. A woman at my side; what a marvellous night, that would become exceptional.

Ecstatic at the cusp of passion, as I awaited intimacy. Imagined closeness, as she climbed into bed. I'm beside my lady. Undressed, aroused, quietly confident but nervous; it'd been such a long time.

The smell of perfume driving me crazy, and pert, perfect breasts as I watched them remove their black stockings.

Silky-smooth legs against mine, entwined as the kissing intensified and I hold my lover's hand and guide ever lower as I caress. Overwhelmed and wild with desire, so wanting to please that vision of loveliness; mine, and I belong to her. I had waited so long and wondered if I would experience tender, intimate moments again.

I wanted that night to last forever. Morning arrived too soon as the curtains opened. The sunshine-rays flooded in and the sun illuminated those beautiful eyes. Filling me with and evoking amorous feelings of love. Alas, that romance didn't last, but I learned, and endured, the loneliness.

No romance or passion during my time at university, either. I enjoyed study, the music and hearing the birds sing outside the university near St Peter's Square as I came home so late.

Lonely and, frustrated by memories, and a girl I met via the CB radio, when I could speak better and knew CB jargon; she didn't want me to leave her. She gave me 50p to buy condoms! I declined an invitation to have sex in the Fozza.

Now I fantasised, wished I could pay for sex! If only I had a motorised wheelchair, I'd go to the red-light district; visit a prostitute. So frustrated and crueller, I'm stuck indoors.

Nobody to tell or help! Just to be near a lady, to talk to one became a dream. So sad that basic but powerful yearning, unfulfilled and a taboo area for me and many disabled people.

Tormenting thoughts — I should have succumbed to Tina in 1993! Said more to her husband. Was I slipping backwards?

My shyness had returned. Drink gave me bold confidence. Dad became my new best friend as he pushed me in my wheelchair to pubs in Bilston Town, and to The Villiers Arms and The Happy Wanderer and drove me to other places.

We visited The Terrace Bar, also known as Waggies, at the Molineux Stadium in Wolverhampton. A great DJ, Charlie, played a favourite song of mine as I arrived: Paul Hardcastle's *Rainforest,* and awesome when everyone sang along to Harry J All Stars, *Liquidator,* and Jeff Beck, *Hi Ho Silver Lining. I hope this place never closes.*

It was a perfect venue for my 30th birthday party, and we went to pubs and discos I visited in my teens. None of my old friends were at those places, just different music, teenage and older groups in their own exclusive circles.

I wasn't a part of any crowd, so I drank just for escape and pined on false hope like in my teens, with one major difference. In my teens, I walked, talked so eloquently; charmed the birds from the trees.

Now the miserable, disabled wallflower in the corner, wilting by over watering. So unfair, as my eyes saw myself in a past dimension, fickle groups, pursuing fun and desire, on the same learning curve I had experienced but in a different era.

Again, like many times in my life, temporary comfort as I drank nearly every night again. A couple of pints combined with my medication were enough.

The sad aftermath following realisation intensified depression. I didn't drink as much as in my mid-to-late, precious, messed up teens. But now older, wiser, and in control!

There were memorable nights at the student's union bar, too, and concerts in Wolverhampton.

In a packed venue, lights, thumping, fantastic music as I sat beside the stage, watching Snap sing *Rhythm Is A Dancer*, a favourite dance song of the 1990s. The lovely lead singer pressed her lips on mine as she left the stage, proving I had the best seat in the house, far better than at the Madonna concert.

I danced with the three sexy, scantily clad dancers wearing silver boots and matching skimpy bikinis. Well, they danced round me, flashing their cleavages and toned belly buttons as I wheeled my chair back and forth to *Move It*, with my name, "Paul" added.

Embarrassed, being lifted by a few bouncers after the REEL 2 REAL singer invited me onto the stage. He saw me at the front amidst the crowd, and changed the words to his song, including my name. Great, mind-expanding fun times, as I planned to continue university nightlife and to socialise.

Also, in 1998, and despite unease, I returned to my base camp, although maybe I shouldn't have after all efforts put into study. Nor did I want to backtrack.

Such a waste, talent, gained skills, knowledge, and unfulfilled potential; growing old, but lacking confidence and impeded by practical problems. Everyone speeding past me into the distance, leaving me behind, abandoned.

Not being where I should be, with a marvellous house, car, money, companion/partner/wife! Superficial compared to what I had experienced, and the greater cosmos, but still niggled.

So what next? Writing seemed a natural progression; it was

what I most enjoyed at university. So I added creativity to my factual scientific writing; even wrote poetry: The Lighthouse and The Desperate Beggar inspired from coma. Excited and refreshed by such diversification, and further dimensions to what I wrote, as I thought in different ways.

Pete recommended trying to write 14-line, 10 syllable sonnets. A fresh form of writing for me, I found a precise and difficult discipline. I relished grappling with the art-form, instead of more rigid, academic writing. Fascinated to read about chakras, too, the spiritual link between my body and cosmos as I diversified my knowledge.

It was bizarre history repeated itself. As eventually, years after school, I studied science and art. Albeit art expressed in a written form, with words, and I had studied science at school instead of art. So, a full circle, and a remarkable transformation, new goals, ambitions, dreams.

I wrote catchy classified ads, hoping I might find a kindred spirit, or even a mate. And, gained several pen-friends, I wrote so many letters and the odd story, including some about my life as I become immersed in the world of words. Dava wrote to me from Norway, too.

Carried away as I wrote letters, as long as 3,700 words to a pen-friend in Sweden, and other global locations: Russia (St Petersburg), America (California), South Africa, and Australia and other locations.

Even an occupational therapist wrote to me. She drove up to see me from down south. Lovely, and she asked me to visit Egypt with her; she'd take care of me. A tempting adventure and I loved to travel, but the plan seemed too ambitious.

Still, I searched, and hoped for an answer; something to strive toward to combat the loneliness and quench deep desires. The internet helped open my mind to another passion.

My fascination in UFOs and aliens rekindled in cyberspace, as I met a lady online, via the college computers. Uncanny she was called Angel, and that she was a UFO investigator from South Africa.

Eminently, in emails from then on, and from college, Pete

became Agent PY. I kept him updated, but didn't mention any significant details regarding exchanges of emails with Angel.

I craved to meet her and investigate UFOs, too. An ideal career as I'd learned about physics and space, and matched lifelong fascinations. Alas, mobility again impeded ambition. I still dreamed and became excited with fresh interests and new pursuits.

And, my internet mission to find romance in faraway lands extended as I gained and wrote to pen-friends. Still niggled, though, as I remembered other adventures; past romance and greenery of Scotland, fond memories as I went back in fluctuating time.

30.

A CRUEL ROMANCE

I had fought concerns about how I may feel in the near future, and in retrospect, the decision to leave college may well have seemed spontaneous and irrational. I chose my route at a crossroads of my life and had started on the YTS.

A few weeks into the scheme, I became more settled, but the days seemed longer, the nights lonelier for having loved and lost.

Bowled over and reeling from heartache intensified a sad but awakening period, yet forming new bonds of togetherness felt satisfying. Comfort in drink at night, dossing around, walking the streets bored; YTS by day. A new routine, and refreshing as I looked forward to the novel life change.

I made friends with Ken, a short, stocky, short-haired biker and passionate Leeds United football supporter and enthusiast. Fellow drinker, too, a genuine, kind, no-nonsense sort I liked.

A friend was with me from school, too, Jon, a football player, and colleague. Good friends and had no regrets. Despite realising people, there hadn't had opportunity to attend college.

Some jokers found it amusing, sending eager trainees to the stores for long waits, boxes of sparks, and even glass hammers. Such antics made me feel out of place, and part of me further pondered the somewhat unprecedented change.

It seemed odd, but great to learn new skills. Acquire a new vocation in woodwork, a practical topic I found unappealing at school and wasn't particularly good at, but now exhibited unknown talents and definite flair.

Talents that manifested as I made a beautiful teak bowl, with a considerable amount of effort and time. Did my utmost best, carefully crafted many parts as I concentrated on the quite intricate procedures involved in its construction, and used a range of chisels and a lathe. A construction that made me proud as I amazed myself with what I'd accomplished.

The tutor gathered everyone round, as he and everyone admired my fabulous finished creation, and proudly said with delight, fervour and full of praise. "This is what you can do with a lot of time and effort."

Despite this new acclaim and proud stature, I didn't fancy following woodwork as a career. With hindsight, a narrow-minded, rash decision that disappointed my woodwork tutor, perhaps, as he saw, I had the talent and potential.

A while later, I began an even more complex task of making an octagonal jewellery box, but became despondent one day to find it sabotaged. A chisel shoved through its middle. After that, I lost heart with disappointment and disgust as I contemplated the identity of the jealous, insidious character that ruined my work.

Anyway, by then I had declined a trainee patternmaker placement. I wished to pursue a computing path, a more futuristic career.

Regards to my social scene, I still drank lots of beer, mainly at weekends, and had further refined my home-brew making skills.

We still often walked to that same pub near Tipton. A trendy place with a great disco, buzzing with classy tunes and vibrant people. A place for socialising and meeting a variety of attractive women.

Before, I went out with a girl in my last year at school, pretty, tall with blonde hair, lovely blue eyes and elegant, with a charming manner and personality, well-spoken but quiet. We parted company.

Then one-night, I saw her at the pub as I'm at the bar and my friends promptly told me she was there, and when I scanned the room, I became mesmerised. She looked lovely, even from afar.

Confident and full of myself, partly because of having a few beers, and being slightly drunk but apprehensive as I approached. Debbie's blue eyes sparkled wondrously as I spoke to her with humble hesitance and wanted to choose the right words as I asked her out. Surprised, she said 'yes' right away.

To my great pleasure, Debbie and I started seeing each other again, and I couldn't believe my luck. She was so beautiful and sweet, a dream-girl. I was extremely happy, very grateful for a second chance, and besotted after a relatively short time!

We'd been seeing each other for a while, when an opportunity arose. An opportunity to partake in a course planned with the YTS that excited me as it involved a 10-day trip to Scotland. A place I had never visited but heard of its scenic beauty. So I agreed to go and liked to travel, relished adventure.

Meanwhile, the relationship between Debbie and me flourished. Progress from our fresh start, so I'd miss Debbie.

The night before I left for Scotland, I saw Debbie; met her parents, too. They left us in the house by ourselves, and we had an exceptional, fun evening in each other's company.

Elated to be together, kissing and cuddling on the sofa, whispering sweet nothings to each other, whilst fondly caressing. "Debbie, you're lovely." as I breathed with gasps of breath.

"I like you a lot too, Paul, and this time seems different!" Heart pounding and singing inside, deep within, as I swooned on cloud nine. I had forgotten Jane; Debbie, infinitely better in every way, but I stopped short of pouring my heart out and expressing how intense my feelings were.

"Yes, you're even lovelier this time round," I replied. A truly perfect, romantic evening, and this time would be different. It had to be. She had given me a second chance; the loveliest girl I had ever had or known. So lucky, and I had money from the YTS. Things looking up for me.

The evening soon ended. Inevitably time to say goodbye for 10 days! Again, we hugged and kissed by the door, made sweet endearments; affirmations, like loving partners would.

"I'll be back before you know it," as I left; had to tear myself away from this lovely lady. I didn't want to leave her, as I ventured into a cold, crystal-clear, frosty, uninviting night.

The road and pavement, white but glistened with the reflection of orange light, shining from the sodium streetlights along the route. In ironic defiance, the road sparkled with a light-blue clean, frosty glow as I cautiously rode home on my bike. Conditions, so appealing, but treacherous!

The following day, my work colleagues and I, a motley group of 12, embarked on the long journey to Scotland! A journey in excess of 400 miles to an unknown, mysterious place not far from Glasgow!

Sheer excitement as I contemplated a true adventure, and notice gradual changes in scenery as that northward-bound journey progressed, and our fields of vision evanesced to snow-capped jagged mountains on the horizon, and around us and much greenery, and it grew colder.

Such a long journey, but eventually we reached our destination. We'd travelled so far to a neighbouring country; didn't know what to expect!

We gazed upon a large, grey bricked, ornate, old-fashioned building, our dwelling place for the duration of the holiday. It's overwhelming being in such a different place as we survey the environment with our senses; our new surroundings.

The place and its atmosphere, astonishingly different to anything I had experienced. Before learning, others would be there, Scottish natives of this strange land, like us, doing youth training schemes. *What will they be like? Will they hate us?* Besides, we were foreigners in an unfamiliar country!

Worse than I imagined, some very stern and burly-looking Scotsmen greeted us, who were as authoritative as feared! They escorted our intrepid national posse to a room where we sat around a table. The atmosphere, tense; the encounter distinctively tinged with formality. One warden got straight to laying down the law. Told us the house rules.

Beginning with, "If anybody has any alcohol with them. They must hand it in as no drinking is allowed. If we find any, we will confiscate it and you'll face the consequences."

My face dropped in utter dismay. *This can't be right.* Questions about morality, honesty, and justice entered my mind.

Agitation and desperate with discomfort, my brain raced. I

struggled to unravel my thoughts; to solve my dilemma fairly. *Shall I hand it in or not?* In an instant, I decided to keep quiet.

I'd been a drinker, party animal and comic since I was 15-years-old! *What is this foreign place? Will I survive the 10 days without booze? No way they're taking my precious 'beer booty' from me.*

After the grilling, they showed everyone to their dormitories. Ours, at the top of an elaborate wooden staircase. The room I'd share with two other males, friends, Jon, and Ken. It was small but pleasant, warm and clean with white furniture and a long, vertical window, a single bed, and a bunk bed; I chose top bunk, near the door.

An unmitigated atmosphere of excitement and apprehension as we entered and unpacked. Soon, my roommates and friends may catch a glimpse of the contents of my case. There'd be controversy, disbelief, and much respect.

I tried to conceal the magnitude of the essential items. But couldn't for long; I had bought so much, my case, full of beer. Eighteen cans of lager, crammed in strategically and carefully, almost as if they were clothes.

My friends, now cohorts, couldn't believe their eyes. They understood why keeping a straight face in the room was so difficult. More fully appreciated, me, the party animal, a proud social hardened drinker intent on having fun, always experimenting and trying new things!

Who were the adults to decide, and dictate, to impose such restrictions? My adamance and defiance justified the devious scenario, to safeguard my beer, and despite slight guilt, even though I'd done nothing wrong.

Two roommates had bought four cans each. This kind of eased the restrictive burden on my conscience, revelling in excelling so spiritedly. But I revelled more, as I amused everyone with my excessive tendencies and gall, and great as the instigator of fun.

Pleasure from laughter, strikingly and inexplicably bonded us together by breaking the solid ice of anticipation that had formed on the journey and fortified from our initial encounter with the

Scots in this strange, novel environment.

As soon as they showed us round, and upon concealing my beer in my allotted drawers between socks and other garments, I ventured downstairs. On the creaking floorboards; eager to explore the territory.

A large, heavy, dark wooden door opened onto a large lounge, beckoned by a homely fire, set in a grand, and ornate open fireplace, with a black hearth. A green-clothed pool table on the right, and an enormous dark window opposite the door.

To the side and in front of the window, old-fashioned furniture surrounded the fireplace. Furniture comprising mainly high, studded, padded armchairs that resembled leather. With chair arms embellished with curvy, dark and shiny wood. Chairs all angled inwards, forming a focal point on the fireplace.

Various artworks adorned the walls, murals resembling ghoulish record sleeves of the macabre that I'd seen in record shops. Interesting, but quite alarming; dank yet vibrant, although some colours, drab, as I admired the masterpieces and explored the room. *It's my first evening of 10 in this place. Who will I meet? What kind of people live here?*

And before, I sat in a comfortable, large padded armchair by the fire. *Where is everyone*, as I contemplated my emotions and tried to relax, take in all the information and reflect upon the day's events? Enchanted and lost in thought, whilst I intensely stared deep into the dancing yellow flames of the fire.

My trance state broke because of an attractive girl who came in and sat, perched on the chair next to me, then leaning forward as she turned toward me. "Hullooa, what's your name?" she asked. *Has she said hello?* As she shook my hand, "I'm Cathy." I knew the dialect, Scottish, and with rosy-red cheeks, long, dark, wavy hair, and slender. Fascinated by each other's accents, as we chatted.

What a thrill to meet such a lovely person, so bubbly. Enthralled by her, I considered myself privileged to meet that lady. For a moment, I forgot about the stern wardens, their rules, and the problem of keeping my beer hidden, let alone drinking it.

Worries no longer gnawed at my conscience as I pondered on the desirable eventuality: the holiday won't be as bad as first conceived.

Great, I'm getting on well with Cathy. "Ever been to Scotland before?"

"No, my first visit... but look forward to seeing the countryside."

"Ahh, never been to Scotland, I'll show you round... Fancy coming for a walk?"

"Love to, now?"

"Uh ugh." As she nods and we stand.

"OK, I'll get my coat." Surprised, and cheery to chat to a friendly, hospitable Scottish lass, eager and proud to show me Scotland, put me more at ease, I accepted, being amenable and friendly, intrigued and excited.

By then it was evening, a nip in the air as we ventured outside into the chilly night together onto Scottish soil, but warmer than I expected.

Filled with anticipation and apprehension, and trepidation as we walked, mainly on my part. *My female companion lives in Scotland, is confident and pleased as host; I live in England*, was a foreigner in her land, but more at ease upon seeing greenery all around and many trees; felt the fresh crisp air, but no wind.

We strolled along the road and turned right into a narrow road toward a stone bridge, along the lane. Ever excited by the remoteness and strange emotions, compelled as we venture into the darkness.

No streetlights, just moonlight. Surreal as we stopped on the brow; at the zenith of this bridge, and heard water in a narrow stream, gently trickling beneath us; humbling, audible delight.

In total admiration and awe of the setting, earthly ambience; tranquil and serene — like a fairy-tale, as it seemed wonderful, unreal. But why were my thoughts asking many enticing questions? My mind and heart racing.

Not even the powerful enchantment of the water's wake, and its relaxing effect, could abate my ever-quickening heart rate. Or quell my intense excitement as we became spellbound.

The romance of isolation, in the middle of nowhere, yet somewhere magical, captivating Cathy and me. Beguiled with no escape from destiny. Heady moments and wild with desire, hunger for love.

Emotions, so intense to evoke a sudden and instinctive, surreal moment. Desire, from inner depths within my heart and soul, preceded by the ignition of a kindled spark of romance that launched us on a rocket to the moon! Seemed so as our lips gently met, in a tender, scintillating kiss, with an intimacy and passion never experienced.

Such a warm, sensuous embrace, close pounding hearts. That enchanted moment, romantic novelty driven by powerful attraction but while trying to suppress much guilt, as the mixture of nerves and delight changed to utter delight but tinged with sadness.

The nervous anticipation and tension dissipated upon the electric meeting of our lips, both elated, although a part of me felt terrible as I thought of Debbie so far away.

That kiss instigating the dissolve of cloud nine for me to fall, and caught by another, but did I float along higher, or fall to a lower cloud? Was it love or lust filling my heart from the touch of lips and embrace of hearts?

I fought the uneasiness as we walked hand in hand, full of cheer and amour, like two smitten kids experiencing their first crush. We talked more but more affably as we ventured from the location, vibrant, and anew; glowing auras!

"I can't believe that's just happened." I said.

"Neither can I,... I don't kiss all the boys, you know!"

"Glad to hear that, Cathy."

"Well, only ones like you, handsome."

"Thanks. I don't kiss all the girls either!... You're the only Scottish person I know! And I've kissed you."

Sometime later, I returned to my dormitory with a smug grin on my face. My roommates could tell something good had happened. I couldn't lie even to save my life; I told them what had happened; shocked them with my speed.

Meeting a female and romantically involved after just two hours in this different land! "You dark horse! What's she like? Hey, any more girls for us?" asked Ken.

The next day, Cathy quizzed me about whether I had a girlfriend back home. Her inquisitive nature made me feel great, partly as I had information that she wanted badly! Of course, I told her about my girlfriend. Cathy's face was no longer animated, but stony as she spoke sharply, became forceful and adamant that I should stop seeing Debbie.

Things weren't the same. The previous night of crazy romance seemed unbelievable, but still wonderful. There seemed to be an uncomfortable void. Some warmth between us had sadly dissipated as almost constant pressure built to phone Debbie.

"If you don't phone her, it will be over between us; I won't even speak to you. Choose her or me?" she said tauntingly. Followed by, "What's she like? Is she pretty?"

"Yes."

"So, you like her more than me!" Cathy scowled. "Fine, have your precious Debbie, but you can forget me!" She said as she stormed away along the corridor, sat on the window ledge, a distance away with head bowed. As I glanced over, she looked upward; her face, full of anger.

An alarming and perturbing transformation, presented with a dastardly ultimatum indeed; the situation seemed hopeless! Either I break up with Debbie, and I didn't wish to, or hurt anyone. In fact, I liked her — so lovely — and had already broken up with her once. So heartless, and despicable of me.

The other part of me couldn't face another nine lonely days without being friends with my new flame – passion and romance foremost in my thoughts. Could I keep such a secret, a holiday romance? Will it be anything more? Debbie wouldn't know, but I just couldn't lie to Cathy or Debbie.

Maybe I wasn't thinking with my head or heart. But another part of me, my mind and emotions, realising how much being dislodged from whatever cloud I was on would hurt; I didn't intend to hurt anyone.

Still, with reluctance, I made the phone call. My finger tentatively selected the numbers on the round number dial.

My heart pounded as I dialled the number. Slowly as I could and I even made a couple of deliberate wrong numbers to postpone as long as possible as I quivered and my heart sank, knowing I'd have to hurt the lady of my dreams for a second time, and lose her forever.

Whether a wise or foolish choice, such a dangerous gamble.

"Hello... Debbie!" in a dulcet tone.

"Oh yes, hello Paul, how's your holiday going?" Debbie sounded so sweet, upbeat, and pleased to hear my voice.

"Oh, it's OK, nice place, and I've made a few friends," hiding nervousness as I braced myself into uttering the next words, combating anxiety and reluctance. "Debbie, I need to tell you something!"

"What!" Debbie replied in an ever-sweet tone.

Suddenly and unexpectedly, Cathy grabbed the phone from me and said vehemently, "Paul's seeing me now! You got that!"

Cathy slammed the telephone receiver on the table and stormed out of the room. I picked it up slowly and prepared to speak.

"Debbie, hello! Are you still there?" As I spoke, I heard the phone being put down on me, and a monotonous, all too familiar tone echoed in my ear. "I'm sorry, Debbie," but I was far too late.

And I wanted to say so much. How I was missing her. But how could I say anything sweet? As I thought of the previous night? Cathy's actions made matters even worse. *How could she say those things?*

Suddenly, there was a gap in my heart; I felt terrible about it all. Debbie didn't deserve that treatment. It disturbed and upset me, as I knew my actions would haunt me and play on my mind forever more.

I couldn't even speak to Debbie privately. If I had, I wouldn't end the relationship. How could I? Her lovely face, her beautiful human nature, innate and sensual? I wished we could speak face-to-face.

Cathy rushed to comfort me, sat beside me at the end of the corridor; put her arm around me. Right away, uncertain I had made the right decision, or a horrendous, rash, ill-thought out mistake.

How about after the holiday? Back home, then what would I do? Well, I made my choice. And that kiss under the Scottish moonlit sky; so special. Debbie's kisses, too; she was wonderful.

At least I had my beer too, and regarding the beer situation. A group of us planned an excursion to a nearby village, intent on getting hold of alcohol! We found that there was a bus that stopped nearby. Ken and I planned the excursion. "We need beer. How can we cope without beer?" said Ken in a passionate, agitated tone.

"Now we know they have buses up here... we'll get some. The buses must go somewhere. There's no stopping us!" I said.

"Yes, and villages have pubs, if not. Maybe an off licence," Stuart said.

"I bloody hope so, otherwise we'll have no booze." Ken said as he stomped back and forth, excited, with eagerness to explore and find a beer supplier.

Our intrepid trio waited for the bus, Ken, Stuart and I. It arrived, looking dilapidated and light-blue. Screeched to a halt, and we stepped on, faced the driver.

"Where to?" he asked.

"The nearest village," Ken and I replied. We ran upstairs, and sat in the front seats of the deserted upper floor, and looked out of the window.

"Not much out there," I said as I gazed at a wilderness of darkness, only occasionally interrupted by the orange glow of streetlights that shed their light on grey sparse houses, dwellings in that strange land.

"I hope this knackered old bus doesn't breakdown," I said.

The lads promptly answered, "We don't care, as long as it breaks near a village with plenty of pubs."

"Plenty of pubs and girls," I jocularly replied.

"Yes, but if there are any women, they're ours. You've already got two, you jammy git," Ken said.

We soon arrived at a small village, with only one pub.

Ken, who looked the oldest with a moustache, would attempt to purchase four cans of beer! So, we all walked into the pub, packed full of mainly elderly men. The place grew silent, unnervingly as it seemed everyone was staring at us.

Despite this, Ken bravely asked in a booming, confident voice, "Can I have four cans to take out, please?"

"Sorry, no, I can't serve you." The landlord's firm reply.

The pub became even quieter when its occupants heard Ken's foreign accent. *Panic stations.* Foreigners, and very conspicuous! In desperation I attempted the purchase, asking in my most grown up cool voice, to no avail.

Argh, trapped. The only option, a hasty exit, a desperate, dishevelled man before my time. Our dispirited and ego-bruised troop ventured back on the bus.

The unsuccessful mission put us in sombre moods, dwelling upon the prospect of no beer, and my supply would soon dwindle away! "What the hell is this place? Can't even get served. They're all crazy up here," Ken said.

"I've been drinking since I was 15! No problems back home," I said.

To make matters even worse, upon arrival at the centre, a stern, irate warden confronted us. He told us to go into the main room; we complied. He shut the door behind him.

The landlord of the pub had phoned the police. The warden wasn't happy, but seemed understanding as he said, "If you want any beer, tell us, and we'll fetch it for you."

I think our determination influenced their decision as we explained we'd been drinking for a long time, anyway! Our glum expressions could have played a part and may have evoked some empathy. He warned us not to cause any trouble, otherwise the consequences would be serious.

We could hardly believe it: they'd lifted the alcohol ban. Smug smiles of joy, the holiday wouldn't be as dull after all, the prospect of no beer, bleak, unimaginable; sombre.

From then on, we placed our nightly orders for beer from the village. As the most radical, I ordered more beer – a further eight cans to celebrate our great triumph – in the party animal spirit; had to go over the top!

The contentment of success, compromise helped to achieve and linked with the theme of the week, leadership. Everyone had to work together to solve problems, and fend for ourselves sometimes outdoors and during winter in harsh, cold weather.

Actually, we had to do a range of outdoor activities, such as building a shelter, by a nearby river and traverse across by a rope. Revelling the task as I carried thick, long, heavy logs down a steep grassy slope to the river in the biting, wintry wind, and rain. We lashed these together firmly, to erect in a tripod-fashion to wrap the tarpaulin around.

The ladies made soup from inside the makeshift shelter. Our efforts to build the homely place gratified us and made me proud.

The long-awaited and deserved treat: tasty, hot soup, nourishing, and warming our freezing, stiff hands on the mugs. A satisfying privilege; I'd never been so grateful for a beverage, or so cold.

I'll never forget how gruelling the task was: carrying the logs back up the hill, on my own, balanced on my shoulder. Hands numb and stinging with penetrating cold. Freezing rain, as I hankered for warmth. The exercise evoked a glorious sense of achievement and accomplishing such feats further built character!

By chance, the holiday dates were such, one day would be my birthday. I didn't tell anyone, except for Cathy, and saddened by being away from home, having no cards or presents.

Melancholic emotions affected my mood. It was a new experience for me, not being with my family on my birthday, and, so far away, in another country.

I wondered what would happen on my much anticipated, and special day. On my birthday, as about 30 of us sat at long tables in the massive dining room, I reminisced about previous birthdays at home.

Presents from my family, cake, and candlelight, preceding, making a wish, suppressed my usual vibrancy. Downbeat, and forlorn, but I chose the adventure…

My reminiscent trance, as I adjust my knife and fork, ready to eat. *Wonder what's for dinner?* As many chat, when, suddenly, the lights went off, followed by silence enveloping the room. *How strange... a power-cut, and why is no-one talking?*

What's that yellow glow from the corridor? Glimmers of light emanating from the door, grabbing my attention. Sure enough, it became clear, someone's wheeling in a cake with candles on; the flames pierced the darkness with a yellow, fuzzy, shimmering glow.

The candlelight flickering and swaying beneath wisps of black soot, illuminating Cathy's smiling face with her dark eyes, sparkling, wondrously.

Ah, someone here shares my birthday?

The light went on and silence broken in unison with singing "happy birthday..." A state of shock, astounded by the touching gesture, but embarrassed. Bashful, and so hot, as my face glowed bright-red! *Should I stand, make a speech?*

These people have melted my heart. How can I show my appreciation? Without a doubt, my 17th birthday was the most memorable of my life.

Cathy beamed as she stared at me, but with composed plainness. I knew she had played a part in the scheme. It was a delightful, sweet and heart-warming gesture, emotional, memorable, but still. Somewhere in my mind were prominent thoughts of Debbie and my family in England.

Part of me dreaded that celebratory December day during winter, the thoughts of loneliness and sadness, homesickness. But, sometimes I wish I could have frozen those moments, savouring the beauty of the light and love — like a brilliant star as a warm ember in the cold, dark depths of outer space.

I wouldn't ever forget that glowing light in the darkness; kindness when I was so far from home. But, I was in a magical place – within a fairy-tale that began as I stared at the dancing flames, and kissed beneath the moon. The fairy-tale continued with a tender birthday kiss.

Another night, myself and fellow YTS trainee called Zaffa

embarked on a bold plan. Zaffa, wild and just crazy, cracked jokes, and with a similar sense of humour to myself.

He was funny; strange, as he spontaneously turned his head and spat, as he laughed, or became agitated. But, his predilection for romantic encounters and an unpredictable streak made me wary of him.

There couldn't be a bolder, amorous man near Cathy. My cohort and I crept downstairs, in the midst of the night, via a creaking staircase. To the girls' dormitory, where Cathy was with the other Scottish girls.

In retrospect, a mad mission, and an unbelievably risky escapade fraught with hazards, but I had to be with Cathy; keep her safe. I climbed the short ladder only in boxer shorts.

Got into bed with Cathy on the top bunk wearing a night-dress; she wearily greeted me, astonished, and couldn't believe my presence, but thrilled and excited!

So nervous, we held each other, kissed softly, whispering intimately. Her body, warm, her embrace dreamily seductive, inviting, filled with desire and wanting her so much, and to take it further; felt so good. I wanted to stay there forever in each other's embrace.

My heart raced away, pounding in my chest; was I mad, taking such a risk? Rocks in my head on the day Cathy asked me that? Insecure as I and couldn't bear to lose her, or be apart?

Suddenly, to my horror and everyone else's, we heard footsteps. "Oh, no." I said as the footsteps became louder.

My heart and mind raced even faster. Disarray as I became like a trapped prisoner in that room, on execution day. Punishment seemed imminent, inescapable, as I became frantic; panic-stricken.

Imperative, I construct a plan with lightning-quick thinking to evade detection! The only desperate plan, precariously balance myself in-between Cathy's top bunk bed and the wall. An arm across Cathy, whilst I perched my buttocks on a hot radiator and she held me!

The door opened. "Everything all right, girls?" A female warden asked.

"Yes, we're OK, thanks." The reply in delayed unison.

"OK, goodnight. See you all in the morning."

What a relief. I left Cathy's company soon after that, but adopted extreme caution, as we still had to venture into the main corridor and walk up the creaky stairs.

No, what can we do? They're so noisy, even though we tread as stealthily as we can, and hope to avoid the creaky floorboards, like mischievous prowlers, and intrepid, bold as I swooned; getting away with a bountiful booty, an amorous, wonderful, once in a lifetime, almost magical encounter; anything for a kiss; entwined; to excite and amaze.

On another night, at about 2am, I visited another friend's room. On this occasion unaccompanied, and heard laughter as I approached the door. Some were having a late-night drink and a smoke, and one youth, Zaffa, up to his usual comic antics.

I was quite drunk, acting silly and getting laughs as usual. One lad in the room rolled a spliff. "Best weed this is," he said, with a serious expression and glaring eyes, as he added "it's curtains and straight back home for us; police called and everything if anyone found out."

Anyway, I joined the small jovial party; and avidly watched and waited for my turn to smoke the strange, innocently ominous paper cylinder filled with tobacco and another herbal narcotic substance. As I sucked on it and inhaled, it made me even more intoxicated and relaxed.

I amused everyone, too, put everyone in hysterics. Uncontrollable laughter, some nearly cried, as I mimicked actors with American accents I'd seen on TV. "This is good shit."

Such fun and frivolity, reproducing sound effects, voices, and impersonation, was my party trick.

Laughter abruptly ceased, though, similar to a previous night, the sinister sound of footsteps in the corridor became startlingly audible.

Panic stations — red alert! The cruel irony: we couldn't abandon ship. And had no weaponry; only our wits, while fear and dreadful emotions flooded my mind.

The rather large weird cigarette was gracelessly extinguished in haste. Again, desperate panic, with limited options, I hid behind the door, scared stiff. Standing as straight as I could, not breathing, like a secret agent may have done in the same situation.

Knife-edge suspense, with only a slim possibility of not being detected, necessitated us to change our moods in a flash to allay any suspicion. Never had I been so anxious, despairing, nervous as we all focussed on the doorknob, watched as it turned.

The door opened; only the strictest warden checking on everybody! "All right, lads? Keep the noise down now." Celebrations continued as the door closed and Zaffa exhaled the smoke he'd kept in his mouth; more beer flowed, eased with some hearty but more controlled laughter! The party, not pooped, pleasingly contrary to earlier fears!

Such superb jolly times we all enjoyed at an amazing, unique place. So far from home, and I met many friends. Lovely people and experienced so much.

Sadly, it was time to leave Scotland's scenic beauty and its unforgettable inhabitants. That long-anticipated, dreaded day; the end of the holiday. Looming since the first enchanted night. That, when I imagined, made my heart thump and pine.

The unbearable day I parted from Cathy, here, the clock ticking, an emotional departure, Cathy in tears as I climbed on that minibus and when I left with the torture in my heart, for that girl had a profound and everlasting impact on me. *How can I return alone?*

So special and nothing like anyone I'd ever met before; perhaps the one for me, the one meant to be with me for life! She had to be as I left cloud nine for her. We made promises to meet again.

"I'll come to see you, Paul." Cathy said, with tears in her eyes.

But I wasn't optimistic about this eventuality. Scotland was so far away. I doubted Cathy would visit.

In the minibus, my subdued mood continued; quiet, and a melancholic, universal silence as I reflected on the wonderful holiday in Scotland. Cathy in my thoughts, and the further I travelled, the more intense my feelings became. I wanted to rebel against being separated; the injustice of my aching heart.

That night I arrived home to warm greetings from my family! I'd missed them and felt happy to see them but also saddened because of parting with Scotland, in particular, Cathy. As promised, the phone rang, and I pounced on it.

"Hello Paul, it's Cathy. How are you?"

"OK, but I'm missing you!" I couldn't stop smiling.

"How was your journey?"

"Long and sad."

"I've been missing you, too,... it's been quiet up here."

That long-distance phone call thrilled and delighted me; made me swoon, and hearing cheer and excitement exuded in the phonemes of her voice confirmed reality. The 10 days in Scotland weren't a fantastic dream.

Cathy was a real, genuine person, not an acquaintance assigned to memories of a faraway place. No sorrow of a discontinued fairy-tale; the romance continued, as I clutched the phone so tight.

Pressed the speaker on my ear as I swooned. Her voice, so sweet and hearing Cathy say how much she was missing me, instilled rapturous joy tinged with a strange sadness; I was missing her, too.

It was rather sad when we said goodbye on the phone. Just as it was earlier that day; but differing from the previous occasion, my face beamed a wry smile. Animated with joy. I imagined Cathy putting the phone down and hoped she was smiling, too.

At home, my family had missed me, as I'd been away for ages. The longest ever time away from home. I had missed them, my usual birthday at home, for the first time, and had many stories to tell; as a changed person. Distant as my mind was elsewhere, part of me, still in Scotland, with Cathy.

I kept on thinking about my new friends, and particularly Cathy's laugh, her voice, her wonderful smile, her caress, her kiss. *Is she thinking of me, too? Will I ever see her again?*

I sat on the sofa and admired the Christmas tree Mom had decorated. The bulbs glistened in the array of many coloured lights, and the tree, in all its glory, looked beautiful and radiated a homely, secure presence.

Mom had bought us a video recorder, and my younger brother proudly showed me a clip he had recorded: The Pet Shop Boys singing *West End Girls* on Top of the Pops®. An exciting, real novelty!

Christmas came with its festivities; it was typical to others, a time of harmony and giving. Mom always tried to make Christmas special. I went out with my friends, but lonely, melancholy without Cathy, as if incomplete.

She rang again, though. Soon after Christmas and confirmed she'd come to see me; the date set, and the means: a train from Scotland to England. Still, I couldn't believe it. Was she actually coming? It was hard to take in and ecstatic.

The day soon arrived. Dad and I travelled to Wolverhampton Railway Station to meet Cathy; as we came near the station, I grew increasingly apprehensive with nervous-excitement, but part of me, calm, the part that didn't believe Cathy was really coming. Sure enough, though, she arrived on time, looked lovely in her red winter ankle boots, jeans, and jumper.

We hugged each other; I held her for a while, tightly and prolonged, wanting to savour that moment, as reality was hard to swallow. Elation, and so exuberant, I felt great; my body was full of warm, joyous emotions.

"It's good to see you, Cathy."

"You too Paul, you didn't believe I'd come, did you?"

"I can't believe you're here; you came all that way. I've missed you, Cathy!" as we ease our embrace and hold hands.

My family liked Cathy, pleasantly surprised at her prettiness, her bubbly persona, charm, and friendly nature. Cathy and I were so happy – and our first fabulous night was here – my wildest hopes fulfilled, desires quenched; I wasn't alone.

We knew what was inevitable; love struck, smitten teenagers with a crush. Now, the crush would expand, as the relationship entered additional dimensions, and bridge new boundaries. Soon we'd progress to lovers in a full sense.

The long and eventful day, far from over, as we eagerly walked upstairs. The romantic orange glow of my radiant heater as I pulled back the bedcovers and Cathy and I lay on the bed. Together, in a state of hypnosis, rapturous disbelief as we kissed, held each other.

Such a contrast to when we met in Scotland: no prying eyes or anxieties. No risk of being caught and heightened excitement, more relaxed, ardent. Two smitten lovers that had chosen each other and filled with desire; the same things on their minds.

Passionate kissing ensued as we undressed. Explored each other's body's with our hands.

Ecstatic, overwhelmed with emotions as we became entwined. Ever closer in each other's arms, becoming one! Flesh against flesh, driven wild by the closeness and tingling sensations. As one, and longing-looks — could she read my mind?

"At last... we're together," I said. Our tongues played and teased each other, scintillating kisses.

With every passing second, our activities increased, both with intensity and drive. In perfect harmony, entwined with rapturous desires and yearnings, as we kissed. Ever more intense with thrusts of energy, as sheer passion flowed between us; I gasped with glee. "Oh yes, you're bloody lovely. Are you enjoying yourself?"

She didn't respond in words; breathed deeper and ever faster. Marvellous, electrifying, in perfect time, like a dream, as I quivered with delight and our passions heightened, much to our satisfaction and our pleasure.

We'd both waited so long. I wallowed in the fact Cathy was mine at last. The one for me, had to be, considering the high-stakes emotional gamble I'd reluctantly made; she'd chosen me from everyone else!

I woke up with a superb feeling of elation entirely because of having Cathy, my life love, next to me; the first I woke with too, wonderful.

The day began in a gentle embrace, together. It was a brand-new, bright morning, with Cathy for company, by ourselves, person to person, body to body, in my domain. Ready to share life

– together as a couple – and do lots of fun things.

I ran downstairs, placed a 12-inch record on the stereo turntable, turned the sound up high, amplifying the crackle of dust as I ran upstairs and showered as Level 42, *Something About You,* played. And, Cathy, laughed in disbelief at the top of the stairs.

The song summed up that era. How I felt and would always remind me of Cathy, the mutual excitement, the start of an exciting first day together.

That day, like a prize peacock, I took my bird. My companion, proudly around town as I showed her the sights of Wolverhampton.

We walked hand in hand, window shopping, gazing at items in enormous glass-fronted stores whilst talking and being jovial, but couldn't imagine what was about to transpire, the terrible development about to unfurl.

In the shopping centre whilst Cathy and I walked along, toward Beatties, I suddenly and cunningly release my grip on Cathy's hand in a futile attempt to ease any pain that I may soon feel as I recognised two figures in the distance.

Alas, upon a sorrowful gaze, my heart races; flutters, yet I didn't utter a word or sound as I lower my head, stare at the floor ahead of me; I want to open up and swallow me.

Dreadful silence… *No, and sheer chance*, and it's wonderful to see Debbie and her mother; upon my sorrowful glance, over at the people ordained to pass by us on the opposite side of the shopping alley and amazingly caught Debbie's eye; she looked down and so did I, cheerful, smiling, animated, then less so.

I wanted to rush over, say sorry, but couldn't. Despite disgust with myself, despised as the lowest form of life on Earth. It all felt so embarrassing with no comfort; our paths set.

Debbie looked so beautiful, and sadly, so forlorn. I wished the impossible, to turn back time, nor make the callous call. So that I was still with Debbie. Alas, all chances of making up were now hopeless, irreconcilable.

I would never forget the painful, cruel, crazy awkwardness of that encounter with destiny; as though I had received a sharp pinch that bought a dawning comparison, as I passed and upon feeling the hurt. A lady I knew as quiet, loving, virtuously forgiving in contrast to bubbly vanity, fiery, exciting and untameable, yet both beautiful in distinct ways.

Only when a safe distance was between us, I disclosed to Cathy that Debbie had passed us. I feared if I had have told Cathy we were about to pass Debbie. She may have gone over, gloated or said something malicious or even worse.

She asked, "Why didn't you tell me?" I didn't answer, but knew why. I did not wish to cause any more hurt, and was quiet all day from then on, uneasy, disturbed by my actions, the diabolical way I had treated Debbie, but I had made my choice.

New Year's Eve 1985 would soon be upon us. Cathy and I were looking forward to spending it together. Eager to show Cathy more suburban nightlife than in Scotland and proud in my best pink shirt and second-hand blue jacket from Bedduz.

And, to be with Cathy, as we met my cousin, Dava, and got the bus in Bilston. Sat upstairs at the front for the most scenic view.

Streetlights and colourful Christmas lights added to our excitement as we buzzed in anticipation of a brilliant night, intending to celebrate New Year in style at Cinders in Willenhall.

Prior to our imminent arrival, I became increasingly nervous about gaining admission. As we waited in the fast-dwindling queue, I heard, "Dava." It was one of our older friends, Gilly.

I reluctantly introduced Cathy as we neared the entrance, not wanting to draw the attention of eagle-eyed bouncers, and annoyed by our friend's sudden appearance. "Walk with me," he said, and gesticulated it would be wiser as he looked older. *No way, go away Gilly, Cathy's with me, but appreciative of a friend's support.*

My worst fears came true as the bouncer allowed Gilly and Cathy into the nightclub, but turned Dava and me away. Gilly, the toolbox of spanners in the works.

It all happened so fast! Dejected because of my baby-face, I lived up to my nickname, Embryo! We were dismayed, to put it mildly. Still, we waited 15 minutes in the freezing cold. Dismay and frustration mixed with confusion as Cathy didn't come out.

Why hasn't she emerged from the club? Cathy's with our friend she's just met, not me!

Distraught with disbelief as I realise the inevitable and feel torn. Although I wished to, we couldn't wait around all night. Especially on New Year's Eve, so with reluctance, we travelled back to Bilston on the bus.

Willenhall's not that special as we consoled ourselves, embraced the hope of getting into Harry's, the next best place to Cinders. To enjoy the festivities closer to home, in more familiar territory, but I was like a lost sheep, without Cathy.

We gained entry; drank a few pints of beer for celebration purposes. *Wish I'd brought Cathy here. Why didn't I stick to my hometown?*

My mind was on Cathy. I couldn't rouse myself into enjoying the festive frivolity and merriment, despite the presence of other attractive girls; plenty alcohol, too.

The imminent countdown to the chimes of Big Ben, fast approaching and 1985, soon consigned to history. It wasn't right being separated by a time warp in different towns. Cathy should have been with me, in my arms and slow, dancing, holding hands and her lips upon mine, kissing me at midnight.

We left the club at 2am, revellers into the frosty night; first day of a brand-new year. Urgency in my step, as I strode home briskly, escalating procrastination with constant anxious expectation in my mind, visions of Cathy on my doorstep. Expectation that ominously changed to hope and jaded optimism as I came ever closer to home.

Soon, my expectation and hope turned to concern, bewilderment mixed with a strange type of anger and worry. I turned the corner and saw our front door; Cathy wasn't there waiting. Where was she? Why didn't she leave the club?

I sat, worried and in procrastination, on the sofa, with the light switched on, lost in thoughts. Awaiting a knock on the door or phone call, and at 4.30am the phone rang.

"Paul, I'm lost," Cathy said. Mumbling, as if she was cold or unsure as she described her surroundings and what she could see.

I knew precisely where she was and rushed outside to get my bike from the garage. Raced over to Wolverhampton as fast as I could; I wanted a lot of answers and to rescue my damsel in distress.

Time of the essence and I covered the two-and-a-half miles from Bilston to Wolverhampton in about seven minutes, against a bitter wind, and spotted Cathy the instant I arrived at the Mander Centre, standing by a bench.

She didn't seem distressed, in fact somewhat nonchalant, offish, as she spoke with apprehension and disturbingly, didn't seem at all upset about not being with me for the strike of Big Ben.

I expected a warmer, more affectionate greeting, as Cathy sat on my bike saddle and I turned the pedals, although upset, but contented to find her.

The ride home wouldn't be easy. We were hastily away, venturing into the freezing, bitter cold, the roads deserted and white with untouched, glistening, white frost.

Upon arrival at home, eager for answers to puzzling questions, "I've waited here until after 4am in the morning for you, I've sat here worried, where have you been all night and why didn't you come away from the club, Cathy?"

"Oh, I went in. Thought you were behind me, or in there somewhere, so I brought a drink! It was packed out, you know."

"I wasn't in there. Didn't you realise I wasn't behind you? Or didn't you bother to look?"

"As soon as I realised you weren't in there, I left the club and started walking. I was lost, Paul!" But things just didn't seem to add up, and as I expressed doubts, she started to cry.

Sadly, I wondered how real the tears were, or was I just paranoid? Real tears, but the mechanism that produced them in question: did they truly emanate from the heart? Elements of distrust and concern; was I just a bit crazy, and needlessly insecure?

Still, it was a new year; new start, and at least Cathy's here with me, in my embrace and soon my bed. We soon made up, despite being apart for the night's festivities.

Reunited, kissed and made up, and delighted. A lovely lady with me, next to me, entwined on that first morning of 1986. In bed together, her bodily flesh, cold, but wonderful against my warm skin as she shivered with a mixture of cold and excitement.

And, was unusually quiet but tired.

"Aww, you're cold,… you shouldn't have been out so late; I'll warm you up."

What a wry and sexy smile and a deep, firm kiss from frigid lips. Still, there were ominous thoughts in my mind I dared not entertain. Something seemed missing from the relationship. The closeness, sadly, becoming increasingly more like a gulf. As one, but apart in different worlds.

Like north and south poles of two magnets being held together and then dislodge, to become free, and further and further apart; into different orbits.

Neither of us were bubbly or full of frivolity any more, and while suspicion tinged with a sour taste had intangibly muddied the once pure amiability and affection exuded by Cathy and I.

A day or two later, we went to a party at a friend's house, the same friend who joined us on New Year's Eve. A brilliant party, and heavy drinking, as expected, and honoured. Proud as I introduced the belle of the ball; elated to be with her.

But I couldn't stay with her every second. I chatted in the hallway, in front of the obscured glass living room door; party in full swing as class tunes played and I burst into the room. Rage – fury filled my entire body; my temperament, so hostile, protective, like a primitive caveman without his club.

So certain Cathy was kissing someone. Brimming pride and happiness to incensed rage, shaken by an earthquake of devastation.

Did I want Cathy to stay in my own proverbial cave, to satisfy my every whim, to provide pleasure and to quench all desires?

I needed to fight the person I thought was kissing her and went outside for a fight, whilst exchanging verbal abuse. "You're mad," he said, as Gilly came out, too, blocked a fist from hitting me, de-escalating the situation.

I despised anyone who presented a threat to my happiness and added a further wedge between Cathy and me. At least now I had proof of Cathy's insincerity; her loose feelings for me!

Cathy followed as I left the party; I seethed with anger. "That's the final straw, you've shown what you're really like at long last... a lying cow!... You've never liked me, it's just been total bullshit all the way along." As I walked ahead fast.

"Wait, I can explain Paul."

"Don't fucking bother, I saw you snogging someone else! I'm not stupid![2] Who knows what you'd have got up to without me there! Go back to the party... I'm going home."

I walked away from Cathy at quite a pace, through the garages toward Central Avenue. She followed, denying all-action of infidelity and wrongdoing, but I had seen her with my own eyes through the glass door.

In hindsight, though, perhaps, I was unreasonable — too possessive. Besides, she may have just wanted fun, a novel fling in a novel land with a novel Englishman. Maybe I was just paranoid, insecure, but could I have been mistaken?

I didn't own her! Though, putting myself in the same situation, I wonder what I would have done? I did the same; kissed another in a foreign land! Gambling with hearts, and my heart breaking, as deserved.

What a strange night, fraught with emotions, but we still shared the same bed. Tensions calmed, and fantastic having the belle of the ball in my arms, still with me in the flesh.

We made up yet again and heightened passions didn't seem at all crude; I adored her no matter what she did. She was still fantastic in my eyes. Strange, I knew it would be our last time!

A couple of days later, Cathy departed for Scotland. Sorrow embedded in my heart as we gave each other a prolonged hug, for one last time. The hug was not long enough. Why couldn't I hold on to her forever, as I felt that within my heart? As though nothing could wrench us apart. But, we did part!

I had lost that high-stakes gamble that perhaps never should have been.

---

2. Was my behaviour a shoddy manifestation of an Obsessive Compulsive Disorder (OCD) and paranoia? Maybe I messed up, as I argued, made a fuss!

"You can come up to Scotland to see me, Paul." Cathy said tearfully as we watched the train approach in the distance.

I became quite sad, melancholic, as I watched her walk away and step onto the train. She waved and smiled from a carriage window and the train left, disappeared in the distance. *How can I ever afford the train fare to visit Cathy on my meagre Youth Training Scheme wage?*

Cathy must have liked me very much. Maybe more, to venture to England. Perhaps I simply expected too much, built my hopes too high. We had to live and experience — apart. Alas, events didn't reflect a fairy-tale ending!

I'd adoringly watched that lovely lass in my bedroom, drawing hearts and doodles on a sheet of paper. Ascribing the words "Cathy loves Paul". Words and names inside hearts embellished with Cupid's arrows.

Touching gestures, like a dream, romantic, ego boosting delight, and were true in those moments, the game of love, but toying with affection and feelings.

Maybe we were just unsuited. She also wrote Scottish star football player's names on the paper; she loved football. Both so different – principles, ideas, fun, frolics – versus everlasting romance, yet, perhaps I wanted and asked for the same.

That unforgettable kiss, our hearts became entwined beneath the stars and moon in such an incredible, romantic place, that bridge, and enchanted country lane; how could it not be everlasting? Or that there could be any other?

Still, Cathy was the first I lived with, and woke up beside. No-one had stayed with me before, and she'd travelled so far.

Such unforgettable, precious memories and experiences that if a price tag could be placed, I'd owe her a lot! I learnt a lot from that experience: wiser to some female traits and emotional afflictions of the heart.

To trust someone so early on is a dangerous, high-stakes gamble. Letting go of the things I have for a moment of excitement, foolish. Betrayed loyalty for heartache.

Some may say I made the wrong choice. Beguiled and stunned

by Cathy's charms; falling for her and devoted, but Cathy didn't seem true, at least not true for me, and lived so far away. Debbie, so lovely, nearer, and even gave me a second chance.

Maybe she'd have been the one for a while, perhaps forever. Alas, I had blown all chances. I didn't deserve her. I had chosen short-term fun, exciting frolics, revelled my larkish antics.

That decision would play on my mind in ways I couldn't imagine as I learned the everlasting romance I yearned; hoped for was elusive, perhaps non-existent.

I ventured on a changed character. Still tenacious, but more tentative and less sensitive, more whimsical; and knew not to open my heart so readily as emotions hurt.

I drank more, reluctantly returned to the social scene of the street, and looked forward to a holiday in the summer.

Cathy and I didn't meet again, but reminiscing about such times inspired me to adapt, try harder, be bolder and to travel as I hadn't before, or had the opportunity.

And, I remembered and missed so many things while tormented by realisations of the past, my earlier existence. So different now, but I still hoped for romance.

31.

THE SILKEN WEB

*P*en-friends, writing, the noisy bars and drink, distracting pastimes allowed escape, but I often thought of Cathy, and others from a different era. I knew it'd be virtually impossible to meet anyone in the places I used to visit. It wasn't all doom and gloom as I rediscovered 80s music.

I danced in my new jazzy orange wheelchair at Cheeky Monkey at Wolverhampton's Civic Hall as Depeche Mode, *Just Can't Get Enough*, played. In front of a massive loudspeaker, blasting sound, as I enjoyed the vibes.

And, the internet expanded my horizons and provided an even more powerful means of escape. It amazed me to be in extra dimensions, cyberspace, as I became absorbed. I was oblivious to the hold of those silken strands of that intricate World Wide Web.

Whilst addicted to instant chat, regardless of geographic boundary, and the intensifying fantasy, it seemed the only way.

Tina's deceit closed my heart to English women. I became less trusting, not as forthright in pursuing romance.

There were more dashed hopes, unfulfilled promises, and desires, but I returned with a hardened heart, back to the allures of cyberspace, despite the inexorable march of time.

I didn't imagine my heart would ever open again until I met Cherri online and experienced a strange attraction, feelings of love like never before. Cherri was so sweet and opened my heart after saying she'd take good care of it; never break it!

I sat at my computer, yearning, addicted and infatuated, hoping to see that name light up on the messenger. When not chatting, we exchanged romantic emails, some erotic, describing desires and dreams that were so real.

My writing encompassed a new goal, charm, seduce, beguile and please as lovers in cyberspace. Disregarding the void between — continents and oceans, vast gulfs didn't matter, only the moments. Passion, and mutually giving our all as there was nothing else; the union of minds and souls.

Cherri was married but unhappy, she said in chats as she bared her soul. Her dream, to be with me, marry me, and she'd put an ad in the local paper declaring her love and telling other girls to keep their hands off me. I was hers. She wanted me and only me to herself.

I soon shared that same dream and believed one day we would be together some way or somehow! There could be no other outcome.

Then, an interruption, as we chat, the words appear on screen, "Say goodbye to Cherri."

"No, never. Who is this?"

"Cherri's husband, and I am disconnecting this computer."

The pleas for reason went ignored and my heart breaks as Cherri disappears, goes offline. How noble of him, but unfair; I should have been the rescuer, the valiant saviour of that beautiful lady who'd won my heart, and me forever.

Entwined hearts — wrenched apart. That cruel man didn't have her heart. I did. *My sweet Cherri will be back soon. She'll find a way.* I looked at Cherri every day, that one photo I had, long black hair, kneeling, holding a large pumpkin in a field.

A prize pumpkin on a farm, perhaps, I didn't know. That one photo, the emails, the chats, many hours banked for eternal bliss that would never transpire, at least not from that path.

A trampled path of no return with immense brambles, a continent thick, and an ocean gulf between us. The evil king had the power to trap and keep her, but her heart was mine. I waited hours, days, weeks, months... My internet love didn't return. Hopelessly lost, but found. Was she rescued from me or I from her?

There was Cherri, then Norine, then Kirsty, and such powerful feelings and attraction. Before Tracey, Julie, and others, I chatted with all of them at once in December 1998.

No, forget them! Kirsty was the one! Intense emotions, and declarations of love. Or was it Tracey as Dad drove me many miles to Colchester? Alas, more hurt and false promises.

In the last years and months of the millennium, I chatted with friends online. Mainly women, including a girl from Texas, called Tiffany, who I got to know well. An Englishman had broken her heart, declared his love, and said he'd visit but never did.

Hey, I wasn't a typical Englishman. That brush couldn't tarnish me, although I had experienced similar let downs and heartache, but remained optimistic, perhaps as I considered this to be my only route to romance. Tiffany, though, considered the internet as fantasy. Saying we'd never meet! Was this a challenge?

Restoring this woman's faith and proving a point? Why not? Visiting America had been a lifetime ambition since I watched Champion The Wonder Horse, Six Million Dollar Man, and Hawaii Five-5-0 on TV, as a kid.

I dreamed of experiencing the lifestyle, the fast cars and seduced by the NASA space programme, Cape Canaveral, the link to space and chicks and American accents.

But, all of my adventures were mere memories of my able-bodied existence. Of before my head injury, when radical and bold. Why was I contemplating such a crazy idea?

Now, as a wheelchair user with speech problems and other impairments, getting to and staying in America posed many practical problems. Besides my care needs and meticulous plans, I'd need lots of help and support for any chance of fruition.

From a negative, pessimistic viewpoint, the venture would be beyond the realm of possibility. Knowing this made me more determined to prove the opposite and the cynics wrong, regardless of how wise they were and nagging feelings they were right.

I had been through so much, ever wiser, resilient from arduous times. But grander, bolder aspirations loomed. Time to put the disappointments of my Colchester visit and flawed internet romances behind me, and move on from experiences of English women.

My philosophy became a new millennium, new ambitions.

As the year 2000 arrived, I formulated plans for a fabulous and intrepid adventure. Still, going to the travel agents was scary, despite scaling back my plans. Apprehensiveness, knowing it would be the first step of a daring adventure.

My dad implored me not to book the tickets. "No, don't go in," he said several times, fuelled my resolve. Others said I was a fool contemplating such plans, let alone embarking on that venture. I had to try, although daunted and fearful, as I booked the airline tickets, relished the adventure with boldness, and hoped to return.

I arranged and planned as best I could and tried to prepare my mind for the epic adventure whilst hoping I could prove I wasn't a fool, just maybe crazy. The long-awaited day had arrived, the clock ticking and a flight to catch.

My mind, dizzy, racing with apprehension and anticipation, trying to suppress escalating nervousness as we arrived early at Birmingham International Airport only to learn of a two and half hour flight delay.

Ever more anxious: *I'll miss the second flight*. What a big spanner in the works! All checked in, bags checked and cases loaded on the plane.

Frantic with nervous-excitement as I tried not to ponder the forthcoming choice. Stay or fly?

The sight of huge black-and-white numbers, the same as the anniversary of my birth, was a sign and I considered being born on Friday 13th a special honour. I was on the right path; had to try to not fear leaving Bilston! Yet going much further, bold, but I hoped not foolish.

So, I departed from gate 13. Said farewells to Mom and Dad. I felt drawn to America, knowing that deep in my heart of hearts, I must relish and accept the adventure. What a challenge it was, but the set of events leading to that point. Uncanny and soul-embracing, esoteric, as if guided.

As I'm transferred and strapped into the aisle chair, ha, no escape, backing out or turning back now; daring to leave Bilston, that place I had always been so reluctant to leave.

My fate and total trust were in the laps of the airline staff, others and even higher powers. Those aisle chairs were narrow and rickety, but the staff soon seated me in the left seat of a large middle row seat on the Boeing® 737®.

Yes, and friendly, smart airline staff greeted me to add to the excitement about the takeoff and feeling the G-forces.

As the plane accelerated, I thought of Newton's laws of motion, physics, and formulas in my head, classical and relativistic. Speed, wow, exhilarating as the plane's front wheel lifted, and we became airborne at 10.50am.

A gigantic leap of faith, but I was melancholy, leaving my parents at gate 13. A lump came in my throat. Were they watching their son ascend and disappear over the horizon on that huge plane?

It was wonderful to be out of my wheelchair as an airline passenger. Among seasoned travellers, as the chatter and American accents confirmed the reality. *Few will know I have disabilities until I speak.*

A friendly stewardess wheels the drinks trolley. "Drinks, sir?"

"Err, Chardonnay, please," said the man to my left.

"Alrighty." As the drink she opened, fizzed with bubbles, quick and efficient. She'd done that 1,000,000 times. And I liked her cool American accent.

It's my turn soon, and anxious. *Will my words come out?*

"Drinks, sir?"

Trying to hide nervousness, "Could I have a Chardonnay please and a straw?"

"Certainly, sir." *That's blew my cover as I lowered my mouth to the straw.*

"I've re-scheduled your flight for you," the air steward said as they walked past. *Impressive, and an enjoyable flight. Next stop, America, and we'll soon be over the Atlantic. My first intercontinental flight, first ocean crossing.* As I sat, surrounded by fellow passengers. And, certain I'm the only one beginning an adventure.

Disappointed, that first flight had to end. *Yes, I've made it to America, landed at Chicago O'Hare International Airport; I might not see these super-kind airline staff again.*

Help there, as arranged, tremendous. As I'm transferred into my unfolded wheelchair by the plane door, and helped with my bag, and suitcase transferred onto the next plane.

Great to be at that huge, fantastic airport, despite anxious moments and delays. *Hope I don't miss my next flight to Dallas.*

Tired, nervously excited, *Will the staff understand my strange accent and speech?* I tried to stay calm and explained my concerns. Got it sorted with the helper's support, although Bulgarian, not a native English speaker. We still communicated.

That kind lady, helper, made sure I reached the next departure gate. *A train inside the airport, similar to our Midland Metro at Bilston!* I couldn't believe it as the helper pushed me onto the level-access train and I felt the tremendous heat.

Awestruck by the airport's size (apparently the largest in the world until Atlanta expanded for the Olympics), as she helped me into a room.

"The flight leaves soon. They're boarding now. You must go to the gate," the airline desk staff said.

And, greeted by an agitated, abrupt air stewardess at the plane door, who said to my helper. "Why isn't the wheelchair tagged? It needs a tag!" My great and friendly helper, silent as if scolded by a superior, awkwardness; she looked sad as I waited to board the plane.

It was difficult with the noise of the jet engines. Somehow, I explained that on the first flight, a flight attendant put my chair on board the plane. "OK, it can come on board here, then." *Whew,* at last, as staff rushed around with schedules to meet.

Super staff and a plane to match, a sleek, more compact jet and quick, thrilling speed compared to the earlier flights.

The sun, the heat, yes, I am in America and on my second flight. Easier than catching buses in the UK, although bizarrely, I hadn't been on a bus in England since becoming a wheelchair user.

About 90 minutes later, we arrived in Dallas, plenty of time to get to my departure gate. I hoped to relax, but an ultra-cool black guy approached in what appeared to be an open-top golf buggy and said, "I'm here to get you to your next gate. Where are you from?"

Nice, but slightly annoyed at first as another lovely flight attendant strolled toward me and was about to chat. I was about to tell her about my adventure, but he moved in to aid my plight and impress her. "England."

"Oh, you've travelled a long way. I'm from Nigeria…" that slick charmer said as he rolled out a ramp from the rear of that strange vehicle and wheeled me up onto the platform as the lady passed, smiled, and walked into the distance.

"OK, relax… I'll get you to your departure gate."

Surprised by the buggy's speed, I held the handrail in front of me. The breeze and sights, as we pass many gates. *Dallas is huge, too; have we gone past my departure gate by now?* The buggy slows, and I hear, "We're here."

Relieved to be on schedule, with my next takeoff, imminent, ever closer to my long-awaited destination. I appreciated the swift and exhilarating ride in a vehicle I couldn't believe existed. I wouldn't forget it, or the cool guy.

One more flight to Lubbock, West Texas. I felt so achy, tired and sore, overwhelmed… *Soon time for my flight*, as I sat watching the orange LED signs, fascinated by placenames such as Abilene and Amarillo. *That stewardess may have pushed me here by now. We could have shopped, ate, or drank at a bar or café.*

The next helper was very nice, polite as she pushed my chair outside, presenting a dark-blue Texan sky, beyond bright, white aircraft lights.

It was dusk as they pushed me along, venturing into the open air and Texan soil. Overwhelmed, as I'm welcomed by a thick blanket of warm air, a wall of heat; felt so good… I laughed as a mobile staircase moved into place.

That third flight across Texas was relatively short from Dallas Fort Worth to Lubbock West Texas on a a plane with propellers. Much smaller than the earlier airplanes, but still big as I sat, overawed with triumph.

Euphoric solace as the engines started and the cabin lights

dimmed. Success as I made it, well, nearly, despite feeling totally drained, achy, and sore by that stage.

The propellers, noisier than the earlier jets, but surprising speed as the lights dimmed. Anxious about toilet stops and dehydration, although mostly in air-conditioned cabins, I hadn't drank much on a hot day. So, I enjoyed the chilled drinks on the last flight into the black night sky.

I struggled to rest my mind, compose myself as I recapped the day's events, looked at my watch. *My watch is now six hours behind the UK. How many hours has this epic journey taken so far?* Trying to think, but so tired, energy sapped; an ultimate endurance test, before getting to West Texas.

Exhausted after nearly an entire day of flying, but relieved as Tiffany and her family met me at Lubbock International Airport. They travelled to meet me. It wasn't mere fantasy. Tiffany was shorter than I imagined, and her mom tall.

"Oh Paulie, it's so good to see you. How was your journey? All those delays? The airline called us," said Shelda in a lovely southern accent. Tiffany was delighted to see me; I'd arrived safe, and a firm handshake and a warm greeting from Marvin, who was quieter.

The warm night excited me as we left the airport building, into a huge, deserted car park and soon by a smart, shiny black van, like I had seen in American movies.

"Nice van,... I have been flying for so long." I said as I position my chair.

"Oh, Paulie, take your time. You tell us how to help you!" Shelda said. My legs were stiff, achy, and tired, but we were soon on the road to Lubbock and at Tiffany's house.

Marvin parked in a driveway in front of a garage, beside a lawn. Front door to the right to an open-plan house, as Tiffany helps me into a hall, kitchen opposite, overlooking a large lounge leading to a corridor and adjoining bedrooms. *I need to rest and sleep. Will these lovely people I've just met be able to help me into bed?*

Peculiarly, I felt safe and calm as Shelda and Tiffany helped me into a double bed, tucked me in; tired, but comfortable. Relieved as the lights went out, knowing I could sleep.

"Paulie. Don't worry about anything. If you need anything, just holler. We're only down the hall. And Tiffany's across the way. In the next room," Shelda said.

The door was closed, darkness and silence except for the hypnotic whir of a large ceiling fan and felt the gentle, cooling breeze on my face. Beautiful, peaceful wind chimes with a magical tranquillizing effect. *Where am I? I've made it, but am I really here?*

So weary, I slept soundly and felt at ease. *Is this a vivid dream? Tomorrow, I'll know, as I wake, experience reality. Tonight is too short, but the adventure will begin. Savour these tranquil moments.*

I expected Texas to be swelteringly hot. A powerful sun beaming in cloudless-blue skies, but it was unusually overcast for the first couple of days, cool and rainy. They issued flood warnings on TV. The clouds soon blew over, it became hotter, and I was out in it all.

Tiffany was lovely and so were her parents, sister, niece, and brother-in-law. Shelda washed my clothes, prepared fantastic food for me, fed me well and made me so welcome. I got on well with Tiffany, too.

I appreciated Marvin's help, as he taught me about American money. He emptied many coins on the table from a plastic purse, moved each one with his index finger. "This is a nickel. It's five cents. A dime, that's 10 cents. These are quarters, 25 cents, a quarter of a dollar, same as five nickels."

"These small ones aren't worth much, one cent." Then similar guidance for the paper money, and Shelda referred to a billfo, slang for billfold, a wallet, called that as they fold dollar bills.

I loved staying at that wonderful place with wonderful people. It was like a dream; air-conditioning and the spinning ceiling fans in each room reminded me of Western cowboy films.

I was the strange outsider from way out of town. Yet, looked after as a loved son. Made so welcome; treated me like royalty. I ate like a king and given such delicious, fabulous foods, together around a family table. The warm sun made me feel even better. And, Tiffany and Shelda took me to a pizza place, as much pizza as you can eat for ($2.99 approx. £1.90). My ambitious mission: sample every type of pizza, even dessert pieces, chocolate topped, apple and cinnamon pizzas.

I'd never eaten so much in my entire-life. Fabulous food, plus free drinks, included in the price.

Other places amazed me, too: Drive-through pharmacy, drive-through banks, huge shopping malls and I bought a cool, blue tinted mirror pair of sunglasses from Walmart® and felt more the part as excitement built, because of an exciting excursion.

A trip to Dallas, planned beforehand, by email. I paid for an adjoining room for a weekend stay.

A thrilling prospect, more so after seeing the airport! How strange to return overland by van from West Texas as we set off on an overcast but warm Lubbock morning, the weekend before the Fourth of July. I sat upfront beside Marvin, who drove with Shelda and Tiffany in the back.

Excited, but wary, as I asked Marvin if I could open my window to experience desert-like heat and the wind.

"No, the van will get too hot and snakes may fly in." Soon after, as Marvin pulled into a lay-by, I experienced better. He and Shelda knew how much I liked the sun and the heat.

Pleased, they both held my arms and helped me to walk beside the highway on the way to Dallas. The heat overpowering, the sky, crystal-blue with white wispy distant clouds, great, humbling scenery, flat all around and as far as the eye can see. Tiffany took my photo at that fantastic place.

We were still far from Dallas. That, as we neared; the highways became larger and wider, six lanes and Marvin's navigation through the maze gained even higher respect from me despite heated words for other drivers.

We arrived at the hotel late afternoon, the car door pillar and roof hot enough to fry 1,000 eggs a metre away from the van. The hotel foyer was much cooler and adorned with palm trees, in pots on cool, white marble floors.

Shelda and Tiffany checked in, the same time as a party of cheerleaders. *Is this heaven? Can life get any better than this?* As I waited in the foyer, and hadn't even seen the hotel room.

Excited as we ascended in a lift that opened onto a long-carpeted corridor leading to my hotel room. With a card swipe, my door opened. *A space-hatch, to out-of-this-world — this room's huge, 30ft long?* A grand view from the window at the far end, and a TV halfway along, past a second doorway. *Doubt I'll watch that.*

The hugest bed I had ever seen, in the corner, a king-size, and my own pristine white shower room.

"Paulie, don't worry. We're in the adjoining room, and the door's opposite the bed. If you need us, just holler," Shelda said in her sweet voice.

Swanky, but there was more. As soon as we unpacked, Tiffany mentioned the tub. We got changed and went further upstairs via the lift, intrigued, as we emerged onto a floor where there was a large hot tub.

The bubbling blue water looked so sublime and inviting, instilled excitement tinged with melancholy as I couldn't climb in and reflected on when I could swim. To my surprise, Marvin, and Shelda helped lift me, nervous as I entered, but I trusted them.

The warm water, the bubbles felt wonderful, as we sat in that hot tub. With Tiffany's and Shelda's arms around me, I never in my wildest dreams imagined such a kind family giving me precious experiences, unforgettable moments; in a hot tub in America, Dallas, and the night was young.

Back in my hotel room Tiffany, and Shelda helped me to shower. To my embarrassment, but I couldn't stop laughing. Tiffany laughed, too, and smiled at me in a way I'll never forget.

Incredible, so adorable, and that smile and eye contact conveyed 1,000 wonderful endearing messages in a nanosecond as my heart pounded.

For that instant, I saw beauty and soul; as one, connected for a fleeting but unforgettable moment. As if the stars in the skies twinkled their magical beams upon us and I doubt few humans had ever experienced in the whole of eternity.

Still swooning, as we left the hotel, in best attire, smart clothes on, ready to experience Dallas; at least I hoped I was. Naively, the extent of my knowledge of that place was limited to the TV series I watched as a kid, the tall glass-fronted skyscrapers, cowboys, ranches, and oil. Marvin drove us into Dallas.

It was about 5pm; still boiling hot, as Marvin parked in a pedestrian area. Being among police officers on bikes, wearing cycling shorts, white helmets, black shirts and in black sunglasses made me wary, but reassured, as we stopped nearby at a nice outdoor café, TGI Fridays®. There were so many people on the busy streets. So we sat outside, at the front.

Hungry, as we waited a while for our food. Marvin wasn't happy and grouched as a pigeon pooped on his shirt, making a splodge sound. "Better not moan anymore." Shelda said, as I parked my chair and we laughed.

But, I noticed two pairs of sexy, tanned legs, high heels, and short skin-tight minidresses on two attractive ladies, one in white, the other in pink neon. *Dare I stare, as I'm with excellent company, mustn't appear rude?*

Tiffany glanced up from her drink, glasses on nose. "They're hookers."

Flabbergasted, embarrassed. "No, really?" *I'm blushing. Did I look too long?*

It was a fabulous day, perfect, and still early. As after we ate, Tiffany pushed me in my wheelchair along a flat pedestrian area, deeper into Dallas. Past talented street performers, buskers, jugglers, unicycle riders, and masses of people. Tempting shops at both sides of the pedestrianised walkway, to window shop, taste the culture.

A heavy police presence and undercover cops evoked an instinctive sense: *Stay alert.* But I felt safe, as Shelda and Marvin walked on either side of us and Tiffany pushed me along slowly. So much to see. At the tail of the gentle slope were lots of nightclubs, a hotspot called The Alley.

Dazzling arrays of lights, music boomed from each nightclub as we passed. Exciting, and it's hotter than Lubbock. Enticed, I so wanted to enter one of those superb clubs. The nightlife, wild and wonderful, impressive, and delighted, as Tiffany stopped outside a nightclub door. "We're here now."

It was a surprise Tiffany planned as two tall, sturdy cowboys on the door, dressed in smart shoes, black shirts, and white Stetson hats, greeted us. After showing them our passports from the bag on my chair, one cowboy helped me into that extraordinary and magnificent nightclub.

We headed for the dancefloor. The women, the disco music as Tiffany, bought a cocktail with a colourful paper umbrella and, a beer for me, with a straw. The music, old, but with funky, cowboy themed songs. Laid Back, *White Horse* and other great songs, Madonna, *Into the Groove*. Tunes that made us want to dance.

Tiffany danced round my chair, smiling as I danced in my chair, moving the wheels back and forth. In time with the music as multicoloured lights flashed and lasers shone into dry ice smoke. That night ended too soon. Time flew by in that place.

The following day, we visited the Grapevine Mall and ate at the Rainforest Cafe®. Fantastic, but on the last day in Dallas, I loved a Mexican restaurant and my first Mexican food.

The day became even more memorable, as we visited a beautiful clock made of flowers with a state-symbolic lone star in the centre.

The highlight, though, visiting The Mustangs of Las Colinas. Majestic bronze statues of mustangs running across a stream.

Muscular, powerful, as wild and as free as the wind. Encapsulating a snapshot in time from a bygone age. The march of time and progress won through, but those statues symbolised a momentous reminder of the terrific power of nature, the wind, the air, sky, and earth.

A wonderful place that evoked memories, and I reminisced about a summer evening's walk up a hill in Wales with my second cousin Colin, Jade, and Paula from New Zealand.

Startled by "Neigh, neigh," as we near a grass field, at the side of the road and a horse appears between bushes and hedgerows. Its big eyes looking at us, head champing up and down disapprovingly, but excited to see us as we chuckled and spoke soothing words to the horse.

I remember watching the camper pull away and I ran up the stone steps to the road, waved as the camper passed. My eyes transfixed on it, as if in a trance, smaller and smaller as it ascended until it disappeared into the distance as I continued walking.

The sadness of reluctant farewells to our newly acquainted friends, crueller as I returned to the now vacant piece of grass. Discoloured from lack of rain and sunlight, tyre marks from where the camper had stood.

Melancholy and happy as I gazed at names, and a peculiar New Zealand placename, lovely handwriting on a precious piece of paper.

It seemed unreal. Still, I had ambitious plans, but dreams derided with time as I accepted the remoteness of the chance of making it to New Zealand; the other side of the world.

That was another life, long ago. Another world — I had surpassed those dreams. *Will Tiffany and her family watch me fly away*, and I knew I would find it hard to leave, envisaging a farewell as untimely dreading the goodbye.

I immensely enjoyed Dallas, other places in Texas and the food. The warm sunshine invigorated, made me feel healthier, before a long-anticipated and special day. An honour as we got into the car after dusk. Driving out into the black night enhanced the excitement and drama. It was the evening of the Fourth of July.

We reached an open space and parked overlooking Buffalo Springs Lake in the distance. A perfect spot to watch the fireworks, as the sky on our horizon became brilliantly illuminated. Red, green, brilliant white, blue flashes of light adorning a black sky and reflecting on the water, falling, then fading as more colours burst into life.

A truly spectacular fireworks display. Times like that, *I'm actually in America, in Texas, the Lone Star State*. And, it was great to sample a delicious beer of that same name; on a scorching day as Marvin and I sat in the beautiful garden.

Marvin pulled the ring-pull, opened a chilled can of Lone Star beer for me and one for him. That day was like paradise. So nice as we chatted about cars, and Marvin told me about his long drive from California in a fast car, as I enjoyed that cold, prize beer, smooth and refreshing.

On my last night in Texas, we sat in the garden together. There had been much talk and excitement about a wiener roast and Marvin had joked, teased me all week, "We'll roast your wiener for you." No idea what a wiener was, or what to expect.

The inner part of the firepit glowed with a flickering orange light and felt warm, relieved and cosy as it roasted wieners, sausages. Lapping and dancing flames spewed black, then white, grey wispy smoke that ascended toward the stars in the clear black night sky.

The flame of the yellow citronella candle perfectly matched the ambience and suited the melancholy mood, as I savoured my last ever-dwindling hours in Texas. I'd dearly miss everyone, but not the mosquitoes that got me, caused the inflamed lump on my arm.

I loved Texas, the special people I met and stayed with and hoped to return one day, or that those I visited may visit me. Chuffed, I planned that trip, a daring escapade to prove a point, and to have restored Tiffany's faith regarding the Englishman who never visited.

Accomplishment of that part of my mission proved the internet isn't just fantasy. Reality can arise from fantasy; emotions I couldn't have imagined. But I didn't expect to experience love. Or how wonderful the family would be; Tiffany and her parents looked after me like their own.

They were so kind to me, experiences and heart-touching moments, forged special bonds in a special place. Unforgettable, and I'd remember sharing a Lone Star beer on that hot sunny day in a delightful garden with splendid company. Most of all, I'd miss the southern drawl.

The next part of my adventure, imminent, but I loved Texas, I felt at home there and didn't want to leave, although I had dreamed of visiting the next destination. Another flight from Lubbock to San Francisco, North California, on a superb plane.

On arrival at San Francisco International Airport, again in

awe of such a huge airport, but I was eventually greeted in the arrivals lounge.

"Hi you must be Paul. I'm Laura's dad. May I take you downstairs in the elevator? The car's on the lower floor." In a deep, slow, certain American accent. The lift descended, and the doors opened onto an underground car park.

He pushed me from the elevator and turned. I saw the metal frame of a wheelchair, open-toed sandals and two white legs. I peeked up and saw straggly, strawberry blonde hair and two huge delighted eyes. "It's lovely to meet you, Paul," said Laura.

A tall lady introduced herself. "Hi Paul, I'm Laura's mom. How was your flight?"

Great, but delayed," as I saw the dark-red adapted van, I recognised from pictures Laura had sent.

The whir of an electric motor as Laura's dad activated the motorised ramp that slid from the opened, side doors of the van, retracted the folding ramps with a metallic clonk on the tarmac.

Then helped into the backseat, followed by Laura, who sat next to me. We were soon on our way.

Ventured upward from the underground into daylight. Onto the city roads of San Francisco and pleased to have arrived in another state, but overwhelmed at the change of location.

And, spectacular to travel across the Golden Gate Bridge, but my heart, still in Texas as Laura's dad said, "There's Alcatraz, Paul, across the bay."

Strange to see something I'd seen on TV. Surprised, too, the top of the bridge being obscured by fog; weird. Soon we were heading north on the freeway toward Eureka.

But uneasy, as Laura sat close; I leaned against a pillow on the window, pretending to sleep. "Oh, you must be tired, dear," Laura said.

I became as settled as I could be on that journey, although the feelings within changed as adrenaline and initial excitement dissipated. My stomach felt empty, my heart fluttered, and like a fractured jug letting water out. My heart did the same.

Trying to hold back the tears, as they welled up, accumulated as I stared out of the window. At the scenery, road signs on highways, and thought of Texas, but I felt bad, ungrateful, selfish. *Get a grip, I'm still in America.*

A couple of hours into the journey, there was a surprise, an unexpected stop. "We're in Santa Rosa, Paul," Laura said. Wow, the scenery: sporty opened topped cars cruising the streets with music blasting, nice shops and high-class girls in smart attire.

Very exciting and more at ease to visit my second, ever Mexican restaurant. Sat in that slick place. Studying the menu, as the waiter approached, asked if we'd like any drinks?

"I've heard you like beer, Paul?" said Laura's dad.

"Oh, yes."

"Well, how about a California blonde? It's a smooth beer."

"OK, thanks" as I chose a second beer.

Laura's parents seemed nice, friendly as hosts. But I didn't try to live up to any preconceived expectations as I attempted to socialise and enjoy the meal, the company.

Excitement as we ventured into secluded forest areas of North California and alongside the setting sun. Darkness, my fate is in the hands of my hosts. I tried not to contemplate sinister thoughts. *Where am I being taken?*

As the green scenery faded to blackness, I stared and thought of another place. A place back home, many ventured. Were the forests like the Fozza?

I missed England and Texas. So many trees around us, as I fixated on the bright white light from the headlights piercing a cloak of pitch-black darkness, illuminating the grey tarmac roads between the high trees.

I fought sleep, but succumbed as the sound of an automated garage door opener woke me. We'd arrived in a quiet suburb of Fortuna, Eureka, after six hours, but I still wondered where I was and if I'd ever return home?

The door opened onto a large, smart open-plan room, TV on the right and beanbag cushions. A light-coloured cane chair in front, and by the window a computer desk with computer beside a large, long kitchen. From the kitchen, patio doors opened onto a patio and garden at the rear.

But, startled; wide awake as a cat, as big as a dog, sped across my path, growled as it broke the sound barrier and darted up the cat pole. *I must keep my bedroom door shut.*

Laura teased, "The carer who'll be here in the morning is lovely; looks like Britney Spears, 18, too." Gulp. *Will I be able to even speak when I wake and meet her? The bed is high. We may end up on the floor.*

Trust the trained carers, stay calm, have faith. Anxious, but I slept well. Bright light rays oozed from the edges of the window blind and Laura's and the carer's voice woke me. Unusual, nothing like the southern drawl I grew fond of and missed, as my heart raced.

I hope my words will come out. The door opened and a lovely carer greeted me after she demonstrated how to open the window blind with the remote-control. Nice to meet a friendly native, a slim blonde with highlighted hair, friendly, not a musician.

So, there I was in North California, on a new estate within a quiet area near a small town, a six-hour drive north of San Francisco. Somewhere by the Pacific Ocean, but in the middle of nowhere, surrounded by mountains and tall trees in dense forests.

A spectacular panoramic view, lush green forests, from the front door not as eerie as I feared the previous night another world. It was too far from Texas, and home. I felt isolated, stranded, extraordinarily uneasy.

Had to be on my guard, as Laura and I didn't get on; the situation seemed difficult. Was I just paranoid? Tensions rose to the extent I thought I had to leave. What an awkward situation! Still, I chatted with online friends. And, I could imagine living in a similar house to Laura's, in an idyllic location. *I'd like to live in America, somewhere hot, Texas!* It was a dream.

After a while, I became used to America and California. And the carers, Lisa, and Cecelia, who came daily. We talked about lots of things. Often laughed, particularly with Cecelia. She was great, on a similar wavelength.

Despite becoming accustomed to that place, I missed England

and my family, Mom, and Dad, even though he moaned and pestered me daily to get his old 1980 Ford® Cortina back on the road.

I worried about my family worrying about me, and maybe they were right, to class my adventure, as foolish. But I understood their concerns and worries. I missed my family, too, and my extended family in Texas.

Laura wasn't easy to live with, and likewise. The female I'd written to, chatted with, exchanged emails with online for so long seemed worlds apart from the person I met in reality, and was now staying with as a temporary cohabitant. Perhaps Tiffany was right about fantasy.

I learnt a lot about women that summer! I wouldn't be there long, anyway. So, I tried to get on, stay calm, enjoy that once in a lifetime experience, while I reminded my host how long she'd been asking me to visit and mentioned places like Willow Creek.

My excitement escalated, as there'd been talk about Willow Creek and its beauty. The place's name evoked a special, eerie anticipation, and I'd been told how warm it was there, warmer than by the ocean.

The day to visit had arrived. And pleased, the forecast for Willow Creek was 102F. I sat on the large backseat, Laura in the front passenger seat with the helper Rita driving us to Willow Creek, two hours away.

Through forest areas, long undulating winding roads, descents then ascents over many mountains. As we climbed, the air pressure dropped; I went partially deaf, my ears popped, like on a plane. Incredible, and this added to the suspense and excitement.

We arrived at a small town, turned left, then parked on an enormous field, a few spaced-out trees by wooden picnic tables with fixed benches and 100F. Even a hardened sun-worshipper would've wanted shade from the leafy foliage of one of the willow trees beside the bench we sat.

At the picnic table, we enjoyed the much-needed sandwiches and juice drinks after the travelling across many altitudes. Refreshed and quenched thirst replenished my eagerness to be in the sun and experience 100 degrees. Rita pushed me from the shade, onto the grass.

Away from any trees, and positioned my wheelchair in the middle of the field. "You sure you want to sit here? It's hot?"

"Yeah, thank you, I'll be OK here."

"OK, I'll let you bake... But if you get too hot, shout."

Sweat ran down my face as Rita walked back to the picnic table and shaded haven. So strange it's the total opposite of standing under that ice-cold waterfall at age 12, heat endurance and that same determination. *I won't call for Rita.*

Startled by an engine noise from behind, chatter, the clatter of pots and pans as an enormous camper van appeared to my left, driven across the grass. It parked close by and about five kids of various sizes and ages emerged from the van, a man, and lady. I sense the excitement, eagerness to help, to picnic in that idyllic place.

The man joked as he instructed his children, and the lady, I presumed, was his wife. A large gazebo became assembled, and I observed with astonishment as I watched the most organised picnic party ever in the world's history and human civilisation. *What a lovely family.*

Rita approached from the shaded willow trees, as the man projected his voice with cupped hands by his mouth, "Hello, come on over." I waved as I couldn't project my voice that far, but didn't intend to appear rude, unappreciative, or uncivilised. Rita shouted over, "This is Paul from England!"

"Hello, Paul. Care to join us?"

Although anxious about social interaction, I wished to accept the invite, meet and mingle, but Rita said, "Paul, Laura wants to go now. Ready?" and steps toward the man, "No thank you, we're going now." Rita pushes me across the grass.

"Oh, OK, bye, Paul from England!"

Disappointed to leave early, but on the way back, Rita parked on a grass verge, as she said, "Ah, some wild Elk... See them, Paul?" They were magnificent on the grass close to the black-green backdrop of forest trees.

Their long, powerful, jagged brown antlers, like wild branches of a tree reaching to the sky in the depths of winter, and brown fur and grey bellies; wonderful animals in their natural habitat; what a special privilege.

Very memorable, as was a beach location at Trinidad. As I relaxed by the deep blue Pacific Ocean water as tranquil as a millpond, with black, rocky mounds protruding upward from the serene water.

Breath-taking beauty as curved random waves broke on a panoramic landscape. As hundreds of birds flew overhead in formation like squadrons and majestic sea hawks circled, swooped from the sky.

Another day at a national park in a forest area, I sat in front of a clear-water lagoon, facing a smooth, light-brown rock cliff. A park ranger in a beige, green uniform, yellow ranger badge on his sleeve and wide-brimmed hat came over to me. "Hi, beautiful day," he said.

What an understatement. More like paradise as the sun blazed. The water, tranquil and inviting, I wished I could have swum there.

The most awesome attraction was the Avenue of the Giants. In awe as we drove on a highway running through giant ancient trees, grand sequoia lining both sides of the road.

And amazed as sunlight then intense dappled shade and trees so high, wide and dense, almost blocking out the sun. Sun rays filtering through the dense foliage suspended from massive branches attached to enormous, almighty tree trunks.

It was an incredible and humbling location, as was Moonstone Beach. The placename fascinated and excited me, with dreamy, romantic overtones. I imagined a beach under the moon.

A much-awaited visit and unreal as I sat in the van and faced the ocean. On a beach-landscape, littered with pebbles, a three-dimensional mosaic of stones of various colours and shapes; millions of pebbles.

I became similarly at ease but melancholy as I watched the moon from the window on nights I sat at the computer, chatting to my Texan friends. I was so far away from home and isolated.

Chatting with loved and dear ones in Texas comforted me and helped.

I'll always remember one particular night. At midnight I phoned home and a perfect, beautiful, brilliant white crescent moon sat high in a pitch-black sky.

Profound thoughts as I imagined the early morning sun back home also illuminating the moon I saw at that moment, 8am back in England, moon set and 10pm in Texas, midnight in California.

Mom and Dad sounded so strange, distant! What a bold explorer I had become. A whole ocean and a continent away. Lonely, but the world felt smaller, and I felt closer for seeing the moon.

As a leaving present, Cecelia said she'd take me to a micro-brewery, and we could eat. I looked forward to the outing on my last Thursday, and to meeting her husband, too, who also liked beer.

Eager and more than ready, as Cecelia and her husband arrived. As we approached the destination, the smell of hops reminded me of aromas in a now distant land; evoked uncannily similar memories. The brewery in Wolverhampton, and the smells of beer, bitter, mild, and cigarettes; sounds of pub chatter and occasional laughter.

I often wished to be at the homely, smoky place, near the senior school I attended and my grandad's local Bilston pub, The Prince Of Wales on Queen Street. The street, Dad was born.

Comforting thoughts, although starkly different, and it felt as strange to be in such a far-flung territory. Just as it did as a child.

I felt lucky and proud, now in splendid company, on an adventure, sampling raspberry flavoured beer and Mexican food.

The chicken quesadillas, Cecelia's recommendation, were extra special, delicious, after eating microwaved pizza, sandwiches and $1 cheeseburgers, before then.

After leaving the micro-brewery, Cecelia drove to a supermarket. Sam said, "Let's get some beer... I'll choose a nice beer for you, Paul, Mexican, my treat," as we headed for the beer. Beer, stacked on shelves from floor to ceiling; spoilt for choice.

Overwhelmed with kindness and pleased with Sam's choice as Cecelia drove onto a pier. "This is nice, a harbour Sam and I sometimes come to."

Then euphoric, being welcomed into that special couple's world. Forging the bonds of friendship, especially nice, considering my ebbing mood, loneliness transformed to excitement. At ease with friends, and with a kind of fellow rebel, Sam, as we stayed out late.

In good spirits, as I became tipsy and jovial. We tried to sneak back into Laura's house, but my chair smacked the wall and I burst out laughing. "Hey, Sam, where's my beer?"

"Hey, don't worry, I put it in the fridge for you." I turned and saw Laura, waiting up in the kitchen, arms folded and scowling. *Oh dear.* Part of me felt so bad for having a fun late-night out! What a fantastic night that was!

On my last evening in California, I reflected on my stay. Anxious moments, times of unease, when I used my mental strength and intellect to survive, loneliness, and isolation were hard to bear.

And the highlights: Willow Creek, magnificent trees, beautiful scenery, Pacific Ocean views, and places few may only dream of seeing once in a lifetime. Even as I calmed tensions, I was glad to have survived. What an epic adventure.

Excited, as I woke. *It's my last day, time to return home. I'll miss this idyllic place.* Melancholic, as Cecelia helped me for the last time, and got me into my wheelchair. Last chat, last goodbye, last laughs in that faraway land, as she helped me pack my suitcase.

And, gave me a glass jar full of extraordinary agates, collected from Moonstone Beach, and a small photo of her and Sam with writing on the back. "We Love you, Paul, and will miss you xxxx." Sad moments saying goodbye to the closest friends I had in California.

Cecelia shook my hand, hugged me and a fleeting kiss on my cheek as she left and I sat outside in the sunshine at the front of the house; waved her off as she drove away. With one farewell, suitcase packed and set for my return home.

The day passed swiftly... The clock ticking. Only a long car journey and flight and ever eager, as recent events stirred strong yearnings to be back home. Laura arranged for Rita to get me to San Francisco Airport to catch my early morning flight.

At around 5pm, the phone rang. Laura answered, "Huh, huh, oh no. Huh, huh, I understand," downbeat as she turned her chair toward me, a forlorn expression as she folded her arms, "Rita can't drive you to the airport... A family emergency!"

"Oh, no." Concerned, as I understood the seriousness of the situation.

I held a thought. *I may miss my flight. Might be stuck here! A six-hour drive, but no driver and plane takes off in less than 12 hours!*

"My dad can't drive you back either," Laura said as she put her head in her hands with despair, maybe as she couldn't stand to have me around one extra minute.

She picked up the phone; explained the arisen situation and the dilemma of getting me to the airport. Placed the phone back in the holder on the wall, "I spoke to Cecelia. She has a night shift, so can't help either."

In disconcerting disbelief, I was out of ideas. The phone rang and Laura pounced on it. "Hi, hmm, huh, OK, thanks; see you later." Her face, expressionless, as she hid a smile and said. "Paul, I got you a ride! Sam will drive you to San Francisco; Cecelia's cancelled her shift, so can come, too."

What a heart-warming gesture after nerve-jangling drama. Cecelia and Sam arrived just after 1am. They loaded my suitcase and bag into the van. Laura sat in the front passenger seat as chief navigator and to make sure I didn't escape.

Glad as Cecelia sat with me on the backseat and said, "I'll keep you company and I've bought blankets for us; if we get cold. Sam will get us to the airport. Don't worry."

Sam drove out of the garage, into the night, onto that long street. A hazy, subdued amber glow from the streetlights, ready and sent us on our way. Heralded and on the cusp of a final journey, even more overwhelmed with Sam and Cecelia's kindness.

As I snuggled in the blanket and as that final, long road journey to San Francisco began, I felt an enormous sense of relief. I had made it: weathered storms and sunny moments, unforgettable and life-changing experiences.

I hadn't slept and battled tiredness. Adrenaline and anticipation kept me awake, for a while at least. After chatting with Cecelia, I closed my eyes.

Succumbed to sleep, and woke at dawn as we approached the Golden Gate Bridge. Streaks of dulled golden rays of sunlight as dawn approached and chatter resumed.

We entered the underground car park, into the maze and crowds. This signified a climax to a long adventure. And despite anxious moments and the fight to stay sane, it still wasn't easy saying farewells to friends and Laura, a kind soul, although we didn't get on, and that country. What a rollercoaster.

Most importantly, I dreamed again. Things needn't be just so. But might, if restricted by negativity. With help from kind people, more is possible than we can imagine or hope.

To learn this, and experience those journeys and adventures, instilled confidence. But my boldness to fly to America, and go for it, not let fears and negativity hold me back instilled great pride.

And, an enormous sense of achievement, but my safe return heralded an even greater achievement with gratitude for kindness and my hosts.

I'd always remember special moments and Shelda's words, "They all tried to help me forget I was in a chair." That represented a precious gift in itself, although perhaps for some parts of the adventure I was a foolish, fly, trapped in an intricate and perplexing silken web?

32.

LUST VERSUS LOVE

*O*nline romances, to no avail. I gained wisdom, friends, and dreams, but was still in Bilston. Perhaps I underestimated and misunderstood the very essence of love in the guise of lust and intimate pleasures.

Still, I turned to the internet. Continued the all-consuming quest and the web fantasies while yearning for reality. Of course I wanted both, although I went out with girls again, 'yippee'. A video I watched years earlier, at a university, in my second-year that seemed crazy made sense, too.

The internet and .com-culture took off, became true, more intense, as I became obsessed with chatting. I had the power though, words, descriptive scenes, I could write and revel; sweet romance. Revelled as the internet became an even more alluring communication tool as I had speech problems.

Ever determined to find love. But I grew tired of the internet, the search for amour and experienced let downs and hurt, the waiting and hoping. A strange affinity to cyberspace as I clung on to the fantasy, powerful illusions.

The internet had absorbed and sapped my energy. I needed rest from stresses of that internet world. A world my life had revolved around for so long.

Tired of the falseness and fantasy, and upset by people online, who appeared on various messengers. People I grew to dislike, who weren't nice at all, all over me one minute and ignoring me the next.

I fought the addiction; didn't chat for a while, easing the stress of multiple incoming messages from amorous admirers. While away from the internet, I focused on writing.

Sat back, waited, then returned, aloof, wiser as I honed in on who I knew was genuine. And those who made the false promises. I went along with it; played their games and strung them along as I confirmed plans. Affirmations never to bear fruit.

So, the more discerning me back with a vengeance, with renewed determination. Multiple messengers, instant chat, chat rooms as I became entangled in the alluring, shiny, silken strands of the World Wide Web. Day and night I sat. Aching physically and mentally as I became oblivious to time and a slave to time zones. So cold and so sad.

It wasn't enough; fantasies soured as I yearned for a romantic reality. I went to clubs, bars with friends and my dad sometimes, too, but drank so much, my speech became frustratingly worse, and harder to compete with music at such high volume. No chance, intensifying feelings of loneliness, and forlorn.

If I could speak a little to the women, they'd realise I had a good brain and heart, although unable to dance like the able-bodied nightclub revellers. I'd charm them.

Seduce them if only they came over, spoke to me, gave me a chance to use my charms. Plaguing thoughts from the past of craziness, zaniness, and conquests before coma, cruelly revived.

My former life, when able-bodied, and wilder; leaving school, the YTS, romance, and the cold winter of 1985 long-gone. Summer approached and a long-awaited holiday with friends.

It couldn't come soon enough. The transforming effects of adventures in Scotland and rollercoaster romances changed me: my heart; the ever eager new ultra-confident, ardent, ever-bolder joker became older, wiser and wilder, less restrained. My persona less timid as I rared to go.

So I was excited with friends, on the train towards, beckoning, lush greenery of Somerset as we chatted. Reminiscing about the visit a year earlier; fun, lovely ladies, drink and dance. Bedduz, Brad, and me with my stereo on the table, quietly playing DeBarge, *Rhythm Of The Night,* and other class tunes on the way.

We were soon at the chalet. Getting changed, ready for a wild first night. Eager for the bars and nightclubs, and I'd imagined the fun I might have; the girls I may meet. Thoughts of such dreams fuelled our excitement; intensified hopes and yearnings of frivolity.

I made a special effort. Best trousers, shoes, shirt, tie, and hair combed and styled with hair gel, but still no moustache and tried not to think of this almost obligatory item. Or the crucial question I had pondered, troubled for so long. *Will I get into the nightclub?*

Now is the moment. Here, but alone with my thoughts as I look around, yet stare, contemplate. Stood in the queue, ever closer to the entrance as rhythmic thumping tunes vibrate the floor.

As more confident men with moustaches, dressed in smart suits, wait, and attractive ladies with gorgeous figures in diaphanous beguiling attire; lovely smiles, entice, and charm.

Excited, but anxious as the queue dwindled – as one-by-one my friends were let in – my turn. A bouncer dressed in a smart black tuxedo, matching bow tie and white shirt, asks, "How old are you?"

"Eighteen."

"You don't look 18. Sorry, I can't let you in," said the party-pooping bouncer.

"My friends are in there." *They're younger than me,* to no avail! Anguish and disbelief as I reel with disappointment, a sure dilemma. *Oh, no! Shit!* All the planning and initiative; the life and soul of the party.

Panic-stricken with racing thoughts and shaking with anger and fear, but I calmly walked away into the cool night. Headed towards the reception, my pace quickened to brisk strides, with a desperate plan.

But, I wasn't optimistic as I strolled in, approached the counter, the two men in black security uniforms. "A doorman refused my admission to the club. People say I look young all the time. My friends gained entry; they're not as old as me..."

Suppressing distress and exasperation, as one guard looked at me pitifully. *This has to work.*

"Oh, sorry, sir," as the bemused security man telephoned the nightclub, "Hello I have a gentleman here; you didn't let into the club!" And continued to explain.

Yes! Mission accomplished, as I left the reception holding back a smug grin. Bursting with euphoria, I needed to scream with delight, but jumped into the air. Yet, I felt bad and alone; disturbed. *My younger friends were allowed into the nightclub, but not me. What if my plan falls apart?*

As I traversed the stairs and looked along the long, carpeted corridor, the same burly bouncer waiting, I shivered in nervous anticipation. He seemed an entirely different person. "Sorry about that, sir, in you go!" he said, smiling.

Jubilant to enter that fabulous place with such cool, loud, thumping, funky music; I spotted my bemused friends, forlorn in my absence; looking lost. And great to see Dava, too.

Their moods changed the moment they saw me, joyous but disbelieving eyes set in puzzled faces as I received a rapturous welcome. Brad shook my hand, "Ah, P, how did you get in?"

Dava approached. "P, you are a one!"

I had astounded all with my ingenuity. We laughed, and I looked over at the bar. Surveyed the room with a partially filled dancefloor. The people dancing, those who sat on plastic moulded, lemon-coloured chairs and lush ladies, stunning like heaven on earth.

The barmaids, were even better, gorgeous goddesses, late teens, or early twenties. Dressed in short, figure-hugging dresses embellished with silver sequins which shone with a dazzling array of colours from the light show; hypnotic sights.

"Let's get the beers on!" Dava said. So, to the bar, and I swiftly drank my £1 pint of beer, expensive compared to home; making up for lost time.

My friends and I were soon on the dancefloor, dancing our best moves, surveying the lush ladies. Most of them looked so mature compared to me, at least.

The following morning, "Yes, we made it!" I said with fervour and joy as my eyes opened. *We're actually here,* as I reminisced about the wonderful night. The excitement, music, lights, and bevy-of-babes I hankered to know.

I stayed calm as I opened my first can of beer of the day and poured it into my cornflakes in a cereal bowl. Daily beer, sodden cornflakes, addicted and for amusement, as one laughed and said, "Alcy."

After breakfast, we walked around the camp; in pursuit of fun, and often ended up in the arcades. My cohorts preferred to be there, the flashing lights and artistry didn't allure or entice me. It's mad!

Pointless feeding these machines. Virtually no chance of winning more cash to spend on beer, and boring. Besides, I preferred the funfair. The fast-spinning rides and atmosphere appealed to me, and the selection of girls, similar to Bilston Carnival back home, but much better.

Many fond memories, gorgeous girls, and barmaids at amazing bars and lovely west country accents. Then, one next to me, on my bed.

Sexy chuckles and sweet smiles, as soft music played. Loose Ends,' *Hanging On A String,* and similar tunes from my stereo, instilling the romantic mood beside that pretty lady. Tender, deepening kisses, and delighted, "You're quite lush!" she said in a soft tone.

One year on I'm bolder, ultra-confident and totally at ease. Dressed up smart, in best attire to go to the nightclub and bars. As I walked from one bar to another, smiling. Aww, the longing-looks from beautiful lust filled eyes within perfectly painted faces.

In disbelief, as we attracted attention. Sexy looks from almost every female reveller; turning heads, mutual smiles as we laughed, casually spoke to each other, friends as we walked, not rock stars. Just brimming-confidence, and happy as we discovered an art to flirting.

"Hey, wow, did you see her smile at me?"

Unbelievably happy, fantastic in a buoyant, ebullient mood as I entered the main ballroom. Music blared, stage lights shone, while arcade games machines enticed with more lights, colours and sound. The place buzzed as we headed for the main bar, ever nearer to several lovely barmaids.

One of them approached to serve me as I reached the bar. Gorgeous, sexy brown eyes, long brunette hair, styled and glittery, stunning, making my heart race and driving me crazy!

"Lager, a pint please," as I get my wallet and hope to stay and chat, charm and admire. The barmaid's stern look, and surprised as she asks, "Any ID?" My momentarily blank, forlorn expression soon transformed to a gentle smile I could not help.

To my glee, the serious but lovely expression on her face also changed to a beaming sexy smile as she said, "Only joking. Someone as good-looking as you don't need ID!"

Simultaneously smiling, but my face exploded into radiant smiles as I blushed, swooning from that wonderful compliment. The nicest I'd ever had, and unexpected. I needed to take her to bed. Would have married her in an instant, there on the spot!

Elated and intensified delight, wild with desire; driven crazy. More outgoing, kind of carefree, reeling and disheartened from three relationships. Then, the best night of my life? *She's the one!*

Yet, as I drank, and the frivolity continued, a vision in my mind. A wonderful smile, her luscious lips, and I wanted to return to that barmaid. But met two good-looking girls; a blonde, the other brunette, who I chatted with, entertained.

Seduced by a lovely, quiet west country accent, smart and attractive. We walked into the warm night. Ever excited with each step, further away together, toward my chalet, filled with intense desires as we arrived.

Overwhelmed by fantasies, I before lacked confidence to enact. Too shy to even mention as wildness evoked more daring antics. Now I dare, as fantasies become real. All hers and she was all mine. As erotic yearnings acted on, that in the past, were mere dreams. Anything and everything she desired, and likewise, to please.

Constant, unrushed, intense and marvellous. Lovely, velvety-smooth legs around me, soft breasts against my chest. Driven by ravenous, carnal desire; ecstatic sensations as we repeatedly kissed, and I did my utmost to please the loveliest woman I'd ever met.

Unreal passion like an unbelievable dream as we emerged

from the room and outdoors. Animated, gleeful, as we chatted on our way to the club. The night, far from over, I didn't want to end. Visions of that barmaid I wanted to marry, hoped to see again; craved.

Back at the club, we sat together, then danced. I met another lady, a cute, long-haired redhead. We chatted, exchanged compliments that excited me, and as an invitation made my heart pound, we discretely and swiftly left the club together.

I couldn't decline! Erotic anticipation as we kissed, laughed and ran, stumbled on the grass and both fell. "These heels," as she took them off to run faster on the turf as we headed to my chalet.

We had fun, not as wild as earlier, but sensuous and amorous. I liked how it felt... The success of the transformation from an over-sensitive, weak romantic to a cold, insensitive bastard. I didn't want to settle down anymore, just have fun.

It was much easier. Less painful, and more rewarding, but addictive. After yearning, the waiting, disappointments, and heartache, sheer, pure elation, the thrill of being wanted, as the new emotionless me!

I beamed inside with joy as we strolled back to the club, anxious as I entered with that lovely lady. *Hope the first girl or her friend doesn't see us.*

The other girl's friend eventually found me. "Where have you been?"

"Nowhere."

"You lying bastard!" Uneasy, maybe she was right. But, I thought about times of being unlucky in love, intense yearnings quenched. *About time, I had success in the passion department. Niggled and gnawed by heartbreaking disappointments.* Still, I yearned, wanted more, a luscious barmaid.

As I lay on my bed, my mind spun; replaying the unbelievable, fantastic events, bewilderingly wonderful moments I didn't want to let go of, or ever forget, playing in my mind, savouring every moment to prolong the pleasure. Pleasure entwined with sadness. And fear, as I craved more; of loneliness as I wanted love.

I still yearned to be next to one of those lovely ladies in my lonely bed. My glorious conquests felt great, but another part of me felt bad. Saddened in a crumbling world.

Alas, jaded fervour. Still, I didn't surpass the torrid dalliances of an elite few friends. Well, I had to compete. Further saddened, as I only wanted one; it had to be more.

The following day, at the pool, I lay on my towel. Basked with the heat of the sun on my body, as I hear a familiar voice and see a shapely, bikini-clad figure. "Hello, all right. It's warm."

It was the lovely redhead; she rolled out her towel beside me and lay down. "All right," as I contemplated a dilemma.

I took little notice; I wanted to be sociable, but worried. *What if the other girl I met last night walks by and sees us sunbathing together?*

An attractive woman in a bikini, next to me, and scared! I dared not talk or even turn my head to glance across at her loveliness. Such nonchalance, ineptitude as I got up, aloof, and walked away into the shade. The kind of thing a cold-hearted philanderer may do. I didn't care, well I did, but couldn't.

So, a quandary, and cruel of me, boorish, only I hadn't forgotten last night. I yearned for more.

Anyhow, that night by the bar, my friend's and my head turned; a stunning girl had strolled in, scanned the room, spotted us and waved. How awkward, uneasy, it was her.

My friends swooned; one friend said, "Look, P, she's amazing. Go over or call her over?"

"No, not bothered." Although I thought, *Shit, I blanked her today, didn't talk to her. Maybe she was the one for me; I've blown any further chances. If I rekindle anything, I'd become even shallower.*

Was she hoping I'd succumb? My friend said, "Mind if I call her over then?"

"No." despite imminent awkwardness.

I didn't realise how intensely awkward and bad I'd feel as my friends drooled like ravenous wolves that didn't know she could beguile and tame them with one brief stare from those blue eyes. Still, they did their utmost to woo and charm, enchant, seduce that lovely lady.

Beauty, such a powerful enchantress, luscious glowing red lips I had kissed, a beautiful body I'd felt against mine... Oblivious to her seductive charms, her power, or the prize I had won.

Few can imagine the loveliness I had. My reality, now a dream as others tried to entertain, impress her, seeking pleasure. I didn't compete; I forfeited that right.

I wanted to say sorry about earlier, but couldn't socialise, do small talk, or improvise with my usual tomfoolery; lost my charm. Drained by lust, tired of charades and sober. *We could've stayed in the chalet longer. The first girl was lovely, too.*

I gazed over at the luscious barmaids. Mesmerised by comely eyes and dazzling flashes, like flickering stars of multicoloured light from their figure-hugging, sequin-laced dresses, as I tried to disregard the flirty banter; the laughter.

Although I couldn't decide if I wanted to hear as I focussed on my drink, picked it up, downed it in one. And drifted ever further away on my lonely rudderless boat on a vast grey ocean, my escape.

The sequin flashes, glinting, the sun reflecting, sparkling on the waves, and undeserving of company as I became classless, unrefined, but not loutish as I swayed and bobbed with the waves. The ebb and flow between worlds as I escaped and suppressed my senses, and the hopeless, sensitive, romantic within, that night and from then.

So, out of phase; there, but 1,000,000 miles away, everdistant, alone and under the sun. But wanted to be in company; with her, intimacy, not ravenous lust and under the moon.

On the last night, even me, the sensible, level-headed one who knew he'd never inject or snort drugs, as his mind was fast enough, became alarmed but intrigued. A cut off plastic bottle immersed in a bucket of water. What a strange party as I watched the bottle fill with grey smoke from a smouldering brown substance on tin foil suspended from the bottle-top hole. I had to experience the euphoria, succumb.

And had to go beyond the most others dared. As I inhaled, I heard, "He's going for all of it." So potent, instantly, totally intoxicated; I had to lie down as fast as possible. Knocked out, and not even two women messing with me woke or roused me.

The next day I felt really ill, a headache, hungover and so thirsty; needed my daily beer on my cornflakes!

Such brilliant and memorable times. Better than Scotland during the past winter. Then the 1986 holiday, in one sense, was possibly the best of my entire-life. Except for the last wild, not so wonderful night, paradoxically also the saddest.

I had relented. Joined the enticing, easy, self-centred, carefree-game everyone else had been playing, and enjoyed, except for me.

Shallower, emotionless, more flippant, uncaring fun, as I encountered romance like never before. But, my ideas of amazing fun would change with the passage of time.

Part of me ached, wished to dwell in that place forever. A year later, at 18, I became less wild, content and happier, as I danced to Whitney Houston's *I Wanna Dance With Somebody*. As though I was back on track. I'd learned from experience with a job and a car.

Still, it was strange without Dava around. He had joined the Royal Marines®. I missed him; but I was OK; maybe I had an option, after all. Sat in anticipation in the waiting area foyer of the Royal Navy® recruitment office.

Upbeat as I pondered learning a trade and a new career. Contemplated seeing the world, getting away from Bilston.

Deep in thought as I focussed on the dark wood of an open-plan staircase in front of me. A smartly dressed female with short red hair and rosy-red complexion came in and sat by me.

What a smile; I almost blushed as we both said, "Hello." But stood up as a tall naval officer in a smart uniform appeared and escorted us up the staircase to the upper floor and shepherds us into rooms.

We met by chance in the corridor after sitting our aptitude tests. "Fancy a coffee?" she asked.

"That'd be good, but I've brought sandwiches to eat in my car. Join me if you want," as we reached the recruitment office door.

"OK, I'll grab a coffee on the way."

Headed to my car, away from the bustling, milling crowds and into the multistorey car park, the concrete structure shielding us from the sun, cooler, darker, subdued light from dim, pillar lights.

Great to have my car, to sit, chat and eat. To make conversation, "If I join, I may get a ship's anchor tattoo or something." I said.

"I already have one."

"Really, can I see it?"

"Yes," as she opened the top buttons of her blouse and unfastens more. Teasing as I watch her reveal a white, lacy bra, cleavage, and bare, white, flesh of a breast, and a delicately painted, deep blue ellipsis with ornate, wispy curves that reminded me of breaking waves out at sea.

Her nakedness and tattoo, arousing as her seductive eyes, stared at me; enticing thoughts raced in my brain. Excited, too, by the novel and fantastic, transpiring situation, as she leaned toward me, and our lips met.

"I want to do it with you, will you?" She asked.

Incredible, a playful smile, as I replied, "Err,... OK, then." The subdued light added romantic ambience as we chatted, flirted, built excitement for later fun. But had we passed the tests to join the Royal Navy®? At the recruitment office, the same naval officer greeted me; called me into an office upstairs as I arrived.

I had naively planned to aim for an artificer post, only knowing it was a higher status than that of an ordinary seaman. For the more technically orientated. "Take a seat," he said.

I sat in the chair facing him at a large, dark wooden desk.

The officer sat back in his seat. "Congratulations, you passed, but you were two points below the score required for artificer. All I need now... Sign here," as he presented a paper, indicated where to sign.

"For how many years?"

"Twenty-two years' service." *What?* Stunned by the speed of events and directness.

Aghast, as I realised this could be it, and following a silence which lasted a near eternity. The officer said, "I can see you're not sure. So, think about it more. In six months, you can retake the test and try for artificer."

Music to my ears — *Yes, I can go back home, and wouldn't have passed the basic training, anyway.* Was it merely to prove I could join, although I knew I couldn't uproot myself from my home, my parents, Bilston, and its appeal? *What if something happened to Mom or Dad and I was at sea, so far away?*

And, I remembered the sadness of goodbyes, tears at a leaving party, years earlier as a kid at Bilston Lawn Tennis Club. I couldn't understand how Dad's relative could emigrate to Australia; leave loved ones.

I never could as I left that formal place. Downstairs, waiting for me, was my tattooed friend. "All right, did you pass?" Although I guessed from her forlorn expression.

"No, I can't join."

"Aww, can you sit the test again, though?" And, as we leave the recruitment office, "Want to come for a drive somewhere?"

So I drove from that dark, cool, morbid, grey concrete shelter of the multistorey car park with my passenger. Away from Wolverhampton, past Sedgley into unfamiliar country lanes...

"We can go to my house! Nobody's home." As she directed me to ever unknown territory and a housing estate.

As I said, "I'm lost now, I'll never get back!" We arrived, and were soon upstairs.

"Let's see that tattoo again, then."

"OK." As she opens her blouse buttons. Again, revealing a wonderful cleavage and lacy, white bra as she giggles with excitement. The blouse and bra dropped to the floor, followed by her skirt, a magnificent sight.

It was more like a mission, a service with zero-romance I sought to make special. But, she kissed me, and said, "Thanks, I'm not scared now to do it with my boyfriend."

Oh well, she wasn't that nice; and saddened by such an era. Undesirable attitudes in the cold society I was in as I drove back home as a disenchanted soul on the cusp of the eternal winter, coma, and near death; the calm before the storm.

Years on, I knew shallow superficiality and facades were

the only winners but for short-term prizes, and I had no guise or prowess. If only women chose me like they did back then, their prize would be joyous, fulfilling, perhaps everlasting bliss. The internet was easier! But, curiously, one-night, it seemed as if someone had pushed me out of bed.

Frightening, as was being stranded on the hard-cold floor. Unable to get back in bed and no-one heard my shouts. Immense relief as the sun rose and Dad came downstairs. Found me and helped; I was glad to be warm and comfortable again.

I became ill. Wheezy, a headache, weak, achy, shivery and so cold, but sweating, delirious as I'm put in the ambulance. My temperature, almost 40C, as I remembered similar symptoms; in our caravan in Wales, as a child.

Worried, I didn't know what the matter was. Mom's cousin's husband bought me a freshly laid and boiled hen's egg in the hope I'd feel better.

It was delicious and delighted me. A hen had laid it just for me. What a gift, but glad a doctor came and diagnosed scarlet fever; it wasn't easy to get to a doctor in those parts. I soon got well again, and my brother and I had a surprise treat.

A relative from another caravan erected a large white screen on a tripod with the large car battery powering the reels of a projector. The gentle whirr, and clicking of film as Dad turned the gaslights off, and sat by Mom.

Magnificent colour on an enormous screen appeared in the pitch-black darkness. It was amazing, magical compared to the small black-and-white TV we'd been watching. The film, *Sinbad the Sailor*, had us transfixed.

We sat, riveted to our seats by the spectacular special effects, and a white flying horse. I'd never forget that fantastic night of entertainment, or that film. Perhaps not even during coma that seemed so long ago.

I also remembered the hot, unforgettable summer of 1976, the torture, being stuck indoors for the whole six weeks of the school holidays with mumps.

The rare treat of a delicious, chocolate ice-cream from the

ice-cream man I couldn't eat as I became so ill, achy, weak and so bored.

I knew I needed more than a fresh hen's egg to make me better, as I'm so poorly now in hospital, and felt much worse than those times.

And, my chest X-rays weren't good. Uncanny too, in the same hospital ward, same bay, and bed I lay in 1987 after waking from coma. Strange, but so different: Delighted now, touched as a lovely girl, Helen visited, to whom I'd become acquainted in Bilston.

So caring and thoughtful, she bought me a magazine. My heart beat so fast, as that adorable lady kindly fastened the buttons on my pyjama top. Pity she was with someone else. I could but hope and dream.

After two weeks in hospital, I was still unwell, but felt upbeat, boosted by Helen's second wonderful visit, and the prospect of being discharged.

It was good to be home; I missed those hospital visits, though. And, experienced peculiar sensations in my lungs, still wheezy, but with sickness, as I learned, I'd been ill because of walking pneumonia.

Then, in 2001, life becomes unlike it had ever been. In some ways, like how I was at 17, very active, popular, albeit mainly online with ladies, as romance blossomed with another American lady. We chatted every night, talked on the phone, sent each other gifts.

Quite strange and wonderful how things worked out. As after years of chatting online, and all events, women exclaimed love, wanted to marry me!

Such attention and decisions evoked joyous turmoil and much pondering. Whilst I wondered how real the internet was. Disillusioned, as I waited a long time for married ladies, and others on the internet, and for hours at Wolverhampton Railway Station. I waited in vain, duped and believing, as Dad patted me on my shoulder. "Never mind, son. Let's go home now."

I always thought of Cathy; the only lady to turn up and the

emotional farewell. *Maybe I should have waited longer outside Cinders?* But, more than a decade later, my dream-girl entered my life.

So, presented with a profound choice, I must get right! Continued fantasy versus a more substantial reality, a lady far away in America and spending time with her online, hearing her voice on the phone.

Or the one I'd adored the moment I saw her in Bilston, and the wonderful day I sat next to her at college. *Wow, kind, intelligent and sexy – so nice and in black, shiny PVC trousers – no chance.*

Delighted to see her, thrilled to chat in Bilston Town sometimes. We looked at records and perused music selections, chatted and laughed. And our feelings grew with each sweet, endearing, long love letter, romantic text, each declaration of love and display of affection.

Hearing her acclaim love, in person, stunned and filled me with sheer joy as I knew that truly came from a heart. It felt unbelievably fantastic, being adored by a wonderful lady and partner. Ever more intense, ever deeper in love with each delightful meeting.

Magical encounters, and such sweet sentiments, she could kiss me all day, couldn't ever stop seeing me and never will. It couldn't get any better; so lucky, and so happy together, with a lovely, caring, genuine, woman, the one for me, like no other I'd met previously. Above all, she was real!

I had got the girl of my dreams, my angel, and her heart; our hearts entwined as one. Happiness upon finding my soulmate. To be with me for good, after years of hoping, the elusive and possibly futile search for love, romance, adventure, worldwide travel and scouring the globe through cyberspace. It's bizarre and brilliant, I discovered all that and more, so very near to me.

Also, new pastimes would soon feature in my life. Pub quizzes as I became part of a formidable quiz team at The Hollybush and Rose and Crown pubs on the Penn Road. I resumed another passion, chess and joined Wolverhampton Chess Club.

Challenges, goals and new, bolder ambitions, in addition to academic achievement, and travel to places I could only ever dream of before coma brought contentment.

33.

PARENTHOOD

*I*n 1987, at 18, my life on this Earth almost ended. A second chance at living as a sentient being heralded a new dawn. And presented a wonderful gift, after being transformed by coma experiences, and my head injury because of my suicide attempt.

It was a tragic event that could have been more tragic — if I had died; my existence hadn't continued. As a changed person, I lived on to experience other adventures, and to achieve where I didn't earlier.

I relished and embraced unbounded opportunities, under totally different, more testing circumstances, with changed abilities.

Some challenges, goals I have strived for, and avenues I explored; were similar to when I was able-bodied. But required more innovative approaches. Were harder because of disability, so represented tests of motivation, tenacity, and inner strength.

It is ironic and inexplicable, too, that despite becoming a wheelchair user, disabilities and being unable to do so much, I have fulfilled ambitions and achieved things I would never have dreamed of in my superior, able-bodied existence.

So, perhaps all those years ago, my mind restricted me, and was my worst, most formidable enemy. My mind opened and expanded after I became disabled, and with age. Developing with experience as I adjusted, and became ever wiser in the years that followed the event, and as I realised, being in a chair doesn't matter.

Maybe such achievements just prove the determined part of me still exists, an underlying trait from both sections of my life, and even during coma.

After all the adversity and despair, triumph, inner solace, as all I had ever hoped, prayed for, yearned, pined and wished for, now reality. This gave a reason and purpose from anguish and pain.

The periods of endless winter magically abated. Still, there's sometimes sun, blue skies, but clouds aren't so ominous.

I had learned to live and ride that rollercoaster. The slow, scary, twisted parts, sombre and thrilling, joyous parts and glad to be alive against immense odds as a survivor and for all I am.

And, all I can do and have, whilst not dwelling on things I don't have, cannot do and probably never shall, but knowing the futility of searching; yearning for material, immaterial riches that can never be.

If I had embraced those notions in my teens. The event may not have occurred. I may have realised there's often another way. Experience and enduring wise lessons though were necessary to reach a point in the future. As the same person, but changed forever, and for the better.

As a more prepared, human being for me to recognise, realise, appreciate or know, as my motivations, desires, and perception of true beauty refined.

For most of my life in its various parts, my quests were flawed. I was blind to what I sought and yearned for, as it couldn't be found, like a tangible prize as fantasy, and cruel illusions.

At 18, my desires were different, aspirations ever-changing, my mind evolving. But I was unprepared before then, and in turmoil. I didn't know about depression. How powerful and debilitating it could be, or about aspects of mental illness and hormones.

If I had wanted to end my life in 1987, my survival and experiencing that journey had changed the core of my being in inextricable and wonderful ways. As despite there still being times when depressed, illness, disabilities, and times of pain, I love life itself.

In total contrast, my fear is passing on, not being with my

wonderful family any more. Or the world I belong, we are a part.

Life continues. Not only for myself, but for others, the wider world, a world I'm privileged to be part of and experience.

My time on this Earth wasn't up in 1987. A grander plan is inarguably a reason to and why I lived on, and a total reason for everything, including dark, wisdom forsaken times. The mysterious journey continues. Its end is not up to me to decide, for experiences are precious and nurturing, whether painful or pleasurable.

More profound and poignant, being there at the ultrasound scans and hearing our baby son's heartbeat was so special and suffused with boundless emotion. I stayed at my partner's side as my son entered this world.

Experienced ecstatic delight, joy, and elation as Helen placed him into my arms. My children, a son, and a daughter born as I cut the umbilical cord on a September day in 2012.

The most precious gifts any human being could wish for, from a loving partner. Even more precious to create new life — after surviving coma.

To me, proof of heaven on Earth. But, it's a heaven I could not have ever known after I learned happiness settles and calms the inner turmoil, and brings peace, as does appreciating the material and immaterial world.

My life journey, including my arduous ascent of the downward spiral, my emergence from coma, all I am now, and all I have, is surely testament to miracles.

Whether my return is part, or fully ascribable with science, dream or perplexingly undecipherable reality, though, is open for wonder instilling debate.

A debate within an infinitely vast, dancing, dynamic and ever-changing, mysterious universe of chaos and order, randomness, and logic, in which I cannot walk. Yet still dance when I hear birds sing. And my daughter rushes to me and says, with eyes full of wonder, "Daddy, the moon in the sky. Come and see it."

With similar excitement, my nephew also told me about the moon after pulling himself up on my chair when he was three.

I proudly and fondly held him in my arms soon after he was born and felt the same emotions as I saw the love as he held our daughter the day after she was born, his new cousin in his arms.

I look up and smile inside and out with visions of angels in the heavens and amongst us, but also remember the immense sorrow. My nephew ended his own life five weeks later at age 14.

An eternal mystery, heartache with millions of tears from those left behind and untimely sadness I shall never forget.

Sometimes the world is cruel and confusing, but perpetually changes. One more day, one hour, one second and the world is different, changed forever; every moment is unique. But each moment is soon history, as now, an illusion as real as our perceptions.

Thinking the world would be better without me in it was wrong, as my life became astoundingly different. Different after believing there was no hope and wanting to die.

As I lived on, to traverse another path after I experienced the journey of near self-destruction, that brought tantalising realisation of mysteries mortals can never know. It gave me further purpose, and reason, to rejoice the unstoppable countdown and my launch to the stars. Although it simply wasn't my time.

Nor could I turn back time. But, it's uncanny and special my children played in the sand, built sandcastles at Rhyl with their grandfather, my dad. Like I did many decades earlier: New generations in cyclic sands of time.

Then on the 11th August 2019, we passed a blackboard sign written in chalk "...Sunset 8.48pm" outside Baysville Coffee & Grill at Kinmel Dunes on the coastal path to Rhyl. The sun shone on the sparkling, blue sea and rising moon — a perfect day, and our last there.

Simple things, yet so important; special, and on Earth. And, whether the heaven I experienced during coma was part of my subconscious or real, maybe my ethereal soul perceived such things as reality.

Irrespective of religious beliefs, at least within the extents of my mind reached, I became a traveller unrestricted by physical dimensions, beyond the world I knew, and far from love; outside time.

When the pendulum finally stops on this Earth, I hope to return to those other realms, heavenly places. If I don't, and just perish, my life and coma experiences have taught me to savour each moment.

And, to appreciate and relish being a part of a dynamic, intricately beautiful Earth and wider cosmos that can sometimes be akin to heaven.

Section V

SENSE FROM TURMOIL

34.

ACCEPTING THE UNACCEPTABLE

(i). The Dawning

*A*fter seeing a counsellor in 1997, I tried to imagine the situations and conditions that may have surrounded and been factors to cause my suicide attempt.

My state of mind, the thoughts; emotions, possible mental states, the mental pain?

I thought of when I came home for a weekend from rehab in 1989, entered the back garden, and to my surprise, saw the dusty, pale-blue shell of my Vauxhall® Chevette. The car in which I almost perished.

Strange feelings disturbingly changed to morbid curiosity: wanting to sit in the car again to see if I felt any emotions or if any memories returned.

After much persuasion, Dad helped me into the car. Onto the black vinyl driving seat, unfixed to the floor so it rocked. I remembered paying £60 for the car and driving it home.

The driving seat, rickety so, rested on bricks and wooden blocks, but sturdy enough to do 60 mph in second gear. Nervous, but careful, and excited by the engine's power, as Dad would fit this into my Vauxhall® Viva.

As I sat on the seat, no memories, or immediate emotions flooded my mind, but I remembered being a youngster into my teen years. When I cried. Lay on the carpet in front of the gas fire and turned the knob.

Depression and curiosity; wanting to sleep, escape from the

lingering inescapable fear, the dread deep within of future pain of a different kind; despise, self-hate. But I always turned the gas fire off with satisfaction, knowing I had endured and survived.

It felt good to have power, control no-one knew; and an option I hoped would never become a choice. A gratifying but desperate option that instilled a strange comfort, solace in an ever-diminishing cruel world.

Now I imagine the muffled engine sound, sweet, potent paralysing toxins and nausea. My head, woozy, and much sorrow as tears stream down my cheeks and grey fumes envelop me.

My brain starved of oxygen as carbon monoxide (CO) molecules attached to the haemoglobin of my blood as I inhaled. In a split moment, I might have realised, with consciousness rapidly slipping away. Rest from the torments of life.

Were such visions entwined with a past reality, my subconscious mind suppressed, archived deep within, to not recall as factual thought, but as vague memories, imagination with thoughts?

Did I want to just sit and rev my engine? Listen to it, then get out? Make an almighty cry for help? If I got scared or changed my mind, I could open the door! Providing I could still make that conscious decision.

In desperation, had I struggled to get out, escape? Was I trapped and panicking? I wonder as I was told about a bruise on my elbow. Was I hit over the head? Forced into the car? Who did it to me?

Such prevalent questions niggled me for a while; furious about what had happened, I kept on telling my parents: "The people who did this to me need punishing, as they put me in the car." I didn't believe I got into the car of my volition.

Even decades after the event, I vowed to never accept something that wasn't experienced as reality; something so out of character, it seems an impossibility. I knew of an imminence though. After passing the point of no return — and I never went back.

Without doubt, the depression, despair, and irrationality

overpowered, but in a moment, it may have been pure, serene logic!

I glanced up and saw some words on the windscreen written in black felt-tip pen: 'I Luv You All.'

Astonished, it wasn't my writing! I'd have spelled 'love' properly! Even so, seeing those handwritten words shocked and filled me with sorrow. Made me wonder if I had been a sad clown wanting to bring tears instead of joyous laughter. Did I want to laugh last, longest and loudest?

Still, inwardly, I questioned if I had written those words. Someone evil, the people who caused me to be what I had become, wrote those words, a pitiful, poor, fake, suicide note, an attempt to dupe all?

If that, a declaration of love, a brief one for those who loved me. Was it a desperate but calculated protest and two-fingered salute against the world? A two-fingered salute at the wider world that didn't care? The ultimate protest at the world and society I was a part? If so, who cared? Who did it affect?

If I had died, would those words have been any consolation, offered any comfort? The words, the meaning, lacked logic and seem cruel as pure love wouldn't have implied the opposite. Surely, I wouldn't have used my last ounce of energy to write those inept, cruelly pathetic words!

Apparently distraught, upset in the phone call I made shortly before the event to a best friend, Paul, who was also a superhero, and a super man, who had stood at my side when I faced Iceman during coma. I really looked up to him. He was like a real-life protector. I knew he couldn't stop me or save me, though, and called to say, "Goodbye."

The friend who had to go, didn't want to leave me upset. He kept asking if I'd be OK? But would be back in 20 minutes, left me tearful as I looked at photographs of past holidays and romances. I probably convinced him I'd be fine and wouldn't do anything daft.

My brother came home to find the doors and back gate locked; he heard the car engine running in the back garden. My friend returned shortly after, presumably 20 minutes after leaving me on the stairs.

He climbed over the gate to find me in the car. The driver's door, jammed. So, they dragged me out through the hatchback boot.

My friend's dad gave me the kiss of life, mouth-to-mouth resuscitation. Without that, I might have died. For a while, I was angry.

Why did my friend leave me? Why was Dad at the launderette? Could anyone have found me sooner? Or even later, even too late? Maybe it was too late, and it was a miracle I lived.

The day I sat in the car was historic, and thought-provoking. From then and from 1997 onwards, I had many more thoughts regarding why I tried to end my life, and if I actually intended that.

The car was also where we found our tortoise, killed with its shell bashed in, many years earlier. Had kids picked her up and dropped her? The world became darker, less-happy knowing people could be so spiteful, evil.

At school, my beliefs, desires, and fears made me think rebellious non-conformity was the only way to boost my popularity and self-esteem.

The shift in focus, from mental, academic to more physical themes of fitness and endurance, had a cumulative effect. And blighted my ambition; led to meagre contentment.

By the latter years of secondary school, I had basically given up, no point to learning. Still, I had an innate desire to learn, although suppressed, oppressed; a curdling lethargy as I became like a nonchalant but brooding mad scientist with malaise and frustration, with no outlet or challenges to strive for; diminished aspirations.

My ideals were flawed, and efforts misguided, partly as boredom, inner stagnation were factors that led to early depression and associated negativity.

I believe the sewing of some origins of emotions, seeds of rebellion as a child nurtured with time. English bored me, and I read so easily, and very well, but the teacher disliked me. They never chose me to read. My inferiority became manifest, the odd, clever, freak — no place for me.

Is it any wonder I became always game for a laugh? The one who did the most radical things. Things few might think of or expect! Who went the extra mile, sometimes to be different, sometimes to entertain and attract attention? The party animal, the comic, the shy, introverted clown who battled on with moments of zany boldness. The way was zaniness! That's how I dealt with, but never coped with shyness. Shyness that stemmed from my childhood linked to my tendency to worry. All before I counted, possibly attributable to an obsessive compulsion. And, depression as I became ever analytical.

Until I had analysed every aspect to ever more perplexing deep detail. Detail no-one else would ever think of or consider.

The drawbacks were anxiety and emotional overload. With the erosion of time as the more I analysed, the more indecisive I became. And, all intensified further by high-sensitivity. I became too in tune and seldom had the aptitude to discern or see options.

As I dwelled on wrong choices, although they may have been right choices, this instigated further analysis and more indecision; often spending time by myself thinking. Which was good, but detrimental to any great extent for that deep, introverted worrier.

Such deep analysis and ever deeper worry, though, impeded my ability to make decisions, exacerbated stress, and deepened turmoil and wasn't conducive to a characteristic of survival.

The radical, defiant me tried to worry less, but smiling became the most unimaginably difficult and pointless task. How could anyone laugh or even smile? And at what jokes? Who and why?

With a perpetually sad face, I'd become such a wise, rebellious clown who aspired to be the strongman and loved by the glamourous trapeze artist and grew so tired of the circus.

Stuck in another dimension, shrouded by negativity. A world of inane, pointless laughter I had no part in or belonged. Most confused by those who laugh, and more perturbed by increasing intensity.

My mom described how she remembered me just before the event: withdrawn and unpredictable! She wanted me to study, go to university and truly aspire: acquire a topnotch position, not go into a factory job.

The only jobs I could get. Dead-end, prospectless jobs from the government joke shops of that era, which would always be inadequate.

Unfulfilled academic aspirations would always plague me, and the society that created the high-flying dreams, beyond and mockingly out of grasp for those not in the cosmic centre of the universe, London!

I couldn't bear to leave Bilston anyway, even with the means and motivation. Was it that place, though? Or where I shouldn't have been?

Tired of the daily drudgery. Sacrifice of my time; being up at 5.30am every morning. After leaving my unappealing, monotonous factory job, I didn't want to go back. But no other options; trapped, stuck in an ever-diminishing circle.

Dossing around the streets for a few years was sobering and transformative. I became a desperate individual who lost their grip after they battled in vain against inner turmoil. The aspirations I once had had faded away.

Money worries loomed with niggling frustration at wrong choices, non-existent career paths, women, and shunned opportunities of romance.

Atypical in every sense. Frantic chaos and depression presented the belief I was beyond hope; no-one could help or change how I felt. All so wrong, and not how things should have been.

Isolation, loneliness, I didn't know where to turn. No-one to turn to, but no-one can understand, or ease my pain anyway; my mind running faster than the speed of light on a vastly different wavelength to everyone else.

Nobody could help! Even if there were people to turn to, they could not help if they wanted to. They were the happy people.

Me so unhappy, but why didn't I just open up, talk to someone? To me, talking was futile, an utter waste of time that would just prolong my existence? Besides, I spoke a unique language no other could begin to comprehend, or understand the septic depression.

The world is better without me. And everyone, happier! There was no-one there, just pretence and everyone else happy, had it made; they could laugh. I wanted to escape the monotonous, cruel world of hopelessness, barren nothingness.

Every day, meaningless and mundane. Nothing to look forward to, dwelling on and tormented by the past; long-forgotten goals. Instead of praising and being thankful for wisdom gained and not realising the distinctive choice.

Or more to the point, I couldn't see anything but a grim future upon realising I had missed my chance to study; messed up opportunities of an academic nature; too late to try college.

No options or challenges to focus on and strive towards with depression, negativity, hopelessness, and many fears.

But, rigid mindedness meant set ideas, and an inability to put things into perspective. Wasted life! Wasted talent and potential. Nothing I could do, nor way forward or even a dream to chase. Or was it my frame of mind?

Tormented by the crux of loneliness; the main bane of my life; where many desires and yearnings emanate. What was wrong with me? My friends had got steady girlfriends, found their soulmates, engaged even and were so happy, but not me?

Just hurt for me. As a loser in love, I couldn't handle anymore. So many betrothed in the stars. Entwined from the dawn of time. And, I thought of the profoundness and shocking depths of love Shakespeare wrote about so eloquently.

Such romance, but the lovely lady I sought for so long — gone forever, lost on a whim. All I needed, I had, but losing made me more rebellious. I became wilder and wiser, but was never prepared or ready for the ensuing wilderness, and drifted ever further away, beyond reach.

Nothing could be fun. Just consternation and misery, as the best days and nights of my life and other wondrous, pleasurable times may not happen again. Nor even be emulated in an eternity was hard to bear.

Did I really not care as I traded superficial camaraderie for suppressed emotions and embarked on unsavoury influences, like dabbling in the occult?

Alas, not even a plan or a Frisbee club. But it wasn't enough. As I wanted more – to be a passenger on my spinning Frisbee. Launching to the stars and outer space! Wanting to live in fantasy. As I didn't have the things I thought mattered.

Sometimes I thought I was living at the wrong time. The social scene of the day didn't seem right. Maybe because of the alcohol and the drugs, cannabis, a combination bringing paranoia and deepening depression.

Melancholy music influenced my mind and mood, too, and perfect pop star studs in videos with the chicks. The bike crash and injuries, particularly to my head; losing my prized steed changed me too and brought more despair.

I didn't want to be me anymore. Anyone else but me, not a nobody who wanted to be somebody. A someone, anyone else but as a romantic dreamer, a thinker of thoughts too deep for a cruel, shallow world.

Could the only logical reason have been a nervous breakdown? I didn't know I was unbalanced and living on a knife's edge. Analogous to teetering, walking a tightrope across an abyss with no sense of purpose, whilst shrouded, consumed by demons but yearning for an angel's embrace.

All this surely wasn't enough? Well, 22 years after the event, I remembered something else. An unexpected visit from Tom; the night before the event. That always smiling, jokey type had never visited me. Or spoke to me in such an agitated state.

Fear in his eyes and voice as he anxiously spoke, "Chief Thug is really angry. He's beat Brad up and told him to tell you, you're next and when he finds you, he won't stop this time; he knows about you and his girlfriend."

My friend wouldn't make up a story like that. That gang, the violent attack, and the dog set on me for nothing and before knowing about my raunchy rendezvous beneath the stars!

They'd beat me up, OK, but not the dog, which was infinitely scarier. This, I believe, was a triggering factor, but only the seismic trigger. The cataclysmic trigger that rocked the world on my shoulders; amplified and tilted the swinging pendulum of life — in eternal winter.

With each swing signifying the passage of time, as I'm left behind in a perpetuated state of unstable equilibrium: unbalanced turmoil, fighting against the ebb and flow of a cosmic tide.

I was out of tune with the rhythm of the universe and it was a relentless and almighty tide, possibly from an amazingly powerful moon in conjunction with a potent celestial configuration.

Regardless of the tide, the planets, and their moons, there was no defence, antidote, or solutions, or hope! This escalated inner rebellion. And, fuelled my radical, defiant, ever-increasing desire to endure beyond the norm. Which may have set my path on a downward spiral to near oblivion and failed-trajectory to the stars.

I believe a variety of factors formed building blocks for a future protest. The accumulative effect of x number of circumstances. A recipe and unique formula for a lethal catalyst. Alas, marooned and cocooned. Programmed to endure on my path to self-destruct.

In addition to ever deeper depression exacerbating my turmoiled, desperate mental state. Enormous but simple complexity and confutations.

Don't agonise pondering the million what if questions there may be; the many reasons we may never know.

(ii). Escaping Oblivion

*M*aybe no-one could have changed my ways or plans. Perhaps I even set a day. Or there may have been a trigger. A trigger that began an **unstoppable countdown on an intricate clock** to that only date, Thursday 3rd of September, 1987.

If I hadn't been left alone. It may have only delayed the inevitable, as the countdown had begun. If I had waited just a minute. An hour, a day, a month, this would have yielded a totally different situation, a myriad of scenarios.

The near fatal event may not have occurred. Or been merely postponed, but each extended moment may have felt different;

another path, another choice, even though now may seem unchangeable. Composure and calm, rational logic might have helped my plight. But despair displaced rational thought; twisted knowledge and distorted logic within a thick, vast, inescapable black sea of depression.

Was I in my rudderless boat at the mercy of the wind that blew my sails, or implanted in the sand?

Determination, driven by mature wisdom, made me indestructible. Powerful, but this was mere fallacy poles apart from the reality. I was a clever character, but a fragile human, unprepared for the pressures of adolescence; a vulnerable, big kid, on the verge, trying hard to be a man.

Like his peers, as I tussled with emotions stirred and disrupted from delusion-driven rebellion. Fantasies, dreams of what others thought I should become.

Overwhelmed, as I juggled with everything ever faster. Hormones, desires, and pressures of the world, and addicted to alcohol; 10 pints of beer and still standing, then you're a man!

Not quite, without a moustache, hairs on your chest like James Bond and muscles like a bodybuilder, but I was oblivious to my personal war: physical prowess versus mental expansion. The need to maintain a balance between mind and body. Stability and sanity versus despair and chaos.

Where was the love, and how deep? How powerful, and how real? Was it miserably inadequate against the negativity and despair? The hopelessness as the lop-sided pendulum swung. And I became consumed in a deep, inescapable and raging, blackness. Wintry winds akin to a maelstrom extinguishing all beacons, hope itself.

Were the beacons of love too intense, brilliant, blotting out the blackness, but creating confusion and more instability? Had I loosed the rope in a perpetual tug of war? To hurtle on a trajectory to oblivion, enduring and finding a way back from coma, my only slim chance?

Through space and traversing time, on a unique path, that ultimately led to a plethora of experiences. In our experiences, there may be a variety of gifts and sometimes curses encompassing splendid joy or strife. This is irrelevant, though. As both extremes, sometimes interchange with time and perception.

Paths, whether destined or navigable, whether choices or illusions have an ever-moulding effect preparing us for future times. The whole of my life ahead of me from birth, and after I woke from coma.

Where did my life go wrong? Where did it go, right? Or was it just so, but indiscernible?

Life would have been different without alcohol, the magic solace it conjured, temporary contentment and a fake solution to all. I might have tried harder at school. Not swayed from the path of learning.

Sadly, mistimed and misguided aspirations, and chasing wild desires due to pressure to conform to flawed ideals, yielded melancholic emotions, dashed hopes and eroded dreams.

More poignantly, I didn't realise I clearly had mental health problems. As a male, I never contemplated seeing my doctor or seeking help.

When I broke my wrist, trod on a nail and had my bike accident, health professionals promptly treated the visible, physical injuries. My mind, mental health issues, went untreated; I endured, told no-one.

This is a crucial factor why so many die by suicide. Suffer in silence, without reaching out. Or are oblivious to their mental health issues. It is beyond sad, so many perish. The cruel devastation and despair in the wake of unbearable shock-waves. Mystery, and precious memories, as the only inadequate consolation.

Returning from a self-destructive path may seem impossible. It isn't. And, it's possible to recover from depression and mental illness. Hopefully, many can avoid the downward spiral, though. To find a safer way to escape, or even delay such encounters to live on. — continue to exist.

The likelihood of this will increase with better mental health awareness. And, better support for those suffering from mental health issues is vital in a more inclusive society. In a better world, where no-one feels isolated and alone.

As once someone feels it futile to reach out, or that they believe they speak a language no other would ever understand, it may be too late.

I could have easily been a tragic, cold statistic, of which there's an abundance. All are grim and may eventually become an even colder line. A line on a graph, a number with no lasting value, or human essence. A mere enigma for professionals to hypothesise, theorise, chase shadows, hoping for substance.

The National Institute of Mental Health[3] in the U.S. in 2018, suicide rates of males was four times higher than that of females. Suicide ranked as the 2nd highest cause of death for 10-14, 15–24, 25–34 age ranges.

In addition, according to the UK Office for National Statistics (ONS), released September 2019.[4] Since the mid-1990s, and in 2020[5] three-quarters of registered suicides have been males. Analysis of which extends beyond the scope of this book but emphasises a point.

Lives do needlessly end, young, old, all genders in every corner of the world. Yet suicide is only highlighted in news and or on TV when well-known celebrities, pop stars, rock stars, lose their lives to suicide.

Even then, there's little coverage. Brief discussion, and this presents part of the problem. It isn't futile to strive to save and prolong lives that end this way, though.

The modern era imposes even more pressures than 30 years ago, and from a myriad of examples. I'll say: Is it right anyone can look online and watch videos of how to end their lives?

On the plus side, there's now suicide prevention organisations

---

3. NIMH: https://www.nimh.nih.gov/health/statistics/suicide/index.shtml
4. ONS: https://www.ons.gov.uk/peoplepopulationandcommunity/
birthsdeathsandmarriages/deaths/bulletins/
suicidesintheunitedkingdom/2019registrations/
5. ONS: https://www.ons.gov.uk/peoplepopulationandcommunity/
birthsdeathsandmarriages/deaths/bulletins/
suicidesintheunitedkingdom/2020registrations/

like [6]PAPYRUS, and mental health helplines. And, candid blogs on mental health improve and promote discussion. The 3 Dads walking campaign to get suicide prevention on the UK school curriculum, and the forthcoming Online Safety Bill may bode well for the future, too.

Hopefully gambling addictions will become more of a focal point for governments, where well-being becomes paramount, not so much profit.

---

6.   https://www.papyrus-uk.org

35.

EPILOGUE

(i). Reflections

*T*here's an emotive, almost senseless question this book has endeavoured to answer: "Why did you do it?"

Was I an outcast to them and society? Sometimes, I've thought I was without such comments, but why? Is it because of deep society-embedded taboos? Stigma based dismay of trying to take my own life; end my existence in this world.

The dismay at the utter selfishness, the self-centred cowardice, all I could have been and achieved, high aspirations, healthy, fit, so a waste. My screwed up life! The whole world under my feet and entire-life ahead, to live!

Sometimes I've thought coma experiences, ordeals; all I went through and changed abilities was akin to being punished for not trying at school. Wasted academic potential, and for making light of my abilities?

Opportunities I threw away, shunned, as I didn't heed wise people's guidance or advice. The stinging whip into the right line, the correct path.

Analogous to a bite from a deadly serpent that slithered toward me and reared its vicious head. Prepared, waited to strike as its jaws opened. Poised before the sharp shock of piercing, plunging, unforgiving fangs. Injected with a potent venom, that brings perilous delirium.

Peace, but temporary tranquillity preceding raging turmoil, as my limp, weary body, and soul succumbed to gravity, and pressure, like a leaf in a whirlwind. At the mercy of nature, a game of chance, or my preordained destiny?

At least I imagined, and luckily I woke. Regardless, each of us experiences and endures unique events to evolve, and each of us reacts and deals with situations in different ways.

In a moment, way beyond despair, in sheer mental pain, I just didn't want to live anymore, but I am glad it wasn't the end. For those who may be feeling how I felt: Does it matter if we're on the wrong or right track, if the present merely signifies a tiny part of a journey toward the future?

The dealt cards can be shuffled. So are our lives as screwed up as we believe? Or as gloomy, as if beyond despair, particularly if mental health issues are prevalent and negativity. And, it's noteworthy, I believe some of my emotions echoed thoughts and words of others.

(ii). The Choice

*T*he mind is complex, consciousness of sentient beings, a scientific and metaphysical mystery, and such complexity has confounded and intrigued me as years have passed.

Yet, although painstaking with bewildering mystery, the immense efforts I have made to understand my attempted suicide — strange, illogical, actions beyond my comprehension, has been a cathartic journey. A process of change as I have aged; lived on and evolved; become wiser with a broadened, more adept, stronger mind.

Stronger despite mental health and, although physically impaired, relatively weak to how I was, and still fragile as I endure.

Obviously, I would have preferred not to endure pain and darker times or to become disabled, but those specific experiences, rigours of life, depression and adjusting to disability since I awoke from coma, moulded and refined me.

As has the sharing of experiences, painful to convey, and even more gruelling, with a deep exploration of mind, body, and soul analogous to climbing many mountains, harsh, insurmountable mountains on a vast mountain range.

And to joining the dots in an enormous picture, the squiggly bits, lines, people, events, emotions, but with words depicting a journey through time, my life so far.

The transformation also changed me, as I wouldn't ever wish to be anyone else. That presents a stark revelation of change after wishing to be anyone but me in my previous life. I didn't have to be a sad clown.

Times of deep-depression, when I used to wish I was dead, I failed to grasp the brevity or the everlasting profoundness of death. No longer existing, gone forever, treasured memories the only consolation. That would have been devastatingly unfair.

Did I have that right? Leaving an epitaph memento and remembered by others in distinct ways. Living on, my efforts, all I have met and interacted with, add memories, and represent all aspects and parts of my life, the woes, and joys.

Each individual will interpret this, and my book, in a variety of ways. The essence may be a human's struggle to find purpose, and fathom the complexities of the world. And to find harmony and solace from turmoil, as a lifelong-quest...

A journey, a quest to love, for love, and to feel loved, valued, needed in this world. To mutually give, and above all to strive on, as I didn't when I could have. Yet wishes and desires from the past were perhaps more achievable than I imagined, if I had focused efforts and not been dissuaded from chasing dreams.

I hope many will read my book, but know success depends on definition. Each reader will have unique views. Still, if anything in this book comforts a soul, or helps others to understand. Then it has been worth the toil. Anything more, a bonus.

Many choose to end their lives, and unintentionally and inadvertently leave heartache, with torment and senseless despair. There's often eternal mystery too, and shock as the bereaved loved ones never expected to lose someone they loved in that way. All of which exacerbates the heartache.

With such undesirable aftermaths, the mystery deepens when only a multitude of unique factors multiplied by an immeasurable number of variables cause that exact event.

Such complexity and uniqueness of each sentient being may

suggest it's futile to tell anyone what to do, or dictate whether they're receptive to advice and perhaps no-one might understand or abate such events; change their minds, alter their course. Or know another's physical or mental pain; what they're going through.

There's no magic formula, either, or advice regardless of whether anyone can ever know their time is up, nor a guarantee of a second chance, but there's a clear and presented choice; a prolonged life. Or a tragic, cruel mystery.

A step back from the edge of an abyss, even though it may seem easier to step forward, and the only option and solution, it is not.

In that motive, intending and striving for solace, the turmoil, the mental pain exchanges, continues in another form, another place. Perhaps in the hearts of others. The sad irony may be, those who should have cared didn't. And those we imagined wouldn't care actually missed us more than we could ever imagine and cared the most.

So, why not step back? Look up at the sky? The stars and heavens are always there. Their light still shines, although not always visible tomorrow might be brighter, less grey and better. If not, eventually, the sky will be blue, unlike today.

Live on, embracing, we are on a countdown. Time on Earth cannot yield or stop, but future countdowns can alter, preserving and prolonging the preciousness of unstoppable time, each second, each moment, all-times. We cannot turn back, but can rejoice the now.

Just some may never realise they have a purpose, their importance, or salience; that they're enigmatic; precious, at least to others, even if they believe they're of no value.

So, it follows, society should embrace the uniqueness of each individual, include everyone without division or prejudice, with perpetuation of kindness, respect, and an appreciation everyone is valuable.

Each of us has talents, qualities, and weaknesses, as well as strengths. And if not needed by someone now, they may be in future moments, even relied upon and loved.

No-one should have to endure pressure to fit in, made think they're inferior, unworthy, or insecure; hopeless, believing they have nothing to contribute to the world.

Or experience any negative aspect, if only in their minds. Nor isolated to the extent of loneliness; in such despair they believe there's no point in talking, or to reach out as they're alienated with no support or recognition of mental health.

It's imperative to communicate and interact, even if perceived as futile, as someone, somewhere, might understand, and help with tender compassion for mental pain.

I nearly died because of my own actions, cocooned in a maelstrom, shut off from the wider world, and everyone, whilst oblivious to the infinite number of reasons to live; not to die. There are many reasons I lived on, survived, including writing this book as a reborn being.

This, further and even more poignantly, proves at least one thing. It is wrong to think there's no point. Unwise and premature to think my life should end. Or to assume no-one cares and as I live on, although the person I was became lost forever, I will always be grateful for each second, beholden for every tomorrow.

A future I had no inkling of at the darkest of times; the new beginning, and dawn, and be less fearful of the end, irrespective of whether my rebirth, return from near death, is attributable to science or angels.

In remembrance and a tribute to Marvin, Shelda, and Tiffany Reams, who helped me to believe.

To my dad, David Walters, 1943 to 2020, as he supported and helped me live.

And, to my dear friend Paul, who never got to read this book.

Also, to those who have died by suicide.

APPENDIX A

Anyone and adults	Under 35s and students
Samaritans: Call 116 123 for free 24/7, write a letter or chat online. www.samaritans.org Or Email: jo@samaritans.co.uk	**Papyrus UK:** for people under 35 HOPELINEUK Call: 0800 068 41 41 – 9am to midnight every day. Text: 07860 039967 www.papyrus-uk.org Email: pat@papyrus-uk.org
Campaign Against Living Miserably (CALM): www.thecalmzone.net/ Web chat or call: 0800 58 58 58	**ChildLine:** for children and young people under 19. Call: 0800 1111 – the number won't show up on your phone bill.
The Silver Line: for people over 55, free 24/7 and confidential. www.thesilverline.org.uk Call: 0800 4708090	**Young Minds crisis messenger:** for people under 19. www.youngminds.org.uk Text: "YM" to 85258
Harmless UK: harmless.org.uk The centre of excellence for self-harm and suicide prevention.	**Shout:** Text "Shout" to 85258 Free, confidential, 24/7 text messaging support if you're struggling to cope. giveusashout.org
SOS Silence of Suicide: for everyone. sossilenceofsuicide.org Call: 0808 115 1505 – 4pm to midnight weekends, 8pm to midnight weekdays.	Nightline Association: A student and want to talk? nightline.ac.uk/want-to-talk/

Suicide Prevention UK: www.spuk.org.uk Call: 0800 689 5652	Look up suicide prevention hotlines around the world, in your country.
National Suicide Prevention Helpline UK: Offers a supportive listening service to anyone with thoughts of suicide. Call: 0800 689 5652 (open 24/7).	Or call your GP (Doctor or NHS 111) www.nhs.uk

APPENDIX B

MUSIC (OTHER SONGS I HEARD DURING COMA)

- Westworld, *Silver Mac*
- The Real Thing, *Jellybean*
- George Harrison, *Got My Mind Set On You*
- Bananarama, *Love In The First Degree*
- Billy Idol, *Mony Mony*
- Cliff Richard, *Some People*
- George Michael, *Faith*
- Kiss, *Crazy, Crazy Nights*
- Abigail Mead and Nigel Goulding – Full Metal Jacket, *I Wanna Be Your Drill Instructor*
- T'Pau, *China In Your Hand*
- Alexander O'Neal, *Criticize*
- Freddie Mercury & Montserrat Caballé – Barcelona
- Jan Hammer, *(Miami Vice) Crockett's Theme*
- The Communards, *Never Can Say Goodbye*
- Sisters of Mercy, *This Corrosion*
- The Hooters, *Satellite*
- The Christians, *When The Fingers Point*
- Rick Astley, *Never Gonna Give You Up*
- Pet Shop Boys, *Rent*
- Donna Summer, *Dinner with Gershwin*

ABOUT THE AUTHOR

Paul D Walters is the author of *To Heaven And Back: Don't Die…Live On!* a non-fiction memoir. He wrote his book over many years, as he soul-searched and explored his psyche and the inner depths of his mind as a brain injury survivor after attempting suicide.

His near-death experience of what he calls 'other realms' during coma brought the realisation of beauty, with a defiant desire to live. Writing his book also became a mission to change the world, so there's less heartache.

As well as battling depression, fighting mental health stigma and promoting suicide awareness, he became a qualified editor and copywriter in 2021. And lives in the UK, England, West Midlands in the Black Country with his partner of many years, two children and a cat, called Boots.

Also interested in politics and passionate about the environment, he loves trees, nature, the great outdoors, the stars and the moon, and enjoys 80s music.

Printed in Great Britain
by Amazon

27932206R00209